GLOBAL ACTION FOR BIODIVERSITY

A fine will be charged if not returned by the date stamped above

This book may be recalled before the above date.

GLOBAL ACTION FOR BIODIVERSITY

AN INTERNATIONAL FRAMEWORK FOR IMPLEMENTING THECONVENTION ON BIOLOGICAL DIVERSITY

Timothy Swanson

IUCN
The World Conservation Union

EARTHSCAN
Earthscan Publications Ltd, London

WWF
© 1986 World Wide Fund For Nature

First published in the UK in 1997 by
Earthscan Publications Ltd, in association with IUCN

The views of the author expressed in this book do not necessarily reflect those of
IUCN. The designations of geographical entities in this book, and the presentation
of the material, do not imply the expression of any opinion whatsoever on the part
of IUCN concerning the legal status of any country, territory or area, or of its
boundaries.

A catalogue record for this book is available from the British Library

ISBN: 1 85383 358 4 (paperback), 1 85383 353 3 (hardback)   1001370398

Cover design by Gary Inwood Studios

Typesetting and page design by Gary Inwood Studios

Printed and bound by Biddles Ltd, Guildford and King's Lynn

For a full list of publications, please contact:

Earthscan Publications Ltd
120 Pentonville Road
London N1 9JN
Tel: 0171 278 0433
Fax: 0171 278 1142
email: earthinfo@earthscan.co.uk
http://www.earthscan.co.uk

IUCN Publications Services Unit, 219c Huntingdon Road, Cambridge, CB3 0DL, UK
IUCN Communications Division, Rue Mauverney 28, CH-1196 Gland, Switzerland

Earthscan is an editorially independent subsidiary of Kogan Page Ltd and publishes in
association with WWF-UK and the International Institute for Environment and Development.

Printed on acid and elemental chlorine free paper, sourced from sustainably managed
forests and processed according to an environmantally responsible manufacturing system.

For the next generation, and especially

Andrew

Matthew

Nicholas

Hannah

Drew

Benjamin

Christina

&

Katarina

CONTENTS

TABLES

Figures

Boxes

ABBREVIATIONS AND ACRONYMS

ASEAN   Association of South East Asian Nations
CBD   Convention on Biological Diversity
CGIAR   Consultative Group for International Agricultural Research
CITES   Convention on International Trade in Endangered Species
DDT   Dichlorodiphenyltrichloroethane
EC   European Community
FAO   United Nations Food and Agricultural Organisation
GEF   Global Environmental Facility
IARC   International Agricultural Research Centre
IIED   International Institute for Environment and Development
IPR   Intellectual Property Rights
ITRG   Ivory Trade Review Group
IUCN   World Conservation Union (formerly the International Union for
        Conservation of Nature and Natural Resources)
IUPGR   International Undertaking on Plant Genetic Resources
LUA   Land Use Agency
NASA   National Aeronautics and Space Administration
NGO   Non-governmental Organisation
NPP   Net Primary Product
OECD   Organisation for Economic Co-operation and Development
R&D   Research and Development
RLUA   Restricted Land Use Agreement
RRAG   Renewable Resources Assessment Group
SACIM   Southern African Centre for Ivory Marketing
UNCED   United Nations Conference on Environment and Development
UNDP   United Nations Development Programme
UNEP   United Nations Environment Programme
UNESCO United Nations Educational, Scientific and Cultural
        Organisation
USAID   United States Agency for International Development
WCED   World Commission on Environment and Development
WCMC   World Conservation Monitoring Centre
WWF   World Wide Fund For Nature

FOREWORD

The seed of the idea for an international convention on biological diversity was planted at the Third World Congress on National Parks and Protected Areas, held in Bali, Indonesia, in October 1982. Over the subsequent decade, numerous international meetings, consultations, workshops, symposia, and other such processes led to the development of the well-ripened Convention on Biological Diversity (CBD) that was signed by virtually all governments at the Earth Summit at Rio de Janeiro in 1992. The Convention entered into force at the end of 1993, over 160 countries have ratified it, and its Conference of Parties has now met several times to begin putting the Convention into practice.

However, it has become increasingly apparent that the Convention contains numerous intellectual challenges for those seeking to implement its provisions. Many of its innovations are little more than good ideas remaining to be given practical application. The CBD provides a synthesis of information and perspectives from a number of different disciplines. The Convention begins with a biological foundation, but builds upon it with economics, sociology, and other social sciences to define new ways of doing business. Much of this involves a political process which must begin at the national government level – or even the local community level – before trickling up to the international arena. A solid body of practice needs to be developed before some of these innovations can become integrated into the mainstream of conservation.

So while it is probably too soon to expect very many new protocols under the CBD, it is useful to begin already thinking about the kinds of elements that might contribute to a more thoughtful and detailed definition of activities under the CBD. Tim Swanson, with a long background in applying economics to resource management, brings a unique perspective to the challenges posed by the CBD. One does not need to agree with all of his suggestions to appreciate the stimulating value of putting such ideas before the global community. The ideas contained in this book will help to inform national delegations to the Conference of the Parties and help them to define more carefully the new approaches that will be required.

In the meantime, science will certainly help to inform decision makers. For example, the Global Biodiversity Assessment (Heywood, 1995), published by UNEP in 1995, made it very clear that biodiversity is especially important to provide resilience to ecosystems, enabling them to adapt to changing conditions. If the main costs of biodiversity loss lie in the loss of resilience of the ecosystems affected, biodiversity is valuable to each and every country, not just those which are blessed with great numbers of species. Indeed, one could even argue that the loss of species may impose much higher costs in species-poor systems than in those which are more species-rich.

It is also very clear that the CBD cannot by itself solve the problems of the loss of biodiversity. Rather, international trade agreements may be far more significant, as changing the relative price of resources or removing trade barriers may be a far greater threat to the planet's biodiversity. Thus all international negotiations need to consider their impact on biodiversity, and the ideals of the CBD need to be considered in discussions dealing with economic cooperation, international trade, forests, desertification, the oceans, climate, population, and the many other developments in modern society that influence biodiversity.

Numerous challenges to governments are to be expected in the implementation of the CBD, requiring them to regulate access to genetic resources, develop mechanisms for prohibiting import and possession of materials obtained contrary to legislation of the originating country, develop mechanisms to identify the source of material from which any particular benefit is derived, design ways to ensure that the benefits arising from biodiversity are equitably shared, and so forth. The Conference of the Parties will always be primarily a political forum where governments hammer out compromises. But real progress in implementing the provisions of the CBD will require governments to move ahead to address their own priorities, a step that is being taken in many countries around the world.

As Tim Swanson has pointed out so eloquently in this book, conserving biodiversity and using biological resources sustainably will benefit all of society. Thus activities to implement the Convention need to be supported by all sectors of society, including local communities, the private sector, NGOs, the scientific community, and so forth. The CBD offers a unique opportunity for this diverse mixture of interests to work toward achieving the same broad objectives. While international consensus will often be difficult to attain, building on the common goals of achieving conservation of biological diversity, using biological resources sustainably, and equitably sharing the benefits derived provide a very strong foundation upon which such consensus could be formed. The approaches advocated in this book will help to facilitate such consensus-building.

Jeffrey A McNeely
Chief Scientist
World Conservation Union
rue Mauverney 28
1196 Gland
Switzerland
February 1997

PREFACE

The nations of the world adopted the text for an international convention for the conservation of global biological diversity in Rio de Janeiro in 1992, and now more than 160 nations have ratified this text. The question now arises as to how to give effect to this Convention and its various undertakings. At present the Convention provides a mere framework of aspirations and admonitions in regard to the maintenance of some level of global biological diversity, but there is little in the way of binding language or substantive obligations. How can the international community move toward the development of obligations and institutions which will give effect to the aspirations within the Convention? How can we ensure that the lofty language of the Biodiversity Convention has some real effect at ground level, especially given that much of the biodiversity resource resides in some of the poorest parts of the Earth?

This volume attempts to describe the fundamental nature of the global problem now before the international community and the basic nature of the international agreement that is required to achieve its solution. The problem remains to fill in the gaps of the Convention, and it is essential that this be done by means of international agreements of the most particularistic kind. Now that the Biodiversity Convention has been adopted, the time has come for the agreements necessary for the conservation of this resource to be concluded.

This volume undertakes to set forth a bio-economic framework for analysing the biodiversity problem from which three very particularistic protocols issue for its resolution. The volume derives these three protocols by means of:

- the creation of a common scientific framework for the analysis of the global facets of the biodiversity problem;
- the elision of all concerns ancillary to the global problem, i.e. the segregation of all other parts of the problem which do not absolutely necessitate international action for their resolution; and
- the integration of all of the ancestral conservation movements concerned with diversity into this single framework.

From this particular perspective on the Biodiversity Convention, a particularistic solution may be derived. It is not claimed here that this is the only approach to the Biodiversity Convention, or even the 'first best'; it is merely hoped that a narrowing of the focus of the Convention to matters necessitating international cooperation for their resolution will allow for progress on a small but important subset of these problems to continue. Therefore, this volume takes an admittedly narrow approach to the problem, in the hopes of furthering the international policy debate along these narrow lines.

The volume proceeds to explain this concept by starting with a presentation of the global nature of the biodiversity problem. Chapters 2 through 4 develop the basic nature of the global problem within a bio-economic framework. These chapters describe the decline of global diversity, cultural as well as biological, as the result of the uniform nature of the global development process and the by-product of the progress of this homogenising process across the face of the globe. It is a global process such as this that is indicative of a global problem that necessitates international action for its management. Chapter 5 provides the bridge between the global nature of the problem and the international nature of its solution; this chapter describes the range of movements that have struggled with various facets of this problem over the past decades and the nature of their concerns. Chapters 6 through 10 then describe the nature of the solutions required to address these problems and these concerns, in increasingly particularistic fashion. Chapter 6 commences with a brief overview of the solution concepts, while Chapters 7 through 9 then develop each in greater detail. Finally, Chapter 10 concludes with the presentation of the three protocols to the Biodiversity Convention which this framework deems necessary to address the global facets of the biodiversity problem as presented.

The Biodiversity Convention represents an unprecedented opportunity for the development of institutions concerned with the fostering of alternative pathways to development. It remains an unfulfilled ambition awaiting fruition, and all that remains is the choice to make something real and substantial out of the opportunity. This is an opportunity that should not be wasted.

Timothy Swanson
Cambridge, UK, February 1997

This manuscript was commissioned by the International Union for Conservation of Nature and the World Wide Fund For Nature International, Gland, Switzerland (Jeff McNeely, contracting officer). I wish to thank Kevin Lyonette for initial discussions and Nancy Vallejo for subsequent direction in the undertaking of this project. I am also grateful to Frank Vorhies and Jeff McNeely for ptheir comments on a previous draft. All comments to the author at: Faculty of Economics and Politics, Cambridge University, Sidgwick Avenue, Cambridge CB3 9DD. Fax: (44) 1223-335475; e-mail: tim.swanson@econ.cam.ac.uk.

1

AN INTRODUCTION TO GLOBAL BIODIVERSITY AND ITS REGULATION: AN ISSUE AT THE CORE OF THE ENVIRONMENT AND DEVELOPMENT DEBATE

Introducing the Biodiversity Convention

In 1992 the global community met in Rio de Janeiro to discuss global problems concerning environment and development. One of the end results of the United Nations Conference on Environment and Development (UNCED) was the adoption of a text for an international convention on the conservation of biological diversity. Since that time, over 160 nations have ratified the Convention on Biological Diversity, making it one of the most global of all international treaties. In addition, a secretariat for the Convention has been established in Montreal, and several conferences of the parties have occurred: the first in the Bahamas in 1994, then in Indonesia in 1995 and in Argentina in 1996. The Parties have agreed to continue to hold annual conferences in order to establish the Convention. In a very short period, the Convention on Biological Diversity is coming to life.

Despite all of this activity, it is difficult to assess its substantive achievements to date. This is because the language and the legal content of this Convention are written in a fashion that makes its objectives and commitments exceedingly vague. For example the Convention enjoins Party states 'to develop programmes for the conservation and sustainable use' of biodiversity (Article 6), and to 'establish a system of protected areas' (Article 8). Such commitments, if taken literally and enforced to the limit by all of the Parties, would in themselves transform the plight of biodiversity. In that case nearly all of the world's undeveloped land would be subjected to intensive efforts for its protection and carefully planned development.

This is unlikely to happen without a lot of help. The global facet of the biodiversity problem lies in the fact that much of global biodiversity resides in precisely those states which have the least capacity to support it. In addition, it is not inexpensive to support diverse resources. This requires commitments of lands and management as well as commitment to the resource itself. For example, it has been estimated that in Africa expenditures of up to US$200 per kilometre are required for the protection of large mammals such as the rhinoceros (Leader-Williams and Albon, 1988). This would imply that rhino management would itself absorb the entire park budget for many sub-Saharan countries, and this does not take into consideration the costs of the land used by this species. When this is done it is apparent that the costliness of conservation is a very expensive undertaking for many developing countries (Norton Griffiths and Southey, 1994).

How could the expansive and expensive undertakings set forth in the Biodiversity Convention be financed by such poor and underprivileged Parties hosting much of our remaining diversity? The convention itself is clear on this point: 'The developed country Parties shall provide new and additional financial resources to enable developing country Parties to meet the agreed full incremental costs to them of implementing measures which fulfil the obligations of this Convention ...' (Article 20(2)). In short, the burdens of conservation efforts conducted by poorer countries in the global interest are to be distributed in accordance with the ability to pay, with the construction of international financial mechanisms adequate to this task (Article 21).

Importantly, the development of pure financial transfer mechanisms is not the only basis upon which those countries 'supplying' biodiversity are to be compensated. The convention also states that each Party should take action 'with the aim of sharing in a fair and equitable way the results from research and development and the benefits from commercial or other utilisation of genetic resources with the Party providing such resources...' (Article 15(7)). That is, the benefits from the development and use of genetic diversity are also to be used to provide incentives for the maintenance of diversity. This implies that the suppliers of genetic resources should be accorded a 'share' in the value that results from their subsequent use and development. The idea of sharing benefits from final products implies an agreement to develop a property-rights-based mechanism for rewarding investments in biodiversity conservation for subsequent use.

These few articles in themselves represent the core of a solution to the global problem of biodiversity's decline, but there is a tremendous amount of detail that remains to be filled in. Nevertheless the basic principles around which a solution might evolve have been agreed, and those are the ones listed above. This agreement is at present of the nature of what is known as a 'framework convention'. That is, it identifies the issues being discussed, the parties to the negotiations, and the basic parameters of an agreement, but it goes only a very short distance in the direction of a fully detailed and concrete solution. The purpose of this volume is to provide a substantive basis for the development of an effective international management regime for the conservation of biological diversity. That is, it is an attempt to 'fill in the blanks' remaining within the Biodiversity Convention. And, it is the object of this volume to do so in a manner that will create concrete and permanent incentives for the conservation of substantial amounts of biodiversity.

How is this to be accomplished? There are several hurdles. The initial hurdle facing the Parties to the Convention is some sort of consensus framework for the understanding of the general problem with which they are dealing. Only after a common conceptual framework for viewing the problem is agreed can the nature of a solution be identified. It has been seen again and again in international negotiations that consensus science precedes substantive obligations. For example, it was only after atmospheric chemists agreed the science of ozone depletion that the Montreal Protocol was a real possibility. The need to undertake the same sort of consensus building exercise for biodiversity has resulted in numerous parallel processes (e.g. see Heywood, 1995) but with much less consensus being built.

Why is it more difficult to achieve consensus in the development of an approach to the biodiversity problem than it is for other global problems? Although atmospheric chemistry is a very complicated scientific problem, the science of the biodiversity problem is an even more difficult and complex subject. One reason for this complexity is because it is a social problem embedded within the biological world and so some sort of broad and integrated approach is required in order to deal with it. It is not sufficient to focus on either social or natural sciences alone to understand the biodiversity problem; both are necessities.

Another reason for the complexity of the science of biodiversity depletion is the number of different levels at which the problem may be addressed; this is indicative of the institutional nature of the biodiversity problem. One important level at which the loss of biodiversity must be analysed is the national one where many of the forces and incentives for diversity depletion persist (McNeely, 1996). There is an already-existing and voluminous literature which examines the failures of national policies to adequately consider the values of biodiversity in national development plans or to correct for the externalities in those policies that lead to its depletion (Repetto and Gillis, 1988; McNeely, 1992). There is no doubt that one of the most important functions of international cooperation regarding biodiversity is to spread information on existing 'best practice' in national conservation policies (McNeely, 1988; McNeely et al., 1990). In many cases, best practice national policies will focus on the development of incentives for local communities – probably the most important level at which biodiversity conservation policy must operate (Swanson and Barbier, 1992).

There is a third level at which biodiversity depletion must be considered – the global level. This is perhaps the most fundamental level, because it represents an attempt to understand the ultimate forces that explain national and local policies as well. It is probably the most complex layer of the biodiversity problem since it represents an attempt to explain a huge range of problems and policies worldwide by reference to a single underlying cause. At this level it is very difficult to find consensus; numerous scientists have explained global biodiversity depletion by reference to very different causes: population expansion, trade and economic growth, poorly chosen policies and paths, poverty and inequality (see the range of explanations in Swanson, 1995a). This is the first topic addressed in this volume: the prospects for the development of a scientific consensus on the *global* facets of the biodiversity problem.

The second hurdle for the Biodiversity Convention is equally difficult but for the opposite reason i.e. because it requires a narrowing rather than a broadening of the approach to the agreement. Clearly, with a name as broad as biological diversity, the range of potential subjects for discussion under this heading is virtually limitless: cultural preservation, habitat preservation, species preservation, and so on. There is almost no subject that would not fit underneath one of these headings. This sort of breadth makes it very difficult to achieve real action: the diffuseness of these various objects makes real movement difficult.

There is one clear and effective manner in which the diffuseness of the Biodiversity Convention might be focused. Despite the potential breadth of the Convention, there are very clear boundaries around the set of problems that absolutely necessitate *international* cooperation for resolution. Since there are many other fora within which other facets of the problem might be addressed, the Biodiversity Convention itself should be restricted primarily to the function of addressing those problems that cannot be resolved in the absence of an international agreement. It is at the most fundamental – global – level of the problem that an international scientific consensus must be developed, because it is at this level that an international agreement is required for its resolution. A problem is truly global in nature, as contrasted with pandemic, only when a global institution is required for its resolution. The second hurdle for the institution of the Biodiversity Convention is the agreement of the scientists on the truly global facets of the problem, and the focusing of the Biodiversity Convention on the development of those institutions required to address those facets.

It is argued here that the Biodiversity Convention as an international agreement should be focused on the task of creating the international mechanisms that will make it possible for the poorer countries to conserve their biodiversity: the transfer mechanisms and property rights mechanisms described above. Without the institution of funding mechanisms that channel funds for diversity, the poorer countries will refuse to invest their resources in diversity; without an international agreement to invest in diversity, richer countries would not provide the funding to make this investment possible. The closing of this circle is something that only the Biodiversity Convention is able to do. The development of these international funding mechanisms to foster alternative development pathways (based on investments in diversity) is the truly global facet of the Biodiversity Convention.

The third hurdle for the Biodiversity Convention again concerns the adoption of an integrative approach. Many of the issues raised but not resolved within the Convention (e.g. protected areas, farmers' rights, rights to genetic resources) have long been the subjects of discussion and negotiation in separate fora (McNeely, Rojas and Martinet, 1995). For example, the issues concerning access to materials in the agricultural gene bank system and the rights to compensation for its use have long been debated within the context of the United Nations Food and Agricultural Organisation (FAO). The issues concerning prospecting by pharmaceutical companies for medicinal plants and the rights to compensation were the subject of a Keystone dialogue and numerous other round-table sessions. The subjects of parks and protected areas, their use and management, have been long advanced by the IUCN – The World Conservation Union and its associated conservation organisations such as the World Wide Fund for Nature (WWF). In addition, many separate international conventions already exist on many of the topics listed within the Convention: the Ramsar Convention (for the protection of wetlands); the Bonn Convention (for the protection of migratory species); the Convention on International Trade in Endangered Species (for the regulation of trade in endangered species); the FAO's International Undertaking on Plant Genetic Resources (CITES – for the establishment of farmers' rights and a compensation mechanism to implement them).

The integration of this wide and varied group of movements is necessary for the successful implementation of a global management programme for biological diversity. Each of these various movements has been approaching a common problem from a different angle, and the most effective approach to the management of this global resource will call for their amalgamation into a single cooperative endeavour. Another of the objects of this volume is to demonstrate both the commonality of the problem that these disparate movements have faced, and the common nature of the solutions that they require.

Altogether the prerequisites for the creation of an effective biodiversity convention are a common framework, a common focus and a common object. These are substantial hurdles to be faced when the scientists, constituencies, and even the subjects of discussion are as diverse as they are in this context. The overarching objective of this volume is to present a single, narrow but integrated approach to the Convention that results in concrete and clear-cut proposals. These proposals may not be all things to all people but they are argued here to be the set of proposals that must be pursued if the international facets of the global biodiversity problem are to be resolved. They are the core of a concluded biodiversity convention.

The Scope of the Enquiry: The International Regulation of Extinction?

This is a volume about the conservation of the diversity of life forms that exists on earth. That is, it is a volume about evolved biological diversity, or 'biodiversity'. Biological diversity is important because it is the primary output from a four-and-a-half billion year evolutionary process. The evolutionary process has endowed the Earth with this range of diversity and it is important for many reasons, from the perspective of humans and from the perspective of life itself. This volume is about the conservation of this unique global endowment.

This is also a volume about global development and North-South relations; that is, this is a volume about the uneven character of global development. This is because the historical pattern of global development has resulted in a clear asymmetry in the world, between those states with material riches and those with species richness. For example by some estimates a majority of the Earth's biological variety now resides in the last, vast tropical forests existing in a few 'mega-diversity' regions in the southern hemisphere: the Latin American Amazon, the Central African and the Indonesian forests. Given this starting point, this volume focuses primarily on the conservation of these last great wildernesses. And, given the rights of the states in these regions to control their own destinies, and hence to control the resources within their borders, this volume focuses ultimately on the resource allocation decisions of a handful of southern states, their impact on the global environment, and the capability of the global community to influence those (land use) decisions.

This volume is also about the cumulative impact of global development; that is, it is a volume about the expansion of the human niche, and the appropriation of many others. Over time, general global development has resulted in a systematic narrowing of the variety of life forms on Earth, with the prospect of a much more severe narrowing in the next 100 years; for example, many of the world's leading biological scientists are now predicting losses of a substantial proportion of all life forms on Earth over the next century. In order to understand the nature of the problem of biodiversity depletion, it is necessary to examine how and why global development results in the systematic reallocation of basic resources away from a wide range of the world's species.

Primarily, however, this is a volume about the human institutions required for the management of biological diversity. It concerns the economic incentives that drive the human-made extinction process. It concerns the institutions (primarily domestic) that exist at present that do not adequately manage this process. Most importantly, it concerns the institutions (primarily international) that must come into existence as they are necessary for the adequate management of biodiversity. These are the core concerns of this volume.

The human management of the extinction process might sound like a typically anthropocentric perspective on a problem that concerns primarily non-human life forms. Or, at a minimum, it might appear to most to be a highly impracticable objective. However, the point of this volume is that the human regulation of extinction is something that is already taking place – only on a wasteful and inefficient basis. This is true, even from the human perspective. Therefore, this volume does not make the case for exclusive human dominion over the other species of the planet; rather, it appeals for the reasonable exercise of that power which already exists. It appeals for this through the vehicle of human interest because it is human interests that drive extinctions at present, and these same interests may instead be channelled to the conservation (rather than the elimination) of diversity. Also, human interests are pre-eminent in this volume because the loss of diversity is likely to threaten human production systems, and hence human life forms, long before it constitutes a threat to life itself.

Therefore, the human regulation of extinction is a system that already exists, but it is a poorly managed group of forces and incentives that appear set to generate a near-term mass extinction of species. The issue is whether this extinction process will be allowed to continue through human ignorance and avoidance of responsibility, or not. This volume demonstrates the wasteful nature of the existing system of regulation, and indicates the direction for potential reforms for the conservation of biological diversity.

Biological Diversity: A Depletable Endowment from the Evolutionary Process

Biological diversity, in the biologist's sense of the word, is the natural stock of genetic material within an ecosystem. This stock may be determined by the actual number of genes existing within the system. The number of genes ranges between organisms from about 1000 in bacteria to 10,000 in some fungi, and to around 100,000 for a typical mammal. The greatest number of genes actually belongs to the flowering plants, whose genes often number in excess of 400,000. Genes are important because they determine the particular characteristics of a given organism. They encode the information which determines the specific capabilities of that organism. The greater the variety in the gene pool, the greater is the variety of organisms which exist or which will exist in the near future.

The usual unit of analysis in studies of biodiversity is the number of existing species. This is because biological diversity may be conceived of as the net result of the processes of speciation and extinction. The number of currently described species is around 1.4 million; however, the number of species which have not yet been catalogued far exceeds that number. Best estimates place the total number of species somewhere between 5 and 30 million, with many experts now believing that the total (excluding micro-organisms) is around 12 million (WCMC, 1992). The vast majority of these species are insects and other smaller organisms. Among the more well-studied categories, vertebrates and flowering plants, the numbers are much lower and more certain. For example, it is known that there are about 43,850 vertebrates currently in existence, of which only 4000 are mammals, 9,000 are birds, 6300 are reptiles and 4180 are amphibians. By way of contrast, it is known that there exist at least 50,000 different species of molluscs (Wilson, 1988).

This diversity of species has resulted from the process of 'radiation': the mutation of species and their consequent expansion into unoccupied niches. It is a process that has occurred over many hundreds of millions of years to produce the diversity this world currently contains (Raup, 1988). The fossil record indicates that there is about 4.5 billion years of Earth's biological history. The record of the first 4 billion years, so-called 'deep time', indicates that there was very little adaptive radiation occurring over that very long period. Simple one-cell organisms (blue-green algae) were all that came to exist over the first 2 billion years of the Earth's existence, and only very simple multicellular organisms are found to have evolved over the next 2 billion years.

At the beginning of the next half-billion years (ranging to the present and known as 'shallow time') some unknown event triggered a revolution in adaptive radiation. The evolution of complex organisms, and their subsequent speciation, occurred all in a rush at the beginning of the Paleozoic era. Almost all of the major phyla presently existing appeared at that time, over a relatively short period of one hundred million years. The size and range of the biodiversity resource was determined by this revolution.

Since that time the average rates of speciation and extinction have been approximately equal. Therefore, the amount of biological diversity existing at present, in terms of the number and variety of species, is probably very close to its historical maximum. Nature, at the beginning of the Paleozoic period, endowed the earth with approximately its present amount of diversity and there is very little known about why this occurred.

Of course, extinction has itself been a natural process. Studies of the fossil record show that the natural longevity of any species lies in the range of 1 to 10 million years. The threat to biological diversity arises when the rate of extinction of species far exceeds the rate of speciation. In these eras of 'mass extinctions', there is the potential for a threat to the entire global biology. In the distant past, so-called 'deep time', there have been a number of occasions of such mass extinctions. There are at least five occasions indicated in the fossil record during which over 50 per cent of the then-existing animal species were rendered extinct (Raup, 1988).

Even averaging in these periods of mass extinctions, the natural rate of extinction over deep time appears to have been in the neighbourhood of 9 per cent per million years, or approximately 0.000009 per cent per year. That is, the current stock of biological diversity is the result of several billion years of mostly low frequency mutation and extinction. Mass extinction has been an infrequent 'unnatural' occurrence brought on by exogenous shocks to the Earth's life support system, such as extreme volcanic activity or collisions with meteors.

This brief account of speciation and extinction demonstrates the facet of biological diversity that is of the nature of a non-renewable resource. The *diversity* of biological resources is a one-time endowment from the evolutionary process. Therefore, although individual biological organisms may be treated as renewable resources, the aggregation of differences between these resources i.e. the diversity that they represent, is best conceptualised as a non-renewable resource. Biodiversity exists at the interface between the spheres of renewable and non-renewable resources.

It is also important to note why it is the case that human technology is incapable of resolving this problem. Humans now have control of the rate of speciation as well as that of extinction, through the use of biotechnological methods. However, there is a very substantial difference between that variety which has developed through the process of evolution and co-evolution over a period of six hundred million years, and that which can be created by experimentation in the laboratory.

The output from the evolutionary process, by the definition of evolution, has been selected by reason of its capability to interact within the system, including its biological activity and its role in its ecosystem. That is, the evolution of a particular life form is an indicator of its capacity to act upon and contribute to the other organisms within its environment. Biodiversity is valuable precisely because it is the output from this four-billion-year-old evolutionary process, not for the sake of variety itself. Existing life forms are an encapsulated history of this process and this constitutes an entirely unique body of information.

Another value of biodiversity lies in the fact that evolution has produced this particular range of variety. Although still subject to debate, it is generally agreed that the direction of evolution is life-sustaining – i.e. it has an in-built capacity to create a system that can continue to persist under a wide range of physical conditions. This is attributable to the fact that evolution is built upon the fundamental tenet of adaptation, and the variety that exists is then an indicator of the requisite range of potential responses life requires for meeting changes in the physical environment. The range of existing life forms developed by the evolutionary process then constitutes a uniquely formulated insurance policy against shocks to the life system itself.

Therefore, in biological diversity we are dealing with one of the ancient non-renewable resources, such as the fossil fuels, rich soils and great aquifers; however, in another important respect, biological diversity is very different from these other resources. It is similar to these other non-renewables in the sense that it is a one-off endowment from nature to the earth, in that it cannot be replaced on any timescale that is relevant to humanity. However, it is distinct from these other resources because it is impossible, by definition, to substitute human innovations for this resource. That is, biological diversity is distinguishable from most other natural endowments by reason of the fact that it is valuable primarily by virtue of its naturalness. It is not possible to substitute human synthesised inputs or processes for the important characteristics of biodiversity, precisely because their importance derives from the nature of the evolutionary process that generated them – a process which occurred over four-and-a-half billion years and generated an encapsulated history of biological activity and interaction. Biodiversity management concerns the management of the unique characteristics of this one-time endowment from the evolutionary process.

Human Development and Diversity Depletion

Although the retention of this evolutionary endowment renders important benefits to all life forms and thus to human societies as well, it is clear that the depletion of diversity has also generated important benefits for human societies. Human societies have been expanding and developing for many centuries through a process closely linked to biodiversity depletion. This is because one of the fundamental avenues for human development has been the conversion of the naturally existing forms of assets to other forms more highly valued by human societies (Solow, 1974a). This trade-off, between the benefits and opportunity costs of conversion, constitutes the fundamental problem of biodiversity management. This is because conversion has taken a special form which necessarily implies diversity depletion.

Over the past ten thousand years, human societies converting their resources have done so by replacing the naturally existing slate of species with a selection from the same small menu of specialised species. These are the domesticated and cultivated varieties that have been developed for use in agriculture, and are now substituted for the resident diversity worldwide.

The *global conversion process* is the observable result from the sequential application of this process of the replacement of the diverse with the specialised, in country after country across the face of the Earth. The nature of this conversion process implies two direct consequences: human societies (and their associated species) have expanded via this conversion strategy while, correlatively, all other species have been in relative decline.

It is important to sort out the line of argument concerning causation in global biodiversity decline. First, the fundamental force currently driving the reshaping of the biological world is the human drive for the appropriation of resources and for fitness; basic instincts within any species. Second, one of the basic strategies used by the human species in the course of this pursuit is the conversion between asset forms, implying the replacement of natural forms of assets (natural resources) with human-selected assets. Third, conversion has taken a very special form in the context of the biosphere; the form that it has taken has resulted in the reallocation of base resources towards a very small selection of species (the domesticated and cultivated species). Fourth, this reallocation of resources as a means of conversion has greatly benefited human societies while simultaneously reducing the resources available to the vast majority of species on Earth.

Therefore, the development process has been closely linked with diversity decline over the past ten thousand years. In addition, much of this development gain to date has been squandered on human niche expansion. Over the past ten thousand years, the human population has expanded from about ten million to approaching ten billion individuals. Coincidentally there have been several other population explosions among the specialised species: one-and-a-half billion cattle, one billion sheep, etc.

What are the costs of this process of expansion? While humans and their associated species inherit the earth, all others continue to see their ranges and their populations decline. Although conversion does not necessarily imply the expansion of the human niche, it clearly does imply the expansion of others. This is because the conversion process has taken the particular form of the replacement of the 'diverse' with a selection from the menu of the 'specialised'. This approach to conversion has twin outcomes: it expands the niche of a small selection of (cultivated and domesticated) species, while contracting virtually all others. This has guaranteed the loss of a large portion of the world's natural variety, when used as a strategy for global development.

The loss of any single species is difficult to value (hence the ongoing debate concerning the 'sign of option value'); this is because the retention of a single species implies costliness in opportunities forgone as much as it does options retained. However, there is no ambiguity concerning the meaningfulness of the loss of large swathes of the world's diversity. The homogenisation of the biosphere implies the decline of evolution-supplied diversity. It is the loss of this product (biological diversity), rather than the costliness of the loss of individual species, that is the opportunity cost implicit within the development process and that is the economic focus of this enquiry.

Therefore, the use of a conversion strategy of this nature has created the close link between human development and diversity decline. The question that needs to be addressed is whether there is the necessity of a link between the two. That is, even assuming that human development requires uniformly high population densities across the world (such as presently exist only in Europe and parts of Asia), does this still require that the life forms on Earth be homogenised in the fashion that has occurred previously throughout the developed world?

The issue here is whether it is possible for human societies to develop alternative development paths that build on the existing natural base of diversity rather than on the conversion to the uniform, specialised resources. It is this option – *of development compatible with diversity* – that is the policy focus of this enquiry.

Other authors believe that it is only possible to sustain global resources through a policy of non-development; they advocate a pursuit of the policy of the 'steady-state' (e.g. Daly, 1992). The past twenty-five years have seen some of the first serious questioning of the fundamental human pursuits of wealth and fitness, in the context of the debate concerning the 'Limits to Growth' (Meadows et al., 1972). I have no quarrels with this policy in theory, but I view it as either infeasible or highly objectionable in practice.

A policy of the 'steady-state' would either require all human societies to disavow further growth and development, or it would require that only some societies pursue further wealth and fitness while others maintain or contract. The former option is infeasible, simply because there are many human societies that still exist in a poverty-stricken state. Most of these states would be unwilling to make a commitment to steady-state policies. It would be unfair to commit some societies to perpetual poverty while others live in great surplus.

The latter option (the selective assumption of development constraints) depends entirely on the identity of the states assuming the constraints. As currently practised, this option is unfair and highly objectionable. It gives rise to allegations of 'environmental imperialism' precisely because these development constraints are usually proposed for imposition upon the most undeveloped states. For example, proposals that states such as Brazil, Zaire and Indonesia should not engage in deforestation and conversion are highly objectionable when they come from the already-converted states of the North.

The only equitable alternative is to continue to pursue development in the unconverted states while assuming constraints only in the developed. That is, uneven development constraints are only fair if they encourage development in those parts of the world where it is less in evidence.

How could the developed parts of the world be induced to encourage development primarily within the less developed? This is the economic role of these unique natural resources; they provide the foundation on which the unconverted states may stake their claim to a fair share of the global product. The converted states have had the ability to claim a disproportionate share of global product in the past, by virtue of the relative uniqueness of the converted forms of assets (Krugman, 1974). However, with an ever greater share of the world's societies undertaking the same conversions, the truly unique assets now lie in those states that retain the unique endowments of evolutionary product. It is the recognition of this monopoly over this important asset that will cause the converted states to invest significant funds (and thus assume their own development constraints) for the benefit of the unconverted states.

Therefore, the policy pathway advocated here is for the unconverted states to pursue development in a manner that is consistent with the unique environmental resources they alone retain. This will allow development to continue in those parts of the world that are still 'catching up', while simultaneously inducing the converted states to invest in that development process. This strategy recognises biodiversity as a global resource for its universal flow of benefits, but focuses on its character as an exclusive 'national resource' for use as a mechanism for inducing international transfers. This is the policy pathway selected for reasons of feasibility, sustainability and equity.

The Regulation of Biodiversity: Managing the Global Conversion Process

The management of biodiversity equates with the management of the global conversion process. The objective is to halt these conversions at least at that point where the human welfare losses from the narrowing of diversity exceed the welfare gains from conversion. Although there are many reasons to halt the process prior to this point (thereby preserving more of nature's life forms), even the most ardent believer in growth and development cannot argue with an objective that maximises human benefits. There is no reason why any individual country cannot undertake further conservation in recognition of other values of biodiversity, but there is clearly no reason why the global community should not act to conserve that amount that is necessary for the advancement of common human interests. This volume sets forth a method by which a consensus level of diversity conservation might be agreed and effected, in the belief that human interests will be the common denominator in the ultimate implementation of the Biodiversity Convention.

Once human benefits are taken to be the measure of the value of biodiversity, a straightforward mechanism for the conservation of diversity commends itself. Economic theory suggests that flows of benefits will provide their own incentives for their conservation provided that these benefits are distributed in accordance with the burdens undertaken. In economic terms, it is more exact to speak of investments and flows of benefits. Flows of benefits derive from prior investments, and these investments can be induced by the expectation of these benefit flows. So long as the investing person or community expects to see the flow of benefits channelled through its hands, it will undertake them. In terms of biodiversity, it is important to channel the benefits of diversity through the hands of the people who must invest in order to retain them.

The optimal management of biological diversity equates with the channelling of the values of diverse resources from the global community to the suppliers of those benefits i.e. to those states in the South harbouring significant diverse resources. In that fashion the optimal policy for biodiversity conservation is effected – through a policy geared to harnessing the value of diversity in order to halt conversions – while the burden of diversity conservation is compensated – through the instrument of channelling the value of diversity to its suppliers.

In addition, this manner of diversity management equates with the creation of alternative development paths for states with large areas of remaining wilderness. Development may be made compatible with the retention of diversity; that is, it is not a universal pre-condition to development that the naturally existing slate of biological resources be replaced with a pre-selected slate. Investing in institutions for the appropriation and transfer of the values of biodiversity equates with investment in the creation of these alternative development paths.

For this approach to be effective in conserving biodiversity, however, it is necessary to characterise the nature of the extinction process as it currently exists. Although a wholly natural and life-sustaining process ten thousand years ago, it is now driven largely by social forces (i.e. the conversion process). However, conversion can be effected via a number of different routes: direct mining for rents (affecting e.g. many slow-growing tropical forests); indirect conversion to other land uses (affecting e.g. many virtually unknown plants and insects); and/or the withholding of management of species exploitation (affecting e.g. many of the large land mammals – elephants and rhinos). Each form that conversion may take is an equally effective potential avenue to extinction.

Despite the multiplicity in the avenues to extinction, each is based in the same fundamental source: a societal-level determination of investment unworthiness (i.e. the conversion decision). If a society views a species as sufficiently investment-worthy, then stocks of that species will be maintained (through adequate levels of investment in it and its ancillary resources). If the species is not viewed as relatively investment-worthy, then it will suffer disinvestment (via one of the routes described above) and ultimately extinction. It is through the process of investment and disinvestment (in species and their ancillary resources) that conversion operates.

Therefore, this volume argues that the 'host state' must perceive diversity as investment-worthy, if its citizens are going to take actions to conserve it. Of course, this implies a fairly innocuous vision of the relationship between individuals, society and the state. Specifically, it assumes that the structure of the state is responsive to the needs of its individual citizens, and especially their joint interests. This implies that societal objectives will be inherent in state decision making and that interventions within the state's decision making framework will impact directly upon the ways in which individual decisions are taken in that society.

This set of limiting assumptions necessarily excludes many other potential sources of conflict and inefficiency in resource management; however, the object here is to demonstrate that, even should host states be responsive to the needs of their citizens, this would not imply the existence of resource management and investment policies that are first-best from the global perspective. Environmental problems are inherent in the division of the global environment into many separate states, as much so as they are inherent in the division of a society into many interdependent individuals. Then, the argument is that it is the role of the global community to intervene within the state's decision making framework in order to make diversity investment worthwhile.

This more fundamental approach to endangered species policy recognises that the proximate causes of species decline (poaching, unmanaged exploitation etc.) are equally the effects of the more fundamental causes of endangerment i.e. the failure to acquire a sufficient proportion of the value of the diverse resource to warrant the allocation of resources to the species. A biodiversity policy based on the arguments developed within this volume would imply the need for substantial reforms to the existing regulatory framework.

Specifically, it points to the need to create a 'global premium' that is to be conferred upon states investing in their diverse resources. This premium performs the function of rewarding investments in diverse resources for the non-appropriable services that they render. It also opens the door to the pursuit of these alternative pathways to development, so that states with diverse resources are able to see the advantages to development without the necessity of conversion.

Institution-Building for Biodiversity Conservation

The solution to the environmental problem of biodiversity losses is easily stated in the abstract; it is to compensate the supplier-states for the stock-related services that they render. The more difficult problem by far is the creation and implementation of the institution or institutions that will perform this task.

To a large extent, problem and solution are side-effects of a human world with many national governments. The impacts of state by state conversions are non-internalised on account of multinationality. The difficulties of reinternalising the costliness of these conversions are again a function of this global decentralisation. We now live in an era when the global costliness of a world with many governments is becoming apparent, even without the costliness of direct conflicts.

The international regulation of extinction requires the creation of an international institution for transferring the values of diversity from consumer-states to supplier-states. It is an attempt to provide a transnational mechanism to compensate for services that are known as 'public goods' in the national context. This institutional problem is at the core of the environmental problem of biological diversity.

Specifically, this volume argues that there is a global community of interest derived from the fact that decentralised (multinational) decision making regarding conversion will lead to local outcomes that diverge from global optima. The international regulation of extinction consists of investments by this global community in international institutions whose purpose it is to generate flows of benefits to host states in such a manner that state-level decision making results in local outcomes that more closely approximate the global optima.

Much of this volume addresses the particular characteristics such an institution must have in order to be effective. For example, an effective international institution must provide some manner of assurance of future benefits if it is to impact upon the investment decisions of host states. This is because investment decisions are decisions regarding assets and the anticipated flows regarding them; a state will only deviate from its perceived first-best investment path if the present value of the entire flow of future net benefits from such an alteration would appear to warrant it. Therefore, in order to have a permanent impact on decision making concerning the selection of development paths, it is necessary to make an impact on the perceived benefits from alternative pathways at all times.

This indicates that international institution-building should be directed to the permanent alteration of the terms of trade between specialised and diverse investments. At present the terms of trade are biased toward the specialised forms of resources on account of the relative rates of appropriability and rent capture. International institutions could create enhanced benefit flows to investments in diversity by one of three potential routes: enhanced rent capture (international certification and labelling); enhanced appropriability (international rights registration); or, direct subsidies to nonconversion (international land use planning). The first two regimes operate indirectly, by enhancing the returns to diversity-related investments. The last is direct intervention; it provides a stream of benefits in return for the act of non-conversion (also known as a 'transferable development right'). The latter half of this volume fleshes out the meaning of each of these regimes.

The argument here is that international institution-building must focus on the creation of *alternative pathways to development*, not the acquisition of a society's right to develop. The distinction is fine, but crucial. First, a focus on alternative pathways emphasises the importance of creating a constructive outlet for the fundamental human drive for advancement; purchasing rights to specific routes for advancement leaves this process undirected. Second, the particular pathway emphasised – *development from diversity* – implies an assumption about the specific nature of global environmental problems. The assumption is that these problems derive less from the general scale of all human activities than from the extreme scale of very specific human activities. Environmental systems are able to withstand higher levels of many diverse activities (drawing upon many different resources and systems) than lower levels of human activity concentrated on a single resource sector or system.

It is the uniformity of development as much as its scale that depletes environmental resources. Investing in diverse pathways for development is therefore synonymous with investment in a broad range of these resources and systems. In the past development has been uniform and hence the institutions (domestic and international) fostering development have been uniform. What is required is a diversity of institutions at the top of the system promoting alternative paths to development across the globe; otherwise the uniformity at the top will dictate the prevalence of uniformity throughout. In short, a diversity of international institutions is an absolute necessity if a diversity of social systems and hence natural systems are to prosper in this world.

Concluding the Biodiversity Convention

The Biodiversity Convention represents an excellent and unprecedented opportunity to accomplish the object of biodiversity conservation. It is a convention that has been concluded by virtue of the coalescence of a wide range of disparate interests, all concerned with the same general underlying problem: the increasing homogenisation of the world and the failure to invest in the diverse. Some of these groups expressed this concern by reference to the failure to compensate diverse cultures, others expressed it by reference to the failure to conserve diverse species or the absence of adequate protection for particular habitats or systems. In all of these cases the underlying concern is the same: the absence of any systemic approach to encouraging investment in the value of diversity.

There is no doubt that diversity in all its forms does generate a lot of value worthy of conservation and development. This is true on very standard measures, in terms of its contribution to the same standardised systems that continue to replace it, and also on broader measures and systems of value. A diversity of systems needs to be retained. However, diversity is an attribute necessarily measured relative to what other countries have done, and are doing, and so it cannot be managed properly in isolation. A global management system is an important element of what is required to manage the world's diversity. It will also be important to invest in national-level institutions and programmes which are effective for biodiversity conservation; however, an international institution will be necessary to provide the incentives and the investments required to establish these national-level programmes.

The Biodiversity Convention represents an opportunity that is ready to be seized. It has brought together this wide band of humanity concerned about the loss of diversity in the face of increasing and expanding productivity. It has listed the broad bands of an agreement and the main items on the agenda. All that remains is to fill in the blanks of this convention in a manner that will address these problems in a real and substantive fashion. Then the Biodiversity Convention will have been truly concluded.

2

THE FUNDAMENTAL CAUSES OF BIODIVERSITY'S DECLINE: A BIO-ECONOMIC MODEL

Human Depletion of Diversity: Past, Present, and Future

Biodiversity's decline derives primarily from human interaction with biological resources. Humans evolved a mere four million years ago (on life's timeline of four billion years or so). We existed as one component within the living system for most of the next four million years; however very recently (in the past ten millennia or so) we humans have placed ourselves outside of that system, and commenced the reshaping of the biological diversity that is arrayed 'beneath ourselves'. During this period, the extinction process has become a primarily human-sourced phenomenon.

Of course, extinction has always existed as a natural process as well. Studies of the fossil record show that the natural longevity of any species lies in the range of 1 to 10 million years. The threat to biological diversity arises when the rate of extinction of species far exceeds the rate of speciation. In these eras of 'mass extinctions' there is the potential for a threat to the entire global biology. In the distant past, so-called 'deep time', there have been a number of occasions of such mass extinctions. There are at least five occasions indicated in the fossil record during which over 50 per cent of the then-existing animal species were rendered extinct (Raup, 1988).

Even averaging in these periods of mass extinctions, the natural rate of extinction over deep time appears to have been in the neighbourhood of 9 per cent of existing species per million years, or approximately 0.000009 per cent per year (Raup, 1988). That is, the current stock of biological diversity is the result of several billion years of mostly low frequency mutation and extinction. Mass extinction has been an infrequent occurrence, usually the result of some exogenous phenomenon such as a collision with a comet.

Although extinction is an essential component of the evolutionary process, human-sourced extinctions have become a phenomenon far apart from the natural one. They are now more of the nature of an exogenous, cataclysmic event. Current estimates are that extinction rates are presently three or four orders of magnitude greater than the natural rate, and these estimates are wholly based upon the impacts of human activities (Wilson, 1988).

The coming of the human race has engendered widespread extinctions at the local as well as the global level. When humans first arrived in Australia 50,000 years ago, that continent lost nearly all of its large mammals, snakes, reptiles and large flightless birds at the same time.

Table 2.1 Recorded extinctions since 1600

	Islands				Continents			
	Birds	Mammals	Other	Total	Birds	Mammals	Other	Total
1600–1659	6	0	2	0	0	0	0	0
1660–1719	14	0	2	16	0	0	0	0
1720–1779	14	1	0	15	0	0	0	0
1780–1809	12	1	4	17	0	1	0	1
1810–1869	17	2	6	25	2	3	1	6
1870–1929	35	6	100	141	5	9	14	28
1930–	15	4	9	56	4	9	56	69
No Known Date	1	20	52	73	0	2	15	17

Source: World Conservation Monitoring Centre (1992, p 200)

When humans first migrated to the Americas, about 11,000 years ago, North America lost 73 per cent and South America 80 per cent of their large mammal species. With the European expansions of this millennium, the first mass extinctions of our era occurred on the oceanic islands. Seventy-five per cent of all modern era extinctions have occurred in island species (WCMC, 1992).

A written record of animal extinctions has been maintained since at least the year 1600. These records demonstrate the impact of human societies upon, first, the island species and now increasingly the continental species. These figures must be considered to be very inexact, merely indicators of the species of which we have a written record of their previous existence. The actual number of extinctions is much greater than is indicated by these figures, simply because the vast majority of species are not within the written record. Their extermination occurs without documentation.

The past few hundred years of taxonomists' efforts have resulted in the cataloguing of about 1.7 million species. For a few groups these figures are relatively precise, such as the number of bird species (9881) or mammals (about 4000), but for the vast majority of groups the total number of species is known to be much greater than the number catalogued. Most estimates indicate that there are between five and thirty million species on the Earth (Wilson, 1988, p.5). The vast majority of Earth's life forms live an undocumented existence.

The problem of species' mass extinctions, or the 'biodiversity problem', derives from the postulated impact of human activities upon these uncatalogued species. Given what is known about documented species' density and endemism, some of the world's leading biologists have attempted to infer species losses from a wider range of human activities. These exercises give estimates of current global extinction rates at the level of 5 to 10 per cent per decade. Projected into the middle of the next century, these activities may yield a mass extinction on the scale of any in the fossil record, i.e. there is the possibility of losing 25-50 per cent of all existing life forms.

Therefore, human impacts on biological diversity have been in evidence for at least 50,000 years but never of the breadth or variety of those which are currently being witnessed. In the distant past, human impacts on

Table 2.2 Estimated rates and projections of extinctions

Rate %	Projection %	Basis	Source
8	33-50	forest area loss	*Lovejoy (1980)*
5	50	forest area loss	*Ehrlich and Ehrlich (1981)*
-	33	forest area loss	*Simberloff (1986)*
9	25	forest area loss	*Raven (1988)*
5	15	forest area loss	*Reid and Miller (1989)*

Note: The rates are given as percentage losses of total number of global species per decade. The projections are based upon the extrapolation of this trend at then-current rates through to the total conversion of the examined forested area.

biodiversity were largely restricted to the megafauna: the large mammalian species most closely competing with the human species. This much was predictable as the human niche expanded across the globe. Humans were acting in the classic role of the exotic species: an invader of a previously secure niche held by another closely related species. In the present and near future, biodiversity losses are forecast to occur across the whole breadth of flora and fauna afflicting many species (plants, insects, etc.) for whom the human species is not an obvious competitor. This sort of broad-based destruction of biodiversity seems to be a relatively new, and distinct, phenomenon. Are humans bringing about biodiversity's current decline by reason of the launching of a new assault on all things natural rather than on our closest competitors? Do humans continue to mismanage all resources over which we gain control – as has been postulated in the case of the Clovis hunters of 11,000 years ago? In short, is there some sort of systematic explanation that applies to both the historical and the predicted losses of biodiversity, or do we simply have to interpret each instance of human-sourced extinction as a distinct example of human mismanagement?

The Natural Process of Extinction

Extinction is itself a natural process and the ultimate fate of every species (Futuyma, 1986; Cox and Moore, 1985). Studies of the fossil record show that the average longevity of a given species lies in the range of 1 to 10 million years (Raup, 1988). Over the four-and-a-half billion years of evolutionary history, the mosaic of life forms on earth has been completely overhauled many times over.

This process is necessary in order to preserve life on earth. The continuous and contemporaneous processes of speciation and extinction form the two necessary prongs of the evolutionary process. It is this constant reshaping of the biological diversity on Earth that allows life to continue in the context of a changing physical environment (Marshall, 1988).

Ecologists conceptualise life on Earth as a single body. 'Life' is the conduit through which the energy of the sun flows on this planet. It is constantly shifting and reshaping itself, via the evolutionary process, in order to better adapt to prevailing conditions. The various parts (life forms) come and go in order to maintain the integrity of the whole. Any given life form maintains its place within the system solely by virtue of its current capacity to capture some part of the flow of solar energy.

Some life forms are able to capture solar energy directly, simply by virtue of being allotted a 'place in the sun' on Earth. These are known as the plants, and the fundamental constraint that they face in their competition for existence is territorial. If a plant life form receives an allocation of land, then this is often the only base resource that it requires for survival.

Plants capture the energy of the sun through the process of photosynthesis, and in so doing generate the 'Net Primary Product' (NPP) i.e. the product generated from energy captured directly by life forms on Earth (Leith and Whittaker, 1975). It is estimated that the NPP on Earth is about 225 billion metric tons of organic matter per annum (Ehrlich, 1988). All non-plant life forms must be sustained from this base resource. It is the most fundamental constraint on all other life forms; in order to exist, all non-plant forms of life must receive an allocation of NPP.

This allocation process was a wholly natural one for billions of years. The competition between plant forms for land allocations and the competition between other life forms for NPP allocations lies at the core of the natural process of evolution. These competitions drove the process of evolution, and the evolutionary process gave us the particular set of allocations that human societies 'received' twenty thousand years ago.

Within the evolutionary process, the particular shapes that life takes derive from the relative advantages of these life forms in appropriating some part of the base resource. A species is the name given to a particular form that life takes for this purpose (Barton, 1988). Ecologists conceptualise energy flows to earth as diffusing over uneven gradients, e.g. uneven latitudes and uneven topographies. Given this uneven distribution, base resources will be similarly concentrated; that is, there will be various peaks and troughs across this gradient. A species is defined as the form of life that has established itself as the appropriator of the energy flow across one of these 'resource peaks', or niches. Therefore, the species and its niche are coincident concepts; a species is the particular form that life takes to fit a particular pattern of the energy throughput on Earth (the niche).

There is an in-built rate of turnover for each niche. First, niches are in a state of constant competition through the process of genetic recombination, mutation, and dispersion. At any point in time a new form of life may arise that is better adapted to the existing niche, i.e. there is a better fit to the distribution of the base resource. Then the existing life form may be supplanted.

There is another sense in which this process of adaptation must always remain a dynamic one. This is the result of a continuously changing physical environment. For example, the geography of the planet is dynamic. The tectonic plates of the continents have always moved at an average pace of approximately five to ten centimetres per year. These changes create gradual shifts in continental climates. In addition, the Earth's overall climate is in a perpetual state of change. The mean summer temperature in Europe has cycled about 12 times over a range of 10-15 degrees centigrade during the past million years (West, 1977). The Yugoslav physicist Milutin Milankovich hypothesised that this cycle resulted from the superimposition of three periodic cycles: a 100,000 year cycle resulting from the elliptical shape of the Earth's orbit; a 40,000 year cycle resulting from the Earth's tilt on its axis; and a 21,000 year cycle resulting from the Earth's wobble of the axis of rotation (Hays, Imbrie and Shackleton, 1976).

These in-built mechanisms for environmental variability have generated a system in which the shape and location of any given niche is dynamic. In essence, a niche may be thought of as a peak in the uneven distribution of the base resource, and a species as an outgrowth from the base resource. However, as the topography of the basic resource is not itself a static concept, the process of species definition must also be dynamic.

It is the static result of this dynamic process that can be seen in the distribution of species prevailing at any given point in time, and extinction is the term applied to the changes which occur between static states. The existence of genetic mutation maintains a pool of potential competitors omnipresent. With the shifting of the underlying base resource, these invaders may be provided with an opportunity at any time. If the invader is successful, and so genetically dissimilar as to not interbreed, then the previous occupant of the niche is superseded and its range is restricted. If this same result occurs across the entirety of its range, then the totality of its niche is appropriated, i.e. it becomes extinct.

The prevailing distribution of populations is a snapshot of this dynamic competition. For example, the family of *Magnoliaceae*, genus *Magnolia*, have at present an extremely disjoint distribution. About 80 species exist, with 26 of these in North (and northern South) America and the remainder in southeast Asia. However, the fossil record indicates that this family was extremely dispersed during the Mesozoic (100-200 million years ago), also including within their range all of Laurasia (Europe, Asia) through to Greenland (Dandy, 1981).

It appears that the magnolias have gradually succumbed to interspecific competition, i.e. the pressure of faster growing, better-adapted species capable of better exploiting their former niches. As the environment altered, these competitors appropriated the magnolias' niche throughout Europe leaving only the disjoint distribution that we currently see. If the process of displacement had continued, the magnolias may have lost the entirety of their niche.

This is the nature of the natural extinction process, as demonstrated by four billion years of evolutionary history. It is not so much a process resulting in the removal of a species, in the sense of niche abandonment, as a process of species resolution, in the sense of niche refinement. It is a natural process for life forms to change over time and over space. With changing environments, former inhabitants have lost their 'best-adapted status' to invaders and have been replaced. This is recognised as extinction if it occurs across the entire geographic range of the life form. However, in the natural process, it is more accurately conceptualised as necessary turnover deriving from the better adaptation of life to the current state of the niche.

Obviously, this description of the natural extinction process does not accord well with the prospect of losing half of all life forms in the coming one hundred years, i.e. the problem of biodiversity losses. Adaptation is more of a gradualist process in the aggregate sense, even though it represents millions of starts and stops for individual species. Species resolution is a process that occurs over periods of hundreds of millions of years.

This is not intended to imply that all mass extinctions must necessarily be human-induced; they result from any large-scale shock to the life system. There have been several occasions when the rate of extinction of species far exceeded the rate of speciation. There are at least five occasions indicated in the fossil record during which over 50 per cent of the then-existing animal species were rendered extinct (Raup, 1988). These mass extinctions have always been the result of a sudden and dramatic change in the physical nature of the system, e.g. hypothesised sunspots, asteroids, geothermal activity etc. The dramatic shift of the physical system places a stress on the life system for immediate adaptations. The result of this stress is the loss of many species without their immediate replacement. In essence, this manner of extinction occurs when the niche has been so severely dislocated by a physical event that the species find themselves without the capability to make a claim on the baseresource. The peaks in the base resource have shifted out from underneath them.

The current mass extinction is not being initiated by one of these exogenous physical phenomena creating a shock to the system. There is indeed a tremendous stress being placed upon the life system on Earth, but it is arising from within the system. This is unique in evolutionary history and it is not a part of the natural process of extinction. It is a part of the human societal choice process.

The Human-Induced Extinction Process

The natural process of extinction bears little resemblance to the processes occurring over the past few millennia. To a large extent, there is a discontinuity which exists in evolutionary history, arising sometime in the past ten to twenty thousand years. Since that time, there appears to be another layer to the extinction process. There is a record of an increasing number of extinctions, especially of the large land mammals, associated with human arrival or intensive settlement. The change appears to derive from a technological shift, regarding hunting and cultivation, that occurred sometime during the climatic upheavals of the late Pleistocene. From this point onwards, extinction has been more a process of human choice than a process of gradual adaptation.

There is no evidence of human-induced extinctions prior to the evolution of *Homo sapiens* and the introduction of this species to new continents about 50,000 years ago. Since that time, the coincidence of human migration with species extinctions has been marked. This occurred in Australia (about 50,000 years ago), in the Americas (about 11,000 years ago), in Madagascar (about 1500 years ago) in New Zealand (about 1200 years ago), and on numerous oceanic islands over the past thousand years (Diamond, 1984).

The causes of the more recent extinctions (i.e. over the past two thousand years) have been categorised under three human-induced causal factors: overexploitation; habitat destruction; and species introduction. (Diamond, 1989). However, for the purpose of human choice analysis, it is best to think of all extinctions as arising from one of two fundamental factors: mismanagement or management.

Both potential explanations of the human-induced extinction process are sourced in technological shifts. Extinctions resulting from management derive from technologies (or strategies) that allow one species (or group of species) to appropriate the niches of others. The essence of a management-based extinction is that it occurs by reason of the human species' appropriation of another species' niche.

Mismanagement-based extinctions result from a poor fit between human institutions and biological resources. This issue has been the subject of a significant economics literature, primarily in the area of fisheries economics. Recently this theory has also been applied to the mismanagement of terrestrial resources such as forests and wildlife (Repetto and Gillis, 1988). For example, overexploitation is often theorised to occur when new technology abruptly reduces the cost of harvesting the resource, if social institutions for managing resource access are unable to evolve rapidly enough to forestall the aggregate impact of the new technology. The inability to adapt in time might then result in the complete removal of a given prey species-a jointly irrational step that equates with human niche contraction.

As mentioned above, it is also possible to extinguish another species through the process of niche appropriation. This occurs under conditions of 'mutual competition', i.e. where two or more species share a common food supply or breeding ground. The principle of competitive exclusion states that, where two species depend on a common resource, niche expansion by one implies contraction by the other. It is possible for a mixed equilibrium to evolve under these conditions, but if the only basis for the relationship is competitive, then extinction is the likely outcome for one species or the other (Hardin, 1960).

Niche exclusion and appropriation by humans occurs mainly through indirect and surrogate competition. Of course, niche exclusion can occur directly through the appropriation of another species' resource base for own use (as with the displacement of many American songbirds with the introduction of the European starling). In the case of humans, however, our niche appropriation occurs more indirectly, through surrogates, by the introduction of one human-preferred species in the place of another (as with the displacement of the large African land mammals with selected crops and domesticated livestock).

Niche appropriation, as practised by humans, has consisted of the selection of a few prey species, and the expansion of *their* niches. The discovery of this strategy (domestication and cultivation) and its implementation constituted a very important part of the technological shift that occurred in the late Pleistocene.

Niche appropriation may be used as a strategy to advance either wealth or fitness. In many cases, humans have used the benefits from the expansion of their surrogates' niches for the purpose of their own niche expansion, but this has not always been the case. It is also possible to capture these gains in terms of the reduced allocation of labour to the production of subsistence (and increased allocations of the released labour to other wealth-generating activities) and thus to capture these gains in terms of wealth rather than fitness.

Therefore, there are two competing explanations hypothesised to be at the base of human-induced extinctions: the efficient use of technology for niche appropriation to advance the objects of wealth and fitness accumulation (management) or the inefficient management of technology with consequent degradation (mismanagement). It is clear that a technological shift occurred ten thousand years ago resulting in a new phase of human-induced extinctions; however, whether these extinctions are sourced in the effective or ineffective management of this technological change is more unclear. The remainder of this section examines the evidence.

There is no doubt that human mismanagement has resulted in the overexploitation and extinction of many oceanic species where there is little human competition for the species' niche. Many of the sea mammals (whales, seals, otters) have been hunted to the point of virtual extinction. Stellar's sea cow, a slow and easy target, was indeed hunted to complete extinction. These examples most definitely do provide some evidence for the mismanagement hypothesis. However, there is a very important difference between terrestrial and marine resources; the cost of institutional adaptations is much greater in the context of the latter because no single governance structure applies. In this context, it is predictable that human institutions would adapt slowly to technological changes, to the detriment of the resources.

For terrestrial species, on the other hand, the available evidence (primarily the archaeological record) cannot separate the two competing explanations. This is because both potential explanations, management and mismanagement, have the identical objective consequences. Since species and niche are one and the same, the removal of either has the same consequence, i.e. the extinction of the species. Whether humans are pursuing the species or the niche, the observable consequences are identical. In either case, the species will be depleted and its products may be used in the process; however, in one case the depletion is itself the human choice, in the other the depletion is a by-product of human niche expansion.

The oft-cited best evidence for human mismanagement of terrestrial resources is the coincidence between the introduction of the human species to the American landmass 11,000 years ago and the loss of many of its large mammals; approximately 73 per cent of North American and 80 per cent of South American land mammals disappeared at about the same time as the arrival of Clovis hunters. It has always been assumed that this coincidence implied mismanagement by reason of overhunting, especially as many of the large mammals' remains indicated that they were slaughtered by humans.

However, it was also at this time that substantial climate changes were occurring (Lewin, 1983). These climatic shifts generated a technological shift among human cultures. In particular, it was during such periods of climatic upheaval that the resource management practices known as modern agriculture were developed. The oldest known fossils of domesticated animals are dated to about 12,000 to 15,000 years ago. Widespread changes of diet have been documented for human populations between eight and ten thousand years ago (Davis, 1982; Diamond, 1989). Cultivated grains have been identified back to 6000 years ago (Wright, 1970). Cultivation and domestication at that time implied large scale land use changes, especially the widespread use of fire for clearing forests and brush to create agricultural and pasture lands.

It is apparent that a substantial number of human-sourced extinctions occurred throughout the northern hemisphere ten thousand years ago; e.g. much of the large mammalian fauna was depleted during this period. Despite much previous speculation, it is not possible for the archaeological record, by itself, to segregate between cause and effect in terms of these extinctions. Archaeological evidence cannot say whether these extinctions were the direct result of human mismanagement of the species, or a side-effect of human appropriation of its niche.

However, when the impact of that technological shift on the human species is considered, there is no longer any doubt as to its character. It was at this time (about ten thousand years ago) that the human species' population began to record unprecedented growth. The development of human technologies (cultivation and domestication) in the neolithic enormously expanded the human niche from the capacity to support perhaps ten million individuals to a capacity of hundreds of millions in a relatively short time period (Boulding, 1981). This population expansion commencing at this time is a clear indicator that the technological shift of the late Pleistocene was being capably managed and the benefits used for the expansion of the human niche, and the appropriation of many others.

The fact that this population level has been sustained over these ten millennia indicates that this technological shift has constituted a long-term appropriation of other species' niches. The continuing growth of the human population (expected to stabilise only sometime in the next century) is indicative of the diffusion of these ideas of niche appropriation across all of the human societies on Earth. In short, human population growth is the best indicator of niche appropriation and the history of the past ten thousand years indicates that this era has been one of massive niche appropriation by the human species.

In more recent times, when the historical record is more complete, the source of causation is less difficult to discern. Over the past few centuries, the introduction of alien species has become one of the most significant causal factors in species extinctions. For example, over the past four hundred years, there have been approximately 30 species of frog and lizard extinctions, 22 of which (73 per cent) have been attributed to the introduction of alien species (Honnegger, 1981). This is a pattern of extinction that is common across many species over much of the last few hundred years; the introduction of aliens is listed as the single highest proximate cause of documented extinctions. The relationship between human management, i.e. methods of production, and recent species extinctions is indicated by the fact that most documented plant and animal extinctions are related to the introduction of only seven alien species: goats, rabbits, pigs, cats, and three species of rat (Atkinson, 1989). It has been the human-chosen domesticated species that have been the source of the majority of modern documented extinction cases.

This effect may also be demonstrated by reference to the study of island habitats. Studies of extinctions on islands are particularly important because they represent a microcosm of the forces occurring globally. Just as most species will have nowhere else to go when human technology diffuses to the final corners of the earth, island species have few options when humans arrive and develop their habitats. The importance of a refuge from human development for species survival is indicated by the fact that fully 75 per cent of all documented extinctions have occurred in island habitats.

(WCMC, 1992).

There are two results from island studies that are of particular importance. First, from the fossil record it is apparent that the species diversity of birds on virtually all oceanic islands was reduced by 30 to 50 per cent within the initial period of human occupancy. Since about one-third of all bird species are endemic to islands, this represents a loss of about one-quarter of the world's bird species over the past few thousand years. (Olson, 1989). Therefore, the impact of humans over the past thousand years has already worked one mass extinction. This confirms the plausibility of large scale extinctions as the same forces diffuse as completely on a global basis.

Secondly, it is important to understand the nature of the base forces that have been working this mass extinction. How does the diffusion of human technology impact on a species when abruptly introduced, and how do they react within their threatened habitat? The best evidence shows that species become increasingly concentrated within the least-threatened final refuges.

> Previously it was thought that high islands had greater species diversity because of their montane rain forests. An important observation to emerge from recent studies, however, is that drier, more level lowland habitats, the ones most susceptible to burning and clearing for agriculture, had greater species diversity than steep areas of high, wet forests. On islands, most species that persist in wet montane forests today do so not because this is their preferred habitat, but because it is the only habitat left that has not been too severely modified by man (Olson, 1989).

The diffusion of the technological change associated with human societies might operate globally as it does on these islands. That is, as human technology diffuses to these island systems in the form of land conversions and species introductions, these alterations in turn result in the restriction of the ranges of resident species. If the base resources are all suitable to human appropriation, then the resident species may find themselves without a niche, i.e. extinct. If some part of the base is less suitable for human modification, e.g. the montane rain forests, then the island species become increasingly concentrated in these unaltered habitats, as 'refuges' (Lynch, 1988).

It is probably the case that this same process has been occurring on a global level, over a period of ten thousand years. The global distribution of species is now as much the result of human as natural processes. Human modification of the environment has restricted the range of many species, forcing the majority into a small number of refugia.

The nature of the fundamental force working during this period is clear, i.e. the transfer of niches to human-selected species in order to expand the claim of the human species on the base resource. Beliefs that mismanagement or human population growth cause extinctions confuse cause with effect. The population of a species is only a measure of its niche; the expansion of the human population from ten million to ten billion is the clearest possible evidence of human niche appropriation. Similarly, overexploitation is often an effect of human niche appropriation; the mining of a species whose niche is gone. Both of these phenomena occur as a consequence of niche appropriation.

Over the past ten thousand years, the course of evolutionary history has taken an abrupt turn. Extinction is no longer a force for better adaptation of all life forms, it is a result of human choices. The choice derives from the technological ability of humans to now appropriate wide ranges of other species' niches. This is the evolutionary nature of cultivation and domestication. Humans discovered how to choose particular prey species on which to build the human niche. Once this was accomplished, the route to human advancement (human niche expansion) was the expansion of the range of the selected species. It is human cooperation with these species, for the expansion of their ranges, that has resulted in the restriction and extinction of so many others.

In essence, within the natural evolutionary process, the allocation of a portion of base resource (land or NPP) was determined in a natural competition between various life forms. In the past ten thousand years, this allocation decision has been usurped by the human species. Recognising that it was possible to select a species to which to allocate the base resource, and then use that species, the human species had realised a new form of niche appropriation. From that point on, the competition for base resource allocations was a social process.

The Nature of the Current Threat to Biological Diversity: Base Resource Appropriation

The early, human-induced extinctions have often been of those species which are most closely competing with humans, e.g. the large land mammals. The ranges of many of these species are usually restricted by the introduction of humans, and extinction sometimes results. Large land mammals are the most threatened initially, precisely because they compete most closely with humans in terms of range and resource requirements. The next set of extinctions occurred when other species, with less demanding requirements, have had their ranges vastly circumscribed, or even shifted. As on the oceanic islands, many species have taken refuge in some of the last remaining unaltered habitats, others have disappeared entirely. The third phase of the extinction process, i.e. the 'biodiversity problem', is the result of the workings of the human niche appropriation process toward these refugia. As this technological change diffuses to the final corners of the Earth, there must necessarily be an increasing rate of extinction.

There is an empirically derived relationship, used by biogeographers, which relates the area of the available unmodified habitat to the number of species which it contains (Williamson, 1988). Studies of 'islands' of natural habitat, whether situated in oceans or civilisation, indicate that the number of species doubles with a tenfold increase in the area of the island. Conversely, a reduction in the size of the natural habitat by 90 per cent is likely to result in a halving of the number of species which it will contain. (MacArthur and Wilson, 1967).

Again, the study of islands is instructive for looking at the global impact of conversions. This biogeographic relationship describes a geometric relationship between conversions and extinctions. That is, the rate of species loss is geometrically increasing with the actual amount of the total base resource appropriated by the human species. As the technology for conversions reaches the final refugia, there will be much greater losses of species per square hectare converted than occurred with the first, earlier conversions. This is what has been occurring on the global level, paralleling the island extinctions from which this relationship was derived.

Land use alterations have been working across the globe for the past few millennia. Humans have been modifying lands for ten thousand years; however, the pace and diffusion of these alterations have been quickening in the past few hundred years. Estimates of aggregate natural habitat losses over the past two centuries range from 25 to 50 per cent (Myers, 1979; IIED, 1989). Since the commencement of the documentation of land-use changes (in the past thirty years), the pattern of current land conversions is clear. Two hundred million hectares of forest and 11 million hectares of grasslands were converted to specialised agriculture between 1960 and 1980 alone, all of it in the developing countries (Holdgate et al., 1982, Table 4.1).

Table 2.3 Rates of conversion of natural habitat to agriculture

Developing	1960 (Million)	1980 (Million)	Per cent Change
Sub-S. Africa	161	222	37.8
Latin America	104	142	36.5
South Asia	153	210	37.2
S.E. Asia	40	55	37.5
Developed			
North America	205	203	0.1
Europe	151	137	-10.0
U.S.S.R	225	233	2.0

Source: Repetto and Gillis, 1988

In the developed countries of Europe and the US, there is virtually no human niche appropriation still taking place. This is because the process of conversion has been completed. The proportion of Europe which is unmodified habitat (of at least 4000 sq km in area) is now certifiably zero. In the US, a mere 500 years after the introduction of the first Europeans, the proportion of natural habitat of this dimension is down to 5 per cent. (World Resources Institute, 1990). The conversion process has worked its way through most of the northern hemisphere, and it is now proceeding in the same manner across the south. At the frontier of this technological diffusion, the rate of conversions remains high.

Table 2.4 Recent rates of conversion to specialised agriculture (ten year rate – to 1987)

Conversions to Cropland %		Conversions to Pastureland %	
1. Paraguay	71.2	1. Ecuador	61.5
2. Niger	32.0	2. Costa Rica	34.1
3. Mongolia	31.9	3. Thailand	32.1
4. Brazil	22.7	4. Philippines	26.2
5. Ivory Coast	22.4	5. Paraguay	26.0
6. Uganda	21.4	6. Vietnam	14.0
7. Guyana	21.3	7. Nicaragua	11.8
8. Burkina Faso	19.4		
9. Rwanda	18.6		
10.Thailand	17.1		

Source: World Resources Institute and International Institute for Environment and Development (1990)

As the theory of island biogeography, and the studies cited regarding oceanic islands, would predict, this steady contraction of the available unaltered habitat has had the effect of concentrating the remaining species in the remaining unconverted habitat. It has been estimated that about half of the world's species are now contained in the remaining tropical forests. This is in part the result of the workings of four billion years of the natural process of extinction, but it is also the result of the impact of ten thousand years of human-induced extinctions.

Much of the world's remaining diverse life forms exist in one of these last remaining patches of substantially unaltered habitat. The so-called 'megadiversity states', as identified by the World Wide Fund for Nature, are: Mexico, Columbia, Brazil, Zaire, Madagascar and Indonesia; for example, four of these states alone contain approximately 75 per cent of all primate species. In sum, it is estimated that 50 to 80 per cent of the world's biological diversity is to be found in 6 to 12 tropical countries, including those mentioned above (Mittermeier, 1988).

All of the projections of mass extinctions are based on extrapolations of human land conversion trends into the final refugia of species diversity, i.e. the tropical rainforests. A fairly conservative estimate would seem to be that the diffusion of these technologies into these final refugia is causing current rates of extinction to be about 1000 to 10,000 times the historical rate of extinction (Wilson, 1988). A range of estimates by some of the world's leading scientists projects a possible species loss of between 20 and 50 per cent of the world's total over the next century.

There is no ambiguity with regard to the source of these projected mass extinctions. The basis for these estimates is invariably the rates of conversion of the tropical forest habitats upon which many of the world's species now depend. The problem of biodiversity, as defined by the world's leading natural scientists, is precisely the problem of the continuing diffusion of human technology to the last refugia on Earth. Humans continue to modify the environment in order to replace the pre-existing life forms with those which they have selected. It is this process that commenced ten thousand years ago, and it is its completion that threatens a final human-induced mass extinction. The first acts of niche appropriation had grave effects on those species with wide range requirements (the large mammalian species in particular); other species, however, merely had their ranges reduced or relocated. Each successive act of appropriation has a greater cost in terms of niche appropriation, and thus increasingly grave impacts on individual species. However, the current problem of biodiversity, as a human-induced mass extinction, is one of the appropriation of the last refuges of the unchosen species. As the diffusion of technology converges upon these sites, the number of species on earth will similarly converge upon the number selected for use by the human species. Humans are now displacing vast numbers of species through indirect competition: the redirection of those basic resources such as land which the species requires for its survival. It is this undercutting of species –their removal from their basic resources – that is the primary cause of endangerment for most of the world's biological diversity.

Exceptions to the Rule? Obvious Mismanagement and the Case of the African Elephant

Of course, not all species are disappearing in a quiet and unnoticed fashion; some are going out with a bang. These are the species for which the primary cause of decline is not undercutting but overexploitation. The African elephant is a case in point.

During the decade of the 1980s it is generally agreed that the population of the African elephant declined by about half, from 1,343,340 in 1979 to

609,000 in 1989 (Douglas-Hamilton, 1989). In addition, the trade in ivory, the principal product derived from this species, also doubled between the early 1970s and the early 1980s – from an average of about 550 tonnes to an average of about 1000 tonnes (Barbier et al., 1990). On account of these trends, population modellers predicted the imminent extinction of the species, over a period of about twenty years (Renewable Resources Assessment Group, 1989).

At first glance, the recent decline of the African elephant appears to be a good example of the working of human mismanagement and greed. There is no doubt that the proximate cause of most elephant deaths during this decade was a high-powered weapon, nor that the motivation for the slaughter was the procurement of ivory. During the decade the trade in ivory reached a peak of over 1000 tonnes per annum, after averaging nearer 600 tonnes in the previous decade (ITRG, 1989).

It is also clear that the incentives for overexploitation were in place over this period. During the 1980s the price of elephant ivory soared, reaching prices of more than US$140/kg in Japan, while the cost of harvesting (indicated by the prices paid to poachers) was more in the order of US$5–10/kg (Swanson, 1989a). This meant that the net revenues available from the killing of an elephant and the sale of its tusks created an enormous incentive for the exploitation of the species, despite the fact that shooting elephants was illegal in almost every African state at that time.

Table 2.5 Estimates of African elephant populations

	1979	1989
Cameroon	16,200	22,000
CAR	63,000	23,000
Chad	15,000	2,100
Congo	10,800	42,000
Guinea	1,300	500
Gabon	13,400	74,000
Zaire	377,000	112,000
Central	**496,700**	**275,600**
Ethiopia	900	8,000
Kenya	65,000	16,000
Rwanda	150	50
Somalia	24,300	2,000
Sudan	134,000	22,000
Tanzania	316,300	61,000
Uganda	6,000	1,600
Eastern	**546,650**	**110,650**

	1979	1989
Angola	12,400	18,000
Botswana	20,000	68,000
Malawi	4,500	2,800
Mozambique	54,800	17,000
Namibia	2,700	5,700
South Africa	7,800	7,800
Zambia	150,000	32,000
Zimbabwe	30,000	52,000
Southern	**282,200**	**203,300**
Benin	900	2,100
Burkina Faso	1,700	4,500
Ghana	3,500	2,800
Guinea Bisseau	NA	40
Guinea	300	560
Ivory Coast	4,000	3,600
Liberia	900	1,300
Mali	1,000	840
Mauritania	160	100
Niger	1,500	440
Nigeria	2,300	1,300
Senegal	450	140
Sierra Leone	300	380
Togo	80	380
Western	**17,090**	**18,480**
Totals	**1,342,640**	**608,030**

Source: ITRG (1989)

Could the elephant withstand the impact of these incentives for overexploitation? One factor that determines the resilience of a species in the face of heavy rates of exploitation is its capacity for growth. This is one reason why the world's fisheries continue in existence despite persistent overexploitation; fish generally have the ability to reproduce at phenomenal rates so long as an adequate stock is retained for this purpose. The elephant could not be more different. Its growth rate is relatively slow (RRAG, 1989). It has a life span of 60 years and reaches fecundity at the age of around 13 with 5-year inter-birth intervals thereafter. Studies indicate that a maximum population growth rate of 6 per cent in a well-balanced elephant population is about all that is feasible.

The congruence of these characteristics spells trouble for species such as the elephant. The high price/cost ratio of harvesting combined with the low growth rate of the species makes endangerment the likely economic outcome. In essence, the downward spiral in elephant populations during the 1970s could be explained as the result of an unfortunate coincidence in income and technology shifts. On the one hand the widespread availability of high-powered weaponry across sub-Saharan Africa occurred for the first time as the result of post-independence availability, causing the cost of harvesting to fall precipitously. On the other hand, at the same time, Asian countries such as Japan began to achieve levels of income never seen before and this translated into high prices being paid for ivory. Since ivory has long been available throughout Asia due to the proximity of the Asian elephant (but only in the limited quantities produced by that species), ivory has long been a sign of wealth and status in Japan and other oriental countries. For example, many Asian communities are willing to pay a very high price for high quality ivory for traditional uses in the construction of musical instruments and hand seals.

The African elephant appears to be a good example of a species endangered through overexploitation rather than undercutting. There is no doubt that the elephants were being killed for their ivory, nor that a very high price was being paid for the ivory procured in this manner. In this case it seems at first glance that it is an unfortunate coincidence (Japanese income advances together with African weapon availability) that is causing the endangerment of this important species.

It is important nevertheless to place this species' decline within the context of the broader forces operating across its range. Although the immediate cause of death of each elephant was some hunter's pursuit of its ivory, the more fundamental causes concern the reasons why these hunters were allowed unmanaged access to the elephant herds, and why the ivory being harvested was not being managed better for the benefit of the elephants' 'owners'.

This framework provides an alternative explanation for the decline of the Afican elephant. In short, the African elephant makes little economic sense as a biological asset for investment purposes. Each elephant requires about 0.5 sq km of good grazing land for its sustenance (Caughley and Goddard, 1975). Average life expectancy is about 55 years (Hanks, 1972). Therefore, it represents a substantial commitment of resources to provide for a single elephant's livelihood.

The resources required for the sustenance of the millions of these creatures that recently roamed Africa would represent a substantial portion of that continent's land area. In addition, few elephants are stationary within an area of a few hectares; they travel widely in search of food, and crops are at particular risk. For these reasons there are substantial negative externalities experienced by those living in the rural areas of a country that has a significant elephant population. Also, the management of access to the population would not be as inexpensive as with a more sedentary animal.

Combined with its slow growth rate and the perceived absence of significant international markets for its products, the pressures for the removal of a substantial portion of the African elephant population from the lands of Africa must be intense. The species will very likely be replaced by a more specialised species such as cattle or goats or even grain.

In short, elephants do not demonstrate the sorts of characteristics that make an asset worthy of the substantial investments (of natural and governmental resources) that this species requires for its sustenance. This is the fundamental force underlying its decline. The absence of incentives for investment made the species a candidate for non-management.

It is the case that the prevailing management regime in most African range states has been *defacto* 'open access'. Open access, in the context of terrestrial resources, is largely a function of the efforts and expenditures of

Table 2.6 Park management spending by selected African states (spending levels $/sq km)

Botswana	1984	10
Burkina Faso	1986	132
Cameroon	1986	5
CAR	1984	8
CAR	1986	5
Ethiopia	1984	57
Ghana	1984	237
Kenya	1984	188
Malawi	1984	445
Malawi	1986	49
Mozambique	1984	19
Mozambique	1986	7
Niger	1984	45
Somalia	1984	50
South Africa	1986	4350
Sudan	1986	12
Tanzania	1984	20
Tanzania	1986	18
Uganda	1984	357
Zaire	1986	2
Zambia	1984	11
Zimbabwe	1984	277
Zimbabwe	1986	194

Sources: 'Funding and Financial Control', in Bell and McShane-Caluzi (1984); Cumming, DuToit and Stuart (1990)

the putative owners. That is, open access occurs when the *de jure* owners fail to allocate sufficient resources to create barriers to accessing the species or its habitat. In the case of the African elephant, the *de jure* owners are the governments of the African range states, who without exception claim exclusive title to the elephant as 'wildlife'. However, governmental spending on park and habitat protection has been insufficient to regulate access in all but a couple of states, resulting in *de facto* open access regimes.

This fact has been demonstrated empirically. Poaching pressure and species decline has been shown to be closely related to the governmental spending levels on park protection. In the case of the heavily poached rhinoceros populations of sub-Saharan Africa, spending on management was shown to be inversely related to the decline of the species' population in those localities (Leader-Williams and Albon, 1988). The equation fitted by these authors indicated a zero population change level at spending of about US$215 per square kilometre. The information that is available indicates that the spending on park monitoring is in fact much lower than this in most African states.

Open access regimes are better thought of as implicit determinations to not invest in the particular resources, with the object of converting to others that are perceived to be more productive. That is, it is likely to be the decision to deplete a natural resource that generates the open access regime, not the other way around. Obviously, in the 1980s, few of the range states perceived the elephant as an asset worthy of the investments necessary to maintain existing stock levels.

Unofficial open access policies have been a good method for mining the vast numbers of surplus elephants, from the perspective of an aid-sensitised African government. The criminalisation of the offtake of ivory preserves international appearances, while the absence of resources applied to elephant protection allows the mining to continue apace. There is, in addition, the side benefit of the revenues derived from sales of seized ivory. Virtually the entirety of the trade in ivory during the past decade (ranging between 500 and 1000 tonnes per annum) has derived from poached ivory sales that were 'licensed' after seizure. This arms-length approach to the industry preserves appearances while fostering the removal of the species from the land.

In short, the elephant's decline has been largely the result of an implicit decision to undertake mining on the part of some of the range states. For example, in the 1980s, four countries alone – Tanzania, Zambia, Zaire and Sudan – are estimated to have lost 750,000 elephants between them, equal to the overall continental losses (ITRG, 1989). Table 2.6 indicates that these states spent US$18, US$11, US$2, and US$12 per square kilometre, respectively, on park monitoring in the year surveyed. The decline of the African elephant during the 1980s, and the ivory trade it spawned, was a direct result of these official non-investment decisions.

Other African states, on the other hand, chose to invest in their elephant populations, and with quite different results. In fact, populations increased by almost 100 per cent in one southern African state that invested heavily in its elephants – Zimbabwe. The relationship is not exact, but it is apparent that most instances of elephant population declines were predetermined by government refusals to investment meaningfully in the species.

This approach of 'arms-length removal' is commonly practised throughout the developing world. Throughout most of Latin America, for example, it is declared illegal to trade in all wildlife products, and yet large-scale trade (in tropical birds and crocodilians etc.) flows from the continent (Swanson, 1991b). This is part of a broader range of government incentives put in place to encourage the removal of the diverse in order to encourage development. 'Homesteading' regimes are of this nature; under these regimes, property rights are only substituted for open access regimes on the condition that the land is cleared and used for specialised agriculture. In each case the government is encouraging the removal of the diverse by the implicit subsidisation of its conversion by virtue of a misconceived belief that diverse resources stand in the way of development. Sometimes these subsidies are received in the form of direct subsidies to converted agriculture, as in the case of cattle ranching tax regimes in the Amazon (Repetto and Gillis, 1988). Other times these subsidies are received in the form of enabled overexploitation, as in the case of unmanaged elephant populations in sub-Saharan Africa (Swanson, 1994).

In summary, even in the case of a species such as the elephant that is apparently well-suited to the overexploitation framework for extinction, the underlying rationale is actually one of underinvestment. This has resulted in the mining of the species from arms' length over the past decade. All species do not live 'by bread alone'; other resources are required. Sometimes these other resources are as simple as an adequate breeding stock, as in the case of the world's fisheries. Other times the resources required to sustain a particular species are more complex, as in the case of the African elephant. In these instances it may be necessary to invest not only in land for the species, but also in an entire socio-economic system. The people who live with a species are the ones who determine its level of endangerment in the final analysis, and they must see the species as a living asset to their community if they are to allow its continued existence. This is what proper wildlife management implies: the creation of a system that allows wildlife to coexist within its community. As with an allocation of land, this also implies the assignment of some of that society's scarce resources to the task of management for the continued existence of the species. As in the case of the decline of the African elephant in the 1980s, in most cases of overexploitation it is the withholding of these management resources which is the fundamental cause of the decline of those species which are in use.

Three Causes, One Source

There are three alternative routes to human-caused extinction for terrestrial species. Each of these routes to extinction inheres in the failure of human societies to supply the threatened species with an adequate allocation of necessary resources. Since there are many different resources upon which any given species may rely for its existence, there are many different forms of withholdings which may endanger this species. However, for purposes of simplicity, these different requirements will be categorised into three logically distinct areas. These three routes to extinction are base resource conversion, management resources diversion and stock disinvestment.

Base Resource Conversion
These are resources that are endangered by reason of the loss of a place in the sun, i.e. a parcel of suitable land for their use. These tend to be species of little or no known individual value to humans. These biological resources are not overexploited but undercut. They are lost because humans find alternative uses for the lands on which they rely.

An example of this process is the depletion of many types of virtually unknown life forms (e.g. plants and insects) when land is deforested and converted to other forms of use such as cattle ranching. This branch of the force for extinction is generally termed the 'biodiversity problem'.

Management Resources Diversion
These are resources that are endangered by reason of the absence of adequate management policies for their support. They tend to be species perceived to be of medium value but relatively low growth. Since they are slow growing resources, they are not obviously important assets; society has no incentive to invest in their growth capacity. In addition, on account of their relatively low value, they do not justify a commitment of substantial amounts of national resources for the management of the exploitation process. Then, the nation will allow these resources to be depleted through unmanaged exploitation.

Examples of this process include the depletion of many of the large land mammals, such as the African elephant case study discussed above. Recall that during the decade of the 1980s, sub-Saharan Africa lost half of its elephant population (from 1.3 to 0.6 million). However, on closer inspection of the national population statistics, it appears that four countries alone (Sudan, Central African Republic, Tanzania and Zambia) lost 600,000 elephants between them. It is also clear how these elephants were lost.

41

These four countries fell at the bottom of the tables of African park and protection spending (averaging about US$15 per square kilometre). The decline of the African elephant in the 1980s was the result of these tacit open access regimes.

Stock Disinvestment

These are species that are endangered through the simplest reason of all, i.e. the failure to provide an adequate stock of the species from which it might regenerate itself. This problem was originally pointed out in relation to the great whales. These tend to be species with high price/cost ratios but low growth. In that case, there are incentives to harvest the entirety of the resource (for its high value) and invest the funds in other assets (for their greater growth rates) (Clark, 1973a, 1973b).

An example of this force in action is the deforestation of the tropical hardwood forests in those countries which capture a large share of the forest's value. These trees represent substantial amounts of standing value, but they have very low growth potential. It is economically rational to 'cash in' the hardwoods and invest the returns in other, more productive, assets such as education perhaps or housing. That is, sustainable management of every resource is not always the most economically viable option; it may pay to move some of a society's assets between accounts if some assets pay a substantially greater return than do others.

Although there are these three alternative routes to extinction, they are all consequential forces, not fundamental. Each of these forces is the consequence of the more fundamental determination that the biological asset is unworthy of investment. It is the particular form in which this decision regarding non-investment first impacts a given resource that determines the applicable route to extinction. However, always at the base is the decision that this particular biological resource is unworthy of human investments, and hence that essential resources will be withdrawn.

Conclusion: The Cause of Biodiversity's Decline

It is possible to source biodiversity's decline in a single, very broadly stated problem: the failure to appreciate and to appropriate the values of biological diversity. Although many different forms of life are endangered in the current phase of decline, and many different causes are at work, the problem at base remains the same. Peoples across the globe now perceive development to be a fairly uniform process building upon a standard set of biological resources. Governments now encourage development largely by providing incentives to cause the citizenry to convert their world into one patterned upon that already existing in other, developed, countries. They do this explicitly through the provision of subsidies to standard developed industries (standard agriculture and manufacturing) and they do it implicitly through the withholding of resources to the traditional and non-industrial sectors. It is this relative starvation of resources to the diverse sectors of potentially diverse economies that is working the current biodiversity endangerment. Whether the resource concerned is a noticeable one (such as the African elephant) or an overlooked one (such as the millions of plants and insects in danger in the tropical forest), the problem remains that developing countries do not see these to be resources on which to build a developed economy. It is this perception of 'investment unworthiness' that is the ultimate cause of biodiversity's decline, and this perception is sourced in the belief that national development policies must take a very particular shape and path.

3

BIODIVERSITY CONSERVATION AND GLOBAL DEVELOPMENT: IS IT POSSIBLE TO RECONCILE THE TWO?

The Interrelationship between Biodiversity Policy and Development Policy

The regulation of global biodiversity is going to require a substantial level of intervention in the development process undertaken by individual states. This much cannot be avoided. As was described in the previous chapter, this is an example of one environmental problem that cannot be solved through uncontrolled development, as this is precisely its source. Many other environmental problems do generate their own solutions with adequate national growth and development; for example, sanitary water and adequate air quality tend to be in disproportionately greater demand as living standards increase, and hence adequate income growth often affords the prospect of retrieving previously degraded air and water quality. For this reason, the most cost-effective prescription for many environmental problems brought on by industrialisation and development in many of the poor countries may often be simply 'to grow out of them' (Beckerman, 1995).

This is not the case in the context of the environmental problem of biodiversity for two reasons. First, in biodiversity we have an example of a resource which is generally discriminated against within the process of development, simply because development is usually practised in a very uniform fashion, e.g. the clearing of land and the establishment of agriculture. As will be discussed in further detail below, development is often seen to be synonymous with the conversion of diverse natural resources to a common roster of uniform national resources: cattle ranching, specialised agriculture and the many other forms of activities that are common across most of the world. Therefore, the standard practice of development uniformly discriminates against diversity.

The other reason that it is impossible to allow time and development to work a solution to the biodiversity problem is that it is unlikely that there will be any resources remaining at the point in time at which they are adequately demanded. The problem here is one of foreseeable demands in combination with irreversible supplies. As development proceeds it is likely that the demand for diversity will increase (as it does for other environmental resources), but it is the conversion of biodiversity that often lies at the base of the development process as it is currently practised. Since existing biological diversity is a non-retrievable resource ('only God or 4.5 billion years can create a tree'), the engine of development is often consuming the very resources for which it will generate demand in the near future.

The regulation of biodiversity requires the regulation of the development process as it is practised. In particular it will be necessary to create global incentive schemes that will induce individual developing countries to pursue development in a manner very different from those states before them. It is a very risky strategy to commit to a unique path of development, different from that undertaken by those who have gone before you, and it is unlikely that any given nation would do so in any substantial manner in the absence of sizeable international inducements, and this will require the establishment of international institutions for that purpose. The problem in the past has been that international institutions themselves have developed in the wake of the first countries' development, usually responsive to and supportive of the choices which they have made. If a diversity of development paths is to be pursued, based upon a diversity of resources, then it will be necessary for a diversity of international institutions to exist in order to support these alternatives. It is the object of this chapter and the next to demonstrate generally how the Biodiversity Convention should be conceived in order to fulfil this role.

The Development Process and the Biosphere

Conversion of natural environments has long been part and parcel of the development process. Societies which we know as developed are those which have previously built their economies upon a productive set of assets; societies which we know as developing are those which are still in the process of assembling their asset base. Hence economic development in human societies derives in part from the substitution of more productive assets for the less productive. When this process of substitution is applied to natural resources it is usually known as the conversion process, as in the case of the conversion of forests into ranchlands.

Natural resources may be conceived of as simply *natural assets*: assets whose initial form was determined by nature rather than society (Solow,

1974a). The natural form of any asset is necessarily competitive with other forms in which humans might hold these same assets. Humans can, for example, remove forests for factories or fields. If development is defined as the process by which a given set of assets is selected by society, then development must necessarily imply the decline of natural asset balances, simply because nature initially selected 100 per cent of the assets on which society depended. As humans become more actively engaged in the selection of the form that assets will take, this necessarily implies that the proportion of naturally chosen asset forms must fall.

Conversion in the process of development lies at the root of the endangerment of most biological resources. For example, the decline of many traditional plant and animal varieties occurs when the lands on which they are grown are converted to a specialised modern variety. The loss of many other diverse resources also has its source in the development process, albeit less directly. For example, a tropical forest replete with many diverse resources may be lost on account of logging activities. In this case the natural asset (the forest) is being converted in a less direct fashion through the liquidation of the standing resources. That is, the natural resource is converted to another asset form indirectly through sale with the proceeds then potentially invested in other forms of assets (such as education), resulting in the conversion of the natural asset (to another asset such as 'human capital').

Development is a process which has long been antithetical to biodiversity conservation. This is because it has been based upon the idea of conversion of assets to preferred forms – from forests to factories, from heathlands to health services, from wetlands to water sports. In the past, the natural form of the asset was not seen as providing any special recommendation for its retention; if a market-preferred alternative was available, it was pursued. More recently, local and national land-use planning legislation in the developed countries has allowed for a broader set of values, other than those which are simply market-based, to be taken into consideration in regard to local resources.

These institutions have come far too late for many of the diverse resources that existed in the developed world, and the institutions still do not exist in many of the countries in which they would have the greatest impact on biodiversity. One of the basic objectives of the Biodiversity Convention should be seen to be the development of the necessary institutions for the incorporation of the values of biodiversity within the land use decision making processes of those nations which still host vast amounts of the resource. That is, one fundamental object is to develop institutions that generate incentives for land use management in countries where development has not yet itself generated that institution (since these are many of the same countries which have not yet depleted their biodiversity through development).

The Impact of Development at the Global Level

Economic development is of course a constructive force in nearly every context in which it occurs. Development has been seen to provide not only the basic needs of many societies, but it is now also seen to provide many of the other requirements, such as environmental services, health services and even individual rights (Dasgupta and Weale, 1992). However, the diffusion of the development process on a global basis is also one of the primary forces contributing to diversity losses. The initial, local conversions of natural resources had little impact on the global portfolio of assets, but the aggregation of thousands and millions of these discrete conversions has generated a phenomenon of worldwide importance.

   In effect, the global conversion process may be conceived of as the diffusion of the idea of asset conversion across the globe, from country to country. Some countries commenced the conversion of their habitats thousands of years ago; for example, the forests of Britain were largely removed during the course of the Iron Age. Other countries still retain the vast forests that have been there since time immemorial. The global biodiversity problem comes to our attention at this point in time because these processes of conversion are now working their way towards the last refugia on Earth. The majority of the world's remain species reside in a small number of the world's states. These are the same states that have been the last to have substantial parts of their territories remaining unconverted.

Table 3.1 Countries with greatest species richness

Mammals		Birds		Reptiles	
Indonesia	515	Colombia	1721	Mexico	717
Mexico	449	Peru	1701	Australia	686
Brazil	428	Brazil	1622	Indonesia	600
Zaire	409	Indonesia	1519	India	383
China	394	Ecuador	1447	Colombia	383
Peru	361	Venezuela	1275	Ecuador	345
Colombia	359	Bolivia	1250	Peru	297
India	350	India	1200	Malaysia	294
Uganda	311	Malaysia	1200	Thailand	282
Tanzania	310	China	1195	Papua New Guinea	282

Source: McNeely et al. (1990)

47

Asset conversion that has occurred for millennia on a local and regional scale has now aggregated to become a force at the global level. At base, this restructuring of the global portfolio of biological assets is driven by the desire for human development gains obtained from the conversion of assets to more productive forms. However, as this basic strategy for human development reaches the final refugia of many of the world's species, it is projected that a cataclysmic 'mass extinction' of species may result (Ehrlich and Ehrlich, 1981; Lovejoy, 1980). Development practices which had little negative impact when practised on a small and local basis have now aggregated to bring about massive changes on a global basis.

Therefore, at the very base of the biodiversity problem is the capability of humans to change the nature of the biosphere from its natural to a human-preferred form. The gains from conversion have been causing the restructuring of the biosphere on a regional basis for several millennia. Now, with the diffusion of this strategy to the final terrestrial frontiers, conversion of the biosphere seems set to occur on a global basis.

The Nature of the Global Conversion Process

Reconstruction of the portfolio of biological assets on a global basis is a powerful force, capable of reshaping the whole of the Earth's biosphere. However, it is not in itself sufficient to explain the potential for a mass extinction. For this, an explanation must be found that will generate not only an expected reshaping of the global portfolio of natural assets, but also a narrowing of that portfolio.

Conversion as an economic force explains only why it is the case that the natural slate of biological resources might be replaced by another on any given parcel of land, depending upon relative productivities. It does not explain why a small number of species would replace millions across the whole of the Earth. That is, this force implies conversion but not necessarily homogenisation. In order to explain the global losses of biodiversity, i.e. *a narrowing of the global portfolio*, it is necessary to identify the nature of the force that would generate this homogenisation of the global biosphere.

It is unlikely that a wholly natural process would drive the world toward less diversity. This would require the evolution of both biological generalists (species with superior productivity across many niches) and uniform human tastes (across the globe). In fact, the current drive toward uniformity is contrary to the very idea of evolutionary fitness. Fitness implies competitive adaptation to the specific contours of a certain niche. The evolutionary process generates species that are well adapted to their own specific niches through a process of niche refinement; that is, a surviving species represents a 'good fit' to its own niche (Eltringham, 1985a).

It is equally unlikely that human tastes are so uniform as to demand the homogenisation of biological resources. Communities 'co-evolve' in order to better fit with the system in which they participate. It would be expected that the preferences of predators would be determined generally by their available prey species. In fact, there is ample evidence to support this expectation that human communities would prefer to consume the resources they depended upon traditionally.

This indicates that the depletion of diversity is not a natural phenomenon; rather, it is a socio-economic one. There are good reasons to believe that prevailing methods of production are biased against the maintenance of a wide range of diversity. The idea of agriculture, that originated about 10,000 years ago in the Near East, was centred on the idea of creating species-specific technologies. This implied the inclusion of two new important factors of production in the production of biological goods: species-specific capital goods and species-specific learning.

In terms of biological resources, the capital goods applied in production are the chemicals, machinery and other tools of agriculture. These capital goods usually do not enhance the photosynthetic productivity of the biosphere; rather, they increase its productivity by means of the mass production of large quantities of a homogeneous output from much-reduced inputs from other factors, e.g. labour.

The productivity gains in agriculture go hand in hand with diversity losses; in fact, they are often derived from the reductions in diversity. For example, farm machinery is developed to work in fields that are planted uniformly in a single crop. Chemicals are fine-tuned to eliminate all competitors of a single species. The fields themselves are cleared, for the introduction of the machinery and chemicals of the production process. These capital goods are effective precisely because of the homogeneous environment within which they operate, and they create incentives for conversion by reason of their effectiveness.

At present, this process of conversion is working its way across the developing world having completed its journey through the developed world. The frontier is discernible by reference to the relative rates of conversion and capital good accumulation. For example, the number of tractors in Africa increased by 29 per cent over the past ten years; they increased by 82 per cent in South America; and by 128 per cent in Asia. During the same period the number of tractors decreased by 4 per cent in North America (World Resources Institute, 1990). It is the extension of this previously successful strategy for development to the four corners of the Earth that is at the base of the concerns about what is presently happening to the biosphere.

It is not difficult to ascertain the approximate location of the technological frontier in this context. For example, data on worldwide land use trends document the rates at which conversions of lands to uses in specialised agricultural production have been occurring. Between 1960 and 1980, the developing world in aggregate increased its land area dedicated to standard specialised crops by 37 per cent, while the developed world experienced a small decrease in the same (Repetto and Gillis, 1988). Therefore, deforestation and land use changes continue to occur on large scales in those countries with natural resources remaining to convert; it cannot do otherwise. For example, the amount of wilderness (20 sq km of unaltered landscape) on the European continent is now virtually zero, versus a global average of approximately 30 per cent (World Resources Institute, 1990). These states of the North are the already converted states; it is only a small selection of the states of the South that retain a significant amount of diverse resources.

At present, the forces for specialised conversions have moved to the boundaries of the last handful of states with substantial amounts of unconverted territory: Brazil (and the other Amazonian states), Zaire, Indonesia and a few others. These states are in a rapid phase of development and conversion, following in the paths of all those states that have gone before. One very large part of the biodiversity problem is the extension of this same development strategy to each and every country on Earth no matter how different are their initial conditions. This sameness, extended to countries initially so different, is one of the major reasons that the world is being depleted of diversity.

The Biodiversity Problem in Agriculture: Convergence on Specialised Varieties of Species

The same process is at work within agriculture as is at work against nature. Natural resources continue to be replaced by the sameness that exists within agriculture as it is extended across the globe. Equally, the differences that have always existed within traditionally practised agriculture are also being replaced by the sameness of modern intensive agricultural practices. This has created another facet to the biodiversity problem that is sourced in the same fundamental causes – the problem of genetic erosion in agricultural species. In order to understand the forces driving biodiversity's depletion and their relationship to development, it is instructive to enquire as to how biodiversity depletion has occurred within agriculture as well as within nature.

Within nature the problem of biodiversity depletion has been explained as the workings of the force of specialisation within the natural world. Human societies have selected a small set of species and relied upon these for their sustenance, replacing diversity with the cultivated and domesticated varieties as part of the process of development. Through specialisation societies have been able to achieve productivity gains by combining certain species with specially developed tools and methods of production. The questions remain: why only a couple of dozen distinct species, and why only those which were chosen initially? The answers to these questions give further insights into the general nature of the biodiversity problem, and especially to the nature of the problem within agriculture.

The answer comes from considering the agricultural production process as it has developed across time. Besides the tools and chemicals used in agriculture, the other important factor that has been important in the evolution of modern agricultural production methods has been species-specific learning. With more experience with a particular species it was possible to become even more efficient in its production (by reason of increased understanding of its biological nature, as well as intervention to determine the same). This information became another crucial factor for agricultural production, but it existed only in one form – embedded in the received forms of the domesticated and cultivated varieties.

Agriculture originated approximately 10,000 years ago in the Near East. It consisted of a set of ideas, a set of tools, and a set of selected species. At that time and in that locale, each of these selections was optimal. However, the set of ideas–technology–species were transported out of that region as a single unit as the continuing investments in this combination caused the ideas and tools to become embedded in the chosen species. For example, when the species of sheep and goats were domesticated in the Near East, a lot was learned in the process. It was of course possible that other peoples in other places might take note of the practice of domestication and apply it to the species indigenous to their parts of the world; however, this would require that much of the knowledge associated with sheep and goats be relearned in the context of other species. In most cases it would be likely to be easier to simply adopt the already domesticated species, and the existing learning with it.

In short, a bias was introduced within the decision making process, by reason of the non-rival nature of the information embedded in the specialised species (that would be costly to produce for any diverse species). This is the essential difference between the specialised (domesticated) species and the diverse (wildlife) species. For one group, an information set is publicly available as an input into their production; for the other, it is necessary to construct that same information. The global conversion process has consisted of the extension of these chosen species' ranges. As a consequence, much of the face of the Earth has been re-shaped in order to suit these few species and the tools used in their production. It is the diffusion of this 'bundle' of ideas–tools–species that is at the base of the biodiversity problem.

Therefore, it is not simply the globalisation of the strategy of asset conversion that is determining the global portfolio of species, it is also the special way in which conversion occurs under agriculture. It is the perceived gain from the substitution of the specialised biological resources for the diverse that is generating an ever more narrow portfolio. It is this force, now acting globally, that is shaping the incentives for investment, and hence extinction.

This is a form of *dynamic externality* in operation with regard to decision making; that is, earlier choices regarding conversions are having an impact on the way that later ones are being made. In the context of the biosphere, this bias is creating a natural monopoly for a small number of species. The biosphere is converging upon this small, select group of specialised species as the sole providers of living resources to human societies.

This is seen in the fact that an increasingly narrow roster of species meets all of the needs of humankind. Of the thousands of plant species which are deemed edible and adequate substitutes for human consumption, there are now only 20 which produce the vast majority of the world's food (Plotkin, 1988). In fact, the four big carbohydrate crops (wheat, maize, rice and potatoes) feed more people than the next 26 crops together (Witt, 1985). The same applies with regard to protein sources. The Production Yearbook of the Food and Agricultural Organisation lists only a handful of domesticated species (sheep, goats, cattle, pigs etc.) which supply nearly all of the terrestrial-sourced protein for the vast majority of humans. The number of domesticated cattle on the globe (currently over 1.2 billion or one for every four humans) continues to increase, while the numbers of almost all other species continue in decline.

The same process of specialisation is evident with regard to variety within a species. Not only are human societies becoming more reliant upon a narrower range of species, they are also becoming reliant upon specific varieties of these species. Specialisation works beyond the species level of genetic convergence to produce a technically calibrated uniform biological asset, something which is capable of working well with the specific tools of agriculture: tractors, harvesters, etc. For this reason, the problem of biodiversity concerns the conservation of greater varieties of specialised species as much as it concerns the conservation of any varieties of non-specialised species.

The global diffusion of specialised species within agriculture is demonstrated in Tables 3.2 and 3.3. They present a snapshot portrait of the conversion of various countries to modern high yield varieties in agriculture. Table 3.2 provides a static portrait of the progress of this technological change in the period 1978-81. It shows that some developing countries had already embraced this strategy of specialisation (e.g. Philippines with 78 per cent of their rice production converted) while others were only just initiating the process (e.g. Thailand with only 9 per cent converted).

**Table 3.2 Area devoted to modern rice varieties
(11 Asian countries 1978–1981)**

Country	Year	1000 ha	% of Rice area
Bangladesh	1981	2325	22
India	1980	18495	47
Nepal	1981	1326	26
Pakistan	1978	1015	50
Sri Lanka	1980	612	71
Burma	1980	1502	29
Indonesia	1980	5416	60
Malaysia	1977	316	44
Philippines	1980	2710	78
Thailand	1979	80	09
South Korea	1981	321	26

Source: Hazell, PBR (1985)

Table 3.3 shows the progress of this process within individual states. In those states that initiated modern agricultural specialisation (e.g. the USA), food production is now almost entirely specialised (the majority of food production involving only a few varieties of a small number of species). In the states adopting the strategy more recently, this 'scoping in' process has reduced the number of varieties in production from thousands to a few in a small amount of time.

Hence the biodiversity problem is a problem with its source in the ever-increasing specialisation taking place within the biological production sector. All societies are embracing the strategy of supplying their needs from a mere handful of species, and increasingly it is the same small group of species and varieties that is supplying every society. This means that the biodiversity problem has two interrelated but very different facets: the problem of ensuring an adequate supply of genetic diversity for the supply of specialised industries such as agriculture and medicine and the problem of ensuring an adequate supply of unconverted habitats for the supply of genetic diversity.

The two problems are interrelated in that unconverted habitats are one source of supplies of the genetic diversity required by specialised industries. The two are also distinct because industrially important genetic

Table 3.3 Examples of genetic uniformity in selected crops

Crop	Country	Number of Varieties	Source
Rice	Sri Lanka	from 2000 varieties in 1959 to 5 major varieties today 75% of varieties descended from one maternal parent	*Rhoades, 1991* *Hargrove et al., 1988*
Rice	India	from 30,000 varieties to 75% of production from less than 10 varieties	
Rice	Bangladesh	62% of varieties descended from one maternal parent	*Hargrove et al., 1988*
Rice	Indonesia	74% of varieties descended from one maternal parent	*Hargrove et al., 1988*
Wheat	USA	50% of crop in 9 varieties	*NAS, 1972*
Potato	USA	75% of crop in 4 varieties	*NAS, 1972*
Cotton	USA	50% of crop in 3 varieties	*NAS, 1972*
Soybean	USA	50% of crop in 6 varieties	*NAS, 1972*

Source: World Conservation Monitoring Centre (1992)

diversity can be supplied through means other than non-conversion, e.g. the retention of genetic diversity in 'banks', and because non-converted habitats can generate many other values than those emanating from the specialised industries, e.g. the values from visits or known existence. However, in the first instance, it is important to focus on the need for diversity to sustain the specialised methods of production, in order to establish an overall constraint on the process of conversion. Once again this approach is adopted in order to place a 'floor' under the minimum required amount of biodiversity. There can be no argument (even from the most rabid pro-growth perspective) for the continued pursuit of the gains from specialisation by sole reliance upon a strategy that places those same gains at risk. Biodiversity provides many different values to human society, however its most fundamental value is in the support of the specialised production system which is its greatest threat.

The Uneven Nature of Global Conversion: Human Development and Diversity Depletion

Before we proceed to the discussion of the value of biodiversity, it is important to recognise the benefits received from specialised development to human societies. These conversions from diverse to specialised resources have generated substantial worldwide productivity gains. World cereal production grew at an average annual rate of 2.7 per cent between 1960 and 1983 (Hazell, 1989). For example, the substitution of specialised rice varieties for diverse is estimated to have increased yields by 1.0 tonne/hectare on irrigated lands, and by 0.75 tonne/hectare on non-irrigated lands (CIAT, 1981). Although the conversion of lands from diverse to specialised production methods must reduce global diversity, it is apparent that these losses are compensated for, and driven by, development gains.

The economic relationship between conversion and development is demonstrated in part by the state of human development in the diversity rich states. Almost without exception, these are some of poorest nations on Earth in terms of human wealth. They range between 1 and 7 per cent of the OECD average per capita income. Although non-human species are faring relatively well in these countries, the human species is doing comparatively poorly.

From this perspective, the decline of diversity has been closely linked with the human development process. The conversion of biological resources has taken the form of substituting the specialised species for the diverse, causing diversity to decline. This has generated a gain for that human society, a gain that could be allocated to either increased wealth or fitness. Thus conversion to the specialised species has been a strategy for generating human development gains.

Table 3.4   GNP per capita in the species rich states

Country	1988 (US$)	Country	1988(US$)
Tanzania	160	Papua New Guinea	810
Zaire	170	Thailand	1000
Uganda	280	Bolivia	1099
Ecuador	284	Colombia	1139
China/India	340	Peru	1300
OECD Average	17,400		

Source: The World Bank (1989)

To date, much of the gain achieved from this strategy has been expended on the expansion of the human niche. For the human species, a revolution in niche expansion has occurred over the last 10,000 years. Scientists estimate that the introduction of the ideas of agriculture at that time coincided with a take off in the level of the human population. Since that time, the human population has expanded from approximately ten million to approaching ten billion individuals.

Despite the scale of the human population, it remains the method of appropriation that is the gravest threat to diversity. This has been demonstrated in various ecological studies. The ultimate scarce resource, biologically speaking, is known as Net Primary Product (NPP). This is the total biomass generated by the process of photosynthesis on this planet. It is also the total amount of usable solar energy available for the sustenance of all life forms on Earth. The expansion of the human niche has resulted in the exclusion of most other species from a substantial part of NPP. Ecological studies show that the human species now appropriates about 40 per cent of terrestrial NPP (Vitousek, Ehrlich et al., 1986).

Most importantly, however, the same study argues that the vast majority (90 per cent) of all human niche appropriation occurs indirectly, i.e. for reasons other than direct use. The vast majority of NPP appropriated by the human species is not used but rather lost to other species, by reason of clearing and burning lands in particular. The biodiversity problem is as much a problem of diversity-unfriendly methods of production as it is human niche expansion. Still, these gains are usually routed initially to the expansion of the human niche, and this is indicated by the growth in the human populations on the conversion frontier.

Table 3.5 Population growth in the species rich states (1980-90)
Per cent per annum

Tanzania	3.1	India	2.1
Zaire	3.2	Thailand	1.8
Uganda	2.5	Bolivia	2.5
Ecuador	2.4	Colombia	2.0
China	1.4	Peru	2.3
Papua New Guinea	2.5		
OECD Average	17,400		

Source: The World Bank (1992)

Therefore, development (human development) is a process that has been driven in part by the process of conversion. This has resulted in a remarkable asymmetry in the world. The states with high material wealth have low diversity wealth, and vice versa. The problem of biodiversity stems primarily from the attempts of the remaining, unconverted states to follow this same development path. At present, the margin of the global conversion process rests at the threshold of the last refugia for diverse biological resources. If development continues in the future in these states as it has in the past in all others, then there will be much less global biodiversity about which to be concerned in the very near future.

Conclusion

The diversity of life forms on Earth has been the result of four-and-a-half billion years of niche resolution and refinement. This mosaic of life allows the environment to shift quite a lot while still maintaining some successful life forms. The human species has brought another fundamental force to Earth, i.e. the force of conversion. This force is now reshaping the face of the Earth in the space of a few millennia, as fully as the evolutionary force has done over billions of years. This has become part and parcel of the human development process across the face of the Earth.

The regulation of biodiversity will require the regulation of the development process in those states in which substantial levels of resource conversion have yet to occur. This is the only way forward for the effective international regulation of biodiversity. It will require significant international institution-building in order to foster alternative development paths. However, in its absence, the predictable pursuit of the same pathway by successive states will ultimately engender a world devoid of diversity. For this reason, it is especially important to think of this as an opportunity to diversify existing institutions to foster alternative modes of development, rather than the subsidisation of states for non-development.

If it is accepted that all human societies have an equal right to pursue development, then it is necessary to institutionalise a system of incentives that will cause the unconverted states to believe that it is possible to pursue development within the context of diversity. It will be a very risky strategy for any given state to pursue development in a manner at odds with all those before it, and so the institutions must be both stable and persuasive. Since the international institutions that have gone before have been based on the previous development experiences, the new institutions must also be novel and diverse. This unusual combination of characteristics – novelty and solidity – is necessary for the conservation of biological diversity: solidity to encourage long-term investments and novelty to channel these investments down new development paths. It will only be through the development of a diversity of institutions that a diversity of development paths will be available, and it will only be through the use of a diversity of development paths that diversity in global biological resources will be retained.

4

REGULATING GLOBAL BIODIVERSITY: CHANNELLING DIVERSITY'S VALUES TO DEVELOPING COUNTRIES

Regulating the Global Conversion Process

To a large extent the problem of biodiversity depletion may be attributed to the absence of an international institution dedicated to its conservation. That is, the global biodiversity problem may be conceived of as the set of difficulties that derive from the fact that the conversion process has been regulated on a globally decentralised basis. Historically, each state has been able to make its own conversion decisions regarding its own lands and resources without regard for the consequences for other societies. This creates an important regulatory problem because the cost – in terms of the value of lost services – of each successive conversion is not the same. The global stocks of biological diversity generate a flow of services to all societies on Earth. As we shall see in this chapter, all of us rely upon the stocks of diversity for the maintenance of our various support systems: agriculture, medicine, ecosystems. The first subtractions from global stocks did little to hinder the flow of these services, but the final subtractions from these stocks will render these flows non-existent. As the last refugia for diverse species dwindle, the cost of each successive conversion (in terms of diverse resource services lost to all societies on Earth) escalates rapidly. The absence of any mechanism to bring these costs into the decision making framework of the converting state is a big part of the biodiversity problem.

Although it may be threatening the very existence of a continuing flow of services from global stocks of biological diversity, the depletion of these stocks may nevertheless be to the clear benefit of the individual or society that is undertaking it. This is the nature of the regulatory problem of biodiversity losses – it is a conflict between what is in the interests of the development of the individual country and what is necessary for the protection of production systems relied upon by the global community. The individual country simply wishes to undertake the conversion process, as have all states that have preceded it in this development process, while the global community wishes to internalise the global costliness of the final conversions to these last, unconverted states.

Therefore, the global policy problem of biodiversity losses involves the management of the global conversion process so as to reach the correct endpoint, taking into consideration the 'global externalities' that individual societies do not. That is, it is necessary to ascertain a global stopping rule that will determine when the marginal conversion by an individual country is not globally beneficial, and then alter the decision making framework of that state so that the conversion will not occur.

The development process drives society to convert more and more of its land area tospecialised uses over time. Each such conversion confers a gain upon human society – the value of converting between assets – and thus continues to drive the conversion (and development) process. The pertinent questions then become: what forces might halt the conversion process prior to total conversion? What countervailing force is there to offset the perceived value deriving from specialised conversions?

It is the value of diversity itself that should provide the stopping point in the global conversion process. That is, with successive conversions, the quantities of lands in specialised production will be increasing while the quantities in diverse resources decline; at some point in this process, the relative values of the two uses might switch, so that the use of the land in diverse resources is preferred. It is the value of biological *diversity* that should arrest the conversion process at its optimal point. The stock of global diversity provides important inputs into the processes of biological production, and it is this value (and not the individual values of the biological materials themselves) that is the essential force to be given effect within the biodiversity regulatory process.

Without intervention, it is very unlikely that this force will be of any effect. As indicated, the main source of benefits from diverse resources lies in their 'stock-related values'. In other words, these are benefits that accrue to the world at large, rather than to the state hosting them. Such diffuse values will not in general be taken into consideration in state decision making regarding conversion. If diverse biological resources are systematically undervalued, then they will be too readily converted to their specialised substitutes. This will result in the retention of a quantity of diverse resource stocks that is less than optimal.

Figure 4.1 demonstrates how the non-appropriability of these stock-related values will lead to the mistargeting of the conversion process. That is, this is a diagram illustrating the misdirection of the conversion process over the very long run, as conversions erode the remaining diverse resource stocks, and the impact that this process will have on the relative values of lands in specialised and diverse biological resources.

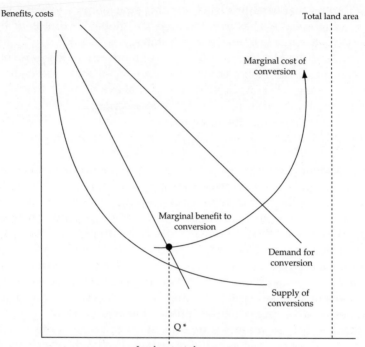

Figure 4.1 The conversion process

This diagram demonstrates that the quantities of lands dedicated to the production of specialised resources in the very long run (allowing all factors to adjust) will be determined by:

- *Domestic Supply of Conversions* (S) – This downward-sloping curve represents the *internalised* marginal cost of converting to specialised resources. This curve is perceived to be downward sloping because of the increasing returns to scale available to capital-intensive methods of production. Each state that decides to convert its resources incurs decreasing costliness because of the fixed costs incurred by its predecessors.

- *Demand for Conversions* (D) – This is the perceived benefit to the marginal state from the conversion of its resources (i.e. reshaping its portfolio from diversity to specialisation). This benefit is declining because there is consumer resistance to the acceptance of specialised substitutes for some naturally diverse resources. It is also declining because the by-products of conversion, i.e. human niche expansion and development, probably yield positive benefits (with consequent population growth, urbanisation and industrialisation) but at a declining rate as these characteristics become less scarce with additional conversions. In short, the downward sloping demand curve takes into account both the declining value of specialised resource flows and the increasing appropriated values of diverse resource flows.

- *Global Marginal Cost of Conversion* (MC) – One of the important marginal costs of the conversion of lands from diverse resources to specialised is the opportunity cost of foregone diverse resource stocks. These costs are included in MC, but not in S, because these represent the full costs rather than the domestically appropriable costs of conversions.

Even accounting for the global values of biodiversity, a large part of diversity would be converted into specialised resources; however, there would necessarily be a stopping point in this process as the value of diversity began to bite. Figure 4.1 indicates this natural stopping point in the global conversion process by the point Q^*. This is the point where the marginal piece of land remains unconverted because the benefits of conversion are no greater than the actual benefits flowing from its retention in its natural state.

The divergence of the S and the MC curves in Figure 4.1 provides the explanation for the mistargeting of the global conversion process. In this scenario, the supply curve for specialised lands is misperceived because of the failure to internalise the full costliness of increasing the land area dedicated to specialised production. The global externalities flowing from reduced stocks of diversity are not being considered in the supply cost of marginal lands, and as these are increasing with each successive conversion (and especially when the final stocks are endangered), the supply curves deviate from one another more substantially with each conversion. The individual or state making the conversion decision considers only this costliness (within a decentralised regulatory framework), and thus an excessive quantity of specialised lands (Q_d) results under a domestic decision making regime. It is possible, even probable, that Q_d would fall at the point of total conversion, in the absence of institutions that render some of these global values appropriable.

The global problem of biodiversity is the result of this decentralised approach to the global conversion process. Each state has converted its lands to specialised resource production without consideration of the stock-related costliness of these decisions. Early conversions were able to be undertaken at low global costliness (because S and MC did not diverge significantly when substantial quantities of other stocks remained). However, as the final stages of the conversion process are undertaken, this divergence becomes increasingly severe and ultimately unbounded. The global problem of biodiversity involves the creation of an international regulatory mechanism which will bring this divergence within the decision making framework of the remaining, unconverted states.

Optimal Biodiversity Policy: The Values of Biodiversity

The divergence between the two supply curves (actual and perceived) in Figure 4.1 represents the value of biological diversity. The area between the two curves represents the total value of biological diversity (ultimately unbounded), while the distance between the two curves at any particular point in the conversion process is the marginal value of biological diversity. That is, the difference between MC and S at a particular point in the conversion process is the value of marginal stock of diversity resources under consideration for conversion. It is the *marginal value of biological diversity* that marks the spot where the conversion process should be halted. In accordance with the pursuit of the global optimum, the policy should be to halt conversions where the benefit from the marginal conversion does not cover its costs. The benefits derived from the marginal conversion are obvious, i.e. the increased productivity derived from the conversion to highly productive specialised varieties. It is less obvious to discern the value to society to be derived from *not* converting the marginal piece of land. An optimal biodiversity policy requires some method for categorising and understanding the opportunity costs associated with uncontrolled conversions.

Diverse resource stocks have always provided value to human societies. Besides their obvious existence values, they also have an important role as inputs into the biological production system, even into the very specialised system that currently exists. Specifically, diverse resource stocks are useful for the *insurance* and *informational* services that they supply for the maintenance of the biological production system that supports human societies.

In essence, unconverted lands contain the output from a four-and-a-half -billion-year-old evolutionary process, which is valuable for the information and insurance contained in the diversity that process has generated. Evolution generates insurance as a core component of that process; the diversity of life forms that exists represents an encapsulated history of the various characteristics that have survived the wide range of environmental conditions that have occurred. Evolution generates information because the range of life forms that exist have co-evolved in the context of biological communities, and the nature of these interactions constitutes a living glossary of the possible forms that biological activity may take. Therefore, diverse resource systems, as the endpoint of this four-and-a-half billion year process, contain irreplaceable information and insurance services.

On the other hand, lands that have been subjected to the forces of human specialisation bear little relation to the biosphere that evolution originally placed there. Specialisation involves a clearing of the natural slate, a homogenisation of the environment, in order to allow for the use of the uniform varieties and their ancillary tools. Little of the information and insurance generated by evolution remains.

Therefore, it is the conservation of the output from the evolutionary process that should be the core concern of biodiversity conservation. These evolutionary outputs may be categorised as information value and insurance values, and the general manner in which these evolutionary outputs serve as inputs into the modern biological production system is sketched out below.

The Informational Value of Biodiversity

The mere existence of greater diversity (irrespective of the specific components of that diversity) also has value. One of the most important services rendered by diversity is information. In fact, in the scientific meaning of the term, the mere presence of variation constitutes information, and uniformity is its absence. For example, the information that I am imparting here in this text has been transmitted through software that will digitise it: transforming all of these words and ideas into a binary code that is entirely made up of zeros and ones. If the software made a mistake and rendered all of my typing into a long string of zeros instead, then there would be no information imparted; the book would consist of nothing but blank pages or, the informational equivalent, the same repeated character string throughout. It is the deviations from such uniformity that provide evidence that potential information exists.

It should also be apparent that not every departure from uniformity has equal informational value; the variety in a digital code that generates words of known meaning contains more information than a digital code that generates meaningless groupings of characters. However, it is clear that much of the variety that is to be found in evolved biological resources will be particularly useful. This is because the process of evolution guarantees that most biological resources will contain biologically active ingredients (Mabberley, 1992). These types of chemicals necessarily result in the context of interaction within a biological environment. Hence, most plants, insects and animals contain chemicals that act upon the higher organisms that interact with or prey upon them.

The activity of these chemicals can be very constructive in some instances, if properly applied. The knowledge that biological resources have evolved in this way is equivalent to knowing the location of a massive unorganised library on the subject of 'active ingredients'. This knowledge does not identify where to look for a specific ingredient with a specific action, but it does narrow the scope of the search quite substantially away from complete randomness in chemical combinations.

The search for active chemical compounds is an ongoing and well financed undertaking in the pharmaceutical industry. In 1988, this industry invested over US$1 billion in the USA alone on 'Biological Screening and Pharmacological Testing' (Pharmaceutical Manufacturers Association, 1992). Although it is possible to synthesise chemical compounds from information derived from the understanding of the biochemical processes of the human body, there appears to be a periodic resurgence in plant screening for the acquisition of this information (Findeisen, 1991). Only about 5000 plant species have been thoroughly screened for medicinal effectiveness, and 40 of these are in use in prescription drugs. One study identified 25 per cent of all US prescription drugs as plant-based. (Farnsworth and Soejarto, 1985). This represents a substantial amount of real economic value in a US$10 billion per annum industry (Principe, 1991). One recent estimate places the value of medicinal plants yet undiscovered at US$275 billion.

The screening process can be rendered even less random by means of the use of the information accumulated by the human communities living in contact with diverse resources. These people gather this information simply by interacting with their biological environment. For example, the important drug *Tubocurarine* was developed from the poison known as curare used on poison-arrows by Latin American peoples (Iltis, 1988).

Indigenous peoples' information is much more useful than a single example demonstrates. A study by Farnsworth (1988) of 119 commercially useful plant-based drugs identified that 74 per cent of them were in prior use by indigenous communities. This is what a biologist would expect, and it provides the impetus behind industrial investments in ethnobotany, the research into indigenous peoples' traditional medicines.

The information emanating from diverse resources is used by industries other than the pharmaceutical. For example, many communities raising traditional non-specialised crops have known of useful traits of these species which were not incorporated into the standard commodities. The most closely related varieties – known as 'landraces' – have periodically been used for improvements to the standard varieties. The crop breeding enterprise is in fact a major international industry, spending US$330 million on the research and development of crop varieties in 1988 (Hobbelink, 1991). Therefore, plant-screening occurs with regard to more than simply medicinal plants.

In sum, biological diversity contains informational value because it maintains a wider choice set. This generates something that economists term a 'quasi-option value', i.e. the value of retaining a wider set of choices in the event that the decision making environment shifts to render the retained choices relevant (Conrad and Clark, 1987).

It remains to explain why it is that a substantial environmental shift will necessarily arrive in order to render retained options of importance. All that is required to generate this sort of value for biodiversity is the occurrence of some sort of unforeseeable change in the environment. The environmental shift that generates this value may be foreseeable in the sense of a generally anticipated event, but it must not be of an entirely predictable nature, i.e. it cannot be something against which very specific contingency plans may be implemented. In this case the only available strategy is the general one of retaining options for the day on which the anticipated but unforeseen occurs.

The very nature of the biological world assures precisely this result. It is the very essence of a dynamic system, in which the processes of mutation, selection and dispersal continuously alter the natural state of nature. In regard to small organisms, such as bacteria, viruses, and insects, these biological processes can occur very rapidly, literally reproducing thousands of generations in a single year. The biological process is evolutionary, not deterministic, and to the extent that it can be understood, it is too complex to predict. Therefore, in a biological world, the retention of a wider set of biological resources must necessarily have positive informational value.

Insurance Value of Diverse Resource Stocks

Diversity also represents value on account of the contribution that it makes to the aggregate value of a production portfolio. Biological assets are necessarily productive assets, in the sense that they naturally generate growth with time. The tendency towards specialisation in biological assets generates a global production method that is increasingly at risk, precisely because it necessarily generates a narrowing of the global portfolio.

Diverse resources have a role as the providers of insurance for ongoing biological production. Again, this role exists in the first instance by definition. This is because insurance services flow whenever the range of productive assets is broadened. If each of a large number of productive assets has a stochastic element to its rate of return, then (to the extent that these elements are uncorrelated) the return to the combined package of assets will have a reduced variance relative to the variances of the individual components. This is known as 'the portfolio effect', and it derives from the fact that chance variations in output from different assets will tend to cancel each other out if the portfolio is large enough.

Since all biological resources are productive assets (in the sense that they grow and reproduce), the retention of the greatest possible diversity will maximise this portfolio effect, thereby assuring the least amount of risk in biological production. The conversion process, on the other hand, substitutes specialisation for diversity, and therefore would be expected to increase average productivity while reducing the portfolio effect. Table 4.1 demonstrates that, on a global basis and over the 23 year period studied, variability in annual production has been increasing along with the average.

This general worldwide phenomenon is much more pronounced in regard to those areas and those crops that have been most affected by the process of conversion to specialisation. For example, maize yields in the US were substantially altered by conversion to uniform seed varieties and

Table 4.1 Impact of worldwide agricultural specialisation on average productivity and variability in productivity (worldwide cereal production)

Years	Average productivity gain (Ave. annual rate over 23 yrs.) 2.7%	Average variability (Coefficient of variation)
1960–1970		0.028
1971–1983		0.034

Source: Hazell, (1989)

agricultural methods in the mid-1950s. In the 20 years prior to this, mean yields were about 57 kg per hectare. However, in the 30 years following this conversion, the average productivity of a hectare in maize production increased by over 100 per cent, to 133 kg per hectare (1955–1985). However, the coefficient of variability itself increased by almost 100 per cent (from 0.06 to 0.105) (Duvick, 1989).

There are two distinct sources of increased variability resulting from increasing specialisation. The first is the loss of the portfolio effect across a geographical region when homogeneous production methods are adopted. In short, when a given territory is converted to the same sorts of crops and methods, the fortunes of all producers then move together. If conditions are favourable to the chosen method, all do better; if conditions are not favourable, all do worse. Since there is no longer as much geographic cancelling out, variability is increased. In terms of the proportion of the variability explained, this is by far the more significant of the two contributors. For example, in the state of India, it was discovered that this factor accounted for at least 90 per cent of all of the increase in yield variability (Hazell, 1984).

This increase in variability is an unavoidable consequence of increased specialisation. Increased correlations between the yields of different sites necessarily result from the replacement of differentiated assets with homogeneous ones. These increased correlations then reduce the cancelling out effects of diversity, and thereby increase variability. The relationship between the loss of biodiversity and the increase in this form of variability is exact.

The second reason for increased variability is the less significant contributor proportionately, but the more serious problem. This variability is inherent in the development of specialised species. The reduction of the diversity of the genetic base of a given crop reduces its own resistance to pests. In essence, the existence of variety within the species serves the same purpose of that variety across productive assets: it provides insurance. With increasing genetic uniformity at the level of the species (with regard to various high yield varieties in use), there is a loss of a portfolio of potential resistance. The specialised, homogeneous crops are consequently more vulnerable to external shocks: pests, droughts, diseases.

For example, in 1970 a particular form of corn blight struck in the US, decimating the crop. Although there were only a few forms of maize susceptible to this pest, a substantial portion of the US crop was planted in a homogeneous strain of one of these types. As a result, approximately 15 per cent of the US maize crop was lost in that year (WCMC, 1992).

As noted, genetic uniformity contributes only a small proportion of total variability in production; however, it is by far the more serious environmental problem on account of the irreversibilities involved. Increased variability due to spatial uniformity can be removed at a single stroke, by the reintroduction of more diverse methods at any point in time. In contrast, increased variability resulting from global reliance upon a small number of specialised species cannot be reversed, unless there is a secure genetic bank to turn to in the event of a failure. The existence of diverse genetic resources provides a portfolio effect across time as well as across space. Any narrowing of this portfolio that we undertake now is unlikely to be able to be undone.

In essence, this intertemporal insurance provides a safety net against the possibility of a fatal flaw in any of the specialised varieties. This manner of insurance can be essential for the safeguarding of a population. Anthropologists have hypothesised that the collapse of the classical Mayan population may have been the result of a maize virus. The potato blight in Ireland in the mid-1840s without doubt resulted in the death of over a million people and threatened the collapse of that society.

Table 4.2 Past crop failures attributed to genetic uniformity

Date	Location	Crop	Cause and Result	Source
900	Central America	maize	potential collapse of the classic Mayan Civilization as a result of a maize virus	Rhoades, 1991
1846	Ireland	potato	potato blight led to famine in which 1 million died and 1.5 million emigrated from their homeland	Hoyt, 1988
1800	Ceylon	coffee	fungus wiped out homogeneous coffee plantation	Rhoades, 1991
1943	India	rice	brown spot disease destroyed crop starting the 'Great Bengal Famine'	Hoyt, 1988
1953–54	USA	wheat	wheat stem rust took most of hard wheat crop	Hoyt, 1988
1960s	USA	wheat	stripe rust in Pacific Northwest	Oldfield, 1989
1970	USA	maize	decrease in yield of 15% – $1 billion lost	NAS, 1972
1970	Philippines & Indonesia	rice	HYV rice attacked by tungro virus	Hoyt, 1988
1972	USSR	wheat	crop badly affected by weather	Plucknett, 1987
1974	Indonesia	rice	the brown planthopper carrying the grassy stunt virus destroyed over 3 million tonnes of rice – from the late 1960s to the late 1970s the virus plagued South and Southeast Asian rice production	Hoyt, 1988
1984	Florida	citrus	disease caused 135 nurseries to destroy 18 million trees	Rhoades, 1991
1940s	USA		US crops losses to insects have doubled since the 1940s	Plucknett, 1986

Source: 'Valuing Biodiversity', in WCMC (1992)

Therefore, biological diversity affords a very significant service in the form of the insurance that it provides. A strategy of specialisation must necessarily entail greater risk-taking. Uniform specialisation at the global level would incorporate irreducible and irretrievable risks into the biological production systems.

The Biological Industries: An Illustration of the Role of Bio-Information in our Economies

The object of this section is to illustrate the nature of the biological/industrial interface in a manner that should make clear both the crucial role of diversity as an input and the intrinsic difficulty of estimating its contribution. There are two industries, pharmaceuticals and agriculture, where the object of the activities concerned is most closely linked to the biological–industrial interface.

Agriculture and medicine should be conceived of as living defence systems rather than static technologies. That is, rather like the sea defence systems of a low-lying country against an inclement climate, these fields of human activity consist of continuing efforts to combat the erosion of human erected defences against a hostile biological world. In agriculture we continue to maintain a system that attempts to keep at bay the always-evolving pests and predators of our primary food crops. In medicine we continue in our efforts to defend against the same as they impact upon human beings more directly. In both cases the defences are neither absolute nor perpetual – as with the Dutch dikes – they are constantly eroding under the pressure of the forces of nature.

As an illustration of the dynamic nature of these technologies, a brief digression is useful in order to describe a situation in which the current equilibrium is most tenuous. A good example comes from the long standing conflict between human society and the parasite *plasmodium*. This is a parasite that has probably been in existence for at least 500 human generations, yet it continues to be one of the primary problems for the species. The parasite gets its name from the fact that it lives on human blood, infesting the victim's liver, digesting haemoglobin and producing toxic by-products that generate waves of fever. The parasite is transmitted between mosquitos and humans, and the related symptoms are the disease known as *malaria*.

Malaria has been infesting human communities for so long that numerous blood characteristics have evolved that confer some forms of immunity to the disease; one of these, known as the 'sickle-cell', is now a significant health problem amongst African Americans although it is a characteristic which confers substantial health advantages in the malarial zones of the world. More recently, human societies have been attempting to erect their own defences against this parasite. In the 1940s two innovations, one from the chemical industry and one from the pharmaceutical, showed promise that bio-technology would soon catch up with the disease. The chemical DDT was applied to the elimination of the mosquitos which bore the parasite. The pharmaceutical chloroquine (itself a development based on natural products research) was administered to already-infected individuals for the elimination of the parasite. The technology was in place for the elimination of both parasite and carrier.

Initial rates of success for the new technologies were astounding. For example, the rates of infection in Sri Lanka fell from millions to dozens in a few years. Such success was fleeting on both fronts, however, as the natural dynamics of the biosphere commenced eroding the technological advantage conferred by these two developments. Some DDT-resistant mosquitos survived the initial applications of that pesticide and returned to previous population levels within a few years. Similarly, if more slowly, the parasite plasmodium has itself been selected for resistance to the chemical chloroquine. Forty years after the initial triumphs over malaria the incidence and virulence of the disease are now as great as ever. It currently afflicts around 300 million individuals, and results in an estimated 2 million deaths annually (Jones, 1994). The defences erected by society against the parasite plasmodium had effect for only 40 years, and the forces of the biosphere have overwhelmed these defences with time.

Even more alarmingly, the resistance that has been developed within the parasite population is of a very general type, rather than a specific form of resistance to the drug chloroquine. The surviving parasites have a high degree of in-built variability and a tremendous capacity for mutation (future variability). In fact many diseased patients are coincidentally infected with numerous strains of the same parasite. This means that any single treatment, medicine or vaccine, is unlikely to be effective against all of the various forms of the parasite, and mutation will provide more forms if they are required. The forces of evolution within the biosphere have, in this context, provided the parasite with a strategy which is likely to prevail not only against existing human defences but also against many of the defences that might be created in the near future. There are few research leads considered to be good possibilities for future success against this disease.

The fight against malaria is an excellent metaphor for the nature of the front-line battle between the human species and its potential biological invaders on all fronts. It illustrates the hubris of human society's static conception of previous medicinal and agricultural successes; any gains (in terms of reduced mortality rates or increased yields) must be perpetually defended. The nature of the biological world assures that these gains must always be under assault. This is true not only in the case of a particular context, such as a tropical disease like malaria, but generally throughout society; wherever humans have successfully appropriated some portion of the world's bounty to themselves (cultivated crops, domesticated species, human populations), there are forces within the biosphere that will place these holdings perpetually under assault.

In short, the existence of a large portion of the biosphere invested in a small number of species (namely, humans and their associated domesticated/cultivated species) *does not* indicate an inherently stable system. This situation in fact represents an opportunity for exploitation by other biological organisms: successful invasion implies massive gains in fitness. Evolution will constantly and perpetually introduce new variants of pests and parasites for the invasion of this niche.

Humans must likewise constantly and perpetually defend this niche against these forces. Agriculture and medicine should be seen as dynamic contests between human societies and nature. Humans continue to expand the niche which must be protected – now approximating 5 billion individuals and 40 per cent of the terrestrial biosphere (Vitousek et al., 1986). This niche is invested in a very small number of species – a few dozen – which would greatly reward the pest or parasite that was able to evade human defence systems and specialise in the exploitation of this niche (Swanson, 1996). Thus human societies must be ever vigilant in the protection of these already-achieved gains; otherwise, these gains will necessarily be eroded by the forces within the biological world. This is the task that society has set for the biosphere-focused industries (or 'bio-industries') that consist of the medical/pharmaceutical industry and the plant breeder/agricultural industry.

Biodiversity as an Input into Bio-Industry

Biological diversity is an essential component in the defence of the human niche simply because it contains ingredients which have been generated within the relevant crucible. That is, it is not just any biological diversity *per se* that is the most useful input into important human industries, but rather it is the information to be gained from the characteristics which have evolved within a living environment that is most likely to make a contribution. Biodiversity is useful to our industries because of the manner in which the existing set of life forms have been selected (within a living, contested system similar to our own), which provides us with an already-vetted library of successful strategies.

Once again the example of the battle with malaria is instructive. Besides the chemical attacks on the mosquito populations, all of the other strategies attempted against this parasite have been attempts to imitate already successful strategies devised within nature. The drug chloroquine is developed from the natural extract quinine discovered initially by local peoples. The drugs currently under research (now that chloroquine resistance is widespread) include an extract from roundwood in use by Chinese communities for over a thousand years, and various alternatives built on strategies which have been devised by living organisms in response to the parasite. For example, sickle-cell characteristics within African populations are effective because they allow the haemoglobin to collapse upon the parasite when attacked, effectively denying it its sustenance. Similar sorts of strategies are in the drug development phase, which attempt to combat the parasite through starvation of fundamental components, such as iron (Jones, 1994).

The same forces which are at work against the human niche are also operating against all other extant life forms. Any organism which persists must do so because it has evolved strategies which are successful in a contested environment: resistance. It is for the retention of these already successful strategies that human societies require biodiversity as an input into their bio-industries.

Any surviving life form may be of some use to humans, either in terms of the explicit information it represents (the observed characteristic or phenotype) or by the implicit, biological coding of that information (its genotype). We can take note of the explicit information and make use of that information to whatever ends we might wish without ever making physical contact with the biological material, or we can make actual use of the coded (genetic) material that produces that effect and transplant it to the desired purpose.

Pharmaceutical industries most often pursue the former strategy (making use of observed strategies in biological material), while agricultural industries most often pursue the latter (Swanson, 1995b). Pharmaceutical companies will often screen diverse plant (and other) life forms in order to ascertain the presence of chemicals with biological activity (e.g. alkaloids in plants) (Fellows, 1995). However, if this information is identified to be of some useful purpose, then the pharmaceutical industry will usually focus on the synthesis of that activity within a laboratory environment from basic chemical constituents. On the other hand, agricultural and plant breeding companies have operated in the past almost exclusively through the identification of a useful trait within a closely-related organism, and the selective breeding for the transport of that genotype into a particularly useful strain. Although the two industries are following the same basic pursuit (i.e. the incorporation of successful resistance strategies into the human economic system), they use opposing techniques to effect this endeavour. One (the agricultural industry) is transporting successful strategies between near relatives using actual genetic material while the other (the pharmaceutical industry) is transporting successful strategies across vast biological distances through the chemical replication of the strategy.

The importance of biodiversity for these human industries is that this living system must contain a library of such successful strategies. The manner in which such strategies are imported into the human defence system is not really crucial, except to the extent to which existing techniques limit the transferability of biodiversity's information. At present the technological frontier in this region of human industry is shifting out rapidly, resulting in rapidly declining constraints on the transferability of this information. Now it is possible to transfer strategies between organisms and living systems in ways that were not imaginable a few years ago. Hence, the advance of the technological frontier in the area of the bio-industries should dramatically increase, rather than reduce, the value of biodiversity.

The Value of Biodiversity: A Case Study of the Plant Breeding Industry

A survey was circulated to the major firms in the seed/agriculture and plant breeding industries. In sum, twenty companies responded, representing the majority of the commercial seed and plant breeding industries by volume of sales. The focus of the survey was on firms involved in plant breeding research and development in the improvement of agricultural crops, but a couple of the firms had a broader range of activities (agrochemical products, agricultural biotechnology). A summary of its primary findings is described below.

The plant breeding companies allocated a mean of 18 per cent of annual turnover to research and development activities. There were a few companies which specialised in R&D which distorted the mean; most companies (73 per cent) spent between 0.5 and 15 per cent of turnover on R&D.

The majority of all agricultural R&D (50 per cent) is focused on the identification and incorporation of characteristics for resistance to disease and pests (50 per cent). Although the usual cycle for development requires 10–11 years, the resistance characteristic is often only viable for 4–5 years. A continual cycle of breeding for new resistance characteristics is required.

Other priorities in agricultural research are much lower, and often indirectly associated with resistance. For example, 8 per cent of all R&D is directed to the development of stress resistance (e.g. extreme temperatures and varied water conditions).

The sources of germplasm researched range from the already heavily exploited cultivars to completely wild species and on to technologically altered species (biotechnology and induced mutation). The most important findings in the study are reported below.

Table 4.3 demonstrates that, on average, 6.5 per cent of all genetic research undertaken in the agricultural industry is focused on germplasm from relatively unknown species (wild species and landraces); 3 per cent of genetic research is being undertaken on wholly wild species.

It is important to emphasise that the figure of 6.5 per cent is not a measure of relative importance of diverse compared to other sources of germplasm; it is instead an indicator of the rate of input from diverse resources required over time to sustain the existing system. The vast majority of research (here, 82.9 per cent) will always be undertaken on those varieties which are already standardised and well-understood and within the system. This is not a substitute for the input of new germplasm; it is merely the continuation of a longstanding programme of research on germplasm that was input into the system much earlier. The figure of 6.5 per cent, relative to 82.9 per cent, indicates that at present the R&D system requires annual injections of 'new' genetic material amounting to approximately 8 per cent of the material currently within the system. In short, these figures would indicate that the stock of germplasm within the agricultural research system tends to depreciate at a rate of around 8 per cent per annum, and must be renewed from external sources at that rate. (This point will be returned to below.)

One other important indicator derived from the table is the extent to which substitutes exist for external supplies of new germplasm. There is only one alternative at present: induced mutation. This technological approach to generating diversity is used to supply about 2.2 per cent of new germplasm, approximately one-third as important as natural sources.

Biotechnology is not so much a substitute for natural diversity as it is a method for transferring characteristics across greater distances (i.e. between less closely related species). New biotechnological methods for transporting germplasm provide about 4.5 per cent of all germplasm, but it is unclear whether this germplasm is ultimately sourced in natural or synthetic diversity. (It is very likely that biotechnological research relies upon natural diversity to the same extent as does general agricultural research, i.e. around 95 per cent.) The survey results corresponding to the plant breeder/seed industry provide a portrait of biodiversity reliance that fits in very nicely with the description provided in the initial sections of this chapter. The stock of germplasm relied upon by society for the maintenance of its agricultural system may be seen as a continuously eroding asset. Research and development is constantly required in order to maintain the current production system against the forces of biological invasion; this is what the industry terms research into 'resistance' and 'stress'. The industry reports that the life cycle of any given product is only about five years in duration, with pests and disease being primary factors for the obsolescence of the product.

In order to combat these biological forces for the erosion of the system, the industry continues to perform R&D on the development of resistance. In order to inform this research (and in this context to provide the raw materials for the development of resistant strains) a stock of germplasm must be maintained for reference. The industry cannot merely resort to the same stock of biological material for an indefinite period of time, as there would be insufficient variety to provide resistance to the wide range of invaders. Instead, the industry must provide infusions of new genetic material from outside of the utilised stock, in order to maintain adequate

Table 4.3 Source of germplasm used for all crops in survey, and by crop group

Source of germplasm	all %	potato %	cereal %	soil crop %	vegetable %
commercial cultivar	81.5	50	87	78.8	95.7
related minor crop*	1.4	8	0.6	1.2	0.3
wild species – *ex situ* genebank	2.5	19	1.2	1	1.4
wild species – maintained *in situ*	1	0	0.7	0.1	0.1
landrace – *ex situ* gene bank	1.6	1.7	1.7	2.3	1.7
landrace – maintained *in situ*	1.4	0	0.7	2.8	0.4
induced mutation	2.2	3.3	0.7	7.2	0.3
biotechnology	4.5	17.7	3.5	6.8	0.1

* minor crop cultivated on a small scale with some improvement over wild ancestors

diversity to maintain the existing equilibrium.

The primary result of this study is that the industry's current rate of utilisation of diverse germplasm indicates a rate of required injection in the order of 7–8 per cent p.a. of the germplasm base. That is, at present rates of replacement, the plant breeder/seed industry is totally renewing the stock of germplasm in use over a period of about 10–15 years. If this is indicative of the rate of depreciation of the existing germplasm pool (i.e. if this rate of injection is necessary in order to forestall substantial losses of agricultural product), then the loss of a pool of diversity from which to draw new characteristics would be disastrous in the near term.

The Value of Biodiversity

The message from this case study is that western society is built upon a biological foundation, and that two of our most important and fundamental industries (agriculture and medicine) are in fact defence systems for the maintenance of this bio-foundation. The biological world provides forces for the continual erosion of these systems, and so we must conceive of these bio-industries as dynamic contests for the maintenance of our foundation in the face of these hostile forces.

If these bio-industries represent the defence systems around human society, then biological diversity represents the basic building blocks upon which these systems are based. In the face of the forces eroding these systems, it is necessary to constantly access new information, new strategies and new biological material for maintenance purposes. Biological diversity provides all of these, partly because it is biological in nature but primarily because the diversity that it represents was formed within the same crucible that is the subject of our concern.

The survey of the plant breeder/seed industries provides a concrete portrait of the extent to which this reliance exists. Plant breeding companies face biological forces that render their products (cultivated crops) obsolescent within five to seven years, and they invest the majority of their R&D funds into the solution of this problem. They are continually researching the stock of germplasm that is associated most closely with the currently utilised species, but this existing stock must also be continually supplemented with infusions of new, more diverse germplasm. The survey indicates that on average about 7–8 per cent of the stock of germplasm must be renewed each year at current rates of depreciation. This means that wild varieties and landraces are being accessed at a rate that completely renews the stock of germplasm every 10–15 years. Without this stock of diversity, the current system for maintaining agriculture could not be sustained.

Therefore, this case study indicates that modern economies are heavily reliant upon biodiversity, not merely for abstract sustainability or for the occasional anecdotal genetic jackpot, but for the simple and continual maintenance of two of our most important industries. Without these resources and hence without these industries, the human niche (and human society as we know it) would be altered beyond recognition. Biodiversity conservation is a simple matter of providing the essential building blocks upon which these basic industries are built.

Conclusion: Channelling Biodiversity's Values

The preservation of human society in the long run (or even the medium run) will depend upon the conservation of an adequate amount of the services endowed by the evolutionary process; human society depends upon the diversity that evolution has generated. It seems that it is not that difficult to make a very practical case that the value of biodiversity is very real and very substantial. However, the nature of the services received from biodiversity makes it difficult for their value to be translated into incentives for investments in stocks of diverse resources. The absence of these incentives is the global problem of biodiversity.

Information is the classic example of a public good. It is so diffusive and non-segregable in nature that it is impossible to appropriate it through a property-based system. The informational values of diverse resources cannot be tied to a particular diverse biological resource, such as a medicinal plant, because the real value lies in the information it disseminates. Therefore, there must be a concern about the inability of host states to capture the informational values of diverse resource stocks. Similarly with the insurance services from diversity, these are values that flow to all who benefit from the biological production system, i.e. all of human society. As with informational value, this value is lost once the first sale of a valuable diverse resource occurs. Although all of human society is insured by the presence of diverse resources, there is no mechanism at present for the channelling of this value to the providers of the insurance.

Therefore, the evolutionary process has endowed the Earth with a stock of biological diversity created expressly for the purpose of generating the services which it does. However, the conservation of this endowment is not something that will appear to be to the individual interest of a person or state because the services which flow from diversity insure the entire life process, not simply the individual involved. The unchannelled nature of these services renders their values non-appropriable by their host states, and this non-appropriability makes these resources compare unfavourably with other resources. Paradoxically, the very breadth and generality of the benefits rendered by biodiversity (i.e. the safeguarding of the life system) render it an untenable resource under human management.

The solution to the global biodiversity problem is a policy that halts the global conversion process at that point where the value of another conversion (in terms of increased flows of specialised resources) is outweighed by the costliness of that conversion (in terms of lost flows *and* *stocks* of diverse resources). A stopping rule that puts this into effect is necessary to halt global conversions at the optimal point.

Such a stopping rule does not currently exist. This is the basis for the international regulation of the biodiversity problem. Since some of the primary values of diverse resources (information and insurance flows) are of the nature of global public goods, there is no consideration of these values in national decision making regarding conversions. Also, since these values flow to the entirety of human society, it will require global action to appropriate them and return them to the host states.

The optimal policy for the global problem of biological diversity is to ensure that the states acting as the providers of diverse resource services appropriate this marginal value of their remaining stocks of diverse resources. The implementation of this policy will halt the global conversion process at the optimal point from the global perspective.

Mechanisms that channel these values through the hands of the host states are what is required for the international regulation of biodiversity. This would translate these 'stock-related' values into 'flow-linked' values. Since terrestrial resources are all sovereign national resources, the decision regarding their conversion must ultimately be made by the host states. In order to influence their determinations, it will be necessary to shape the decision making framework within which the conversion choice is made. These host states must be persuaded that there are feasible development paths compatible with the retention of diversity. An optimal instrument will accomplish this by channelling the value of diverse resource stocks through the hands of the host states. Then, when the value of a piece of land in the production of diverse resources exceeds its value in the production of their specialised substitutes, the process of conversion would be halted. This is how an optimal stopping rule may be implemented with regard to the global conversion process.

5

THE BIODIVERSITY CONVENTION:
A MEETING OF THE MINDS?

The UN Conference on Environment and Development

In 1992 at Rio de Janeiro the United Nations convened a meeting of all of the nations of the Earth. The subject of this world meeting was environment and development, and one of the primary topics on the agenda was the proposed convention on the conservation of biological diversity. Who was in attendance for these momentous discussions? Of course, each of the nations was represented by its negotiating team, and much of the focus was upon the division between the materially richer countries of the North and the more biodiversity-rich countries of the South. Also present were many non-governmental organisations representing a wide range of members' interests: animal rights, indigenous peoples' rights, conservation groups, etc. Of course each of these organisations brought a very different perspective on what was of importance at this conference; more interestingly, so did each of the nations present.

For many years one of the chief divides between nations has been recognised to be the differing perceptions on the problems of environment and development. Since the 1972 UN Conference on the World Environment in Stockholm, there have been attempts to come to terms with the meaning of sustainable development. Initially it was envisioned that a single, universal concept of sustainable development might be created for application to all of the countries on Earth. It rapidly became apparent however that different countries stood at very different points in their development process and hence had very different perspectives on what form of development was appropriate at that point in time and for their particular circumstances. The World Commission on Environment and Development came up with a statement on the meaning of sustainable development that captured this relativist position: sustainable development is 'development that meets the needs of the present without compromising the ability of future generations to meet their own needs'. (WCED, 1987). Each country was left to decide what its current needs might be and how to balance those with the needs of its future citizens.

The problem with this approach to development is that there are certain resources which do not fall neatly within the boundaries of a single country. For these resources some sort of joint international strategy for their use, conservation and development must be agreed. The global ozone layer is clearly one such resource. Global biodiversity is an example of another such resource. At Rio the global community was recognising for the first time the need to establish some common programmes for pursuing the joint management of those resources that can only be managed appropriately on a global basis. There was a need for a meeting of the minds of the nations of the Earth, rich and poor, for the successful coordination and implementation of a global management strategy for biodiversity.

Of course discussions on the international management and conservation of the various facets of biodiversity had been taking place for many years in many distinct fora. Most prominently the International Union for the Conservation of Nature had been bringing together many of the nations of the Earth for many years to discuss a World Conservation Strategy. It had successfully completed two rounds of consultations and drafted two different volumes on the subject. However, as in the case of the World Commission on Environment and Development, much of this work had taken place within the context of a quest for the development of internationally-agreed standards that would be implemented at the national level. There was much less emphasis on the need for direct international action for the conservation of biodiversity. It remained for the Conference on Environment and Development to bring about the meeting of groups focused on this issue.

Over the past 20 years or so, many different groups have been meeting and discussing the same set of issues concerning resource conservation. Sometimes these issues were being raised in the context of wildlife and trade controls, other times the issues were coming up in the context of agriculture and gene banks. In any event the issues were always very much the same: how could domestic resources be managed in a manner to protect global interests in them? How could the benefits of such management be shared equitably? How could the costs of such management be shared? What institutions would be responsible for responding to these problems and implementing the solutions?

Just as important as bringing together the nations of the Earth, the Biodiversity Convention also provided the opportunity for a meeting place for all of the various groups who had been working in parallel on this set of issues. A meeting of the minds is necessary for the conservation of global biodiversity, not only between North and South, but also between all of the various movements that have been working on these issues.

The Objectives of the Biodiversity Convention

The objectives of the Biodiversity Convention are 'the conservation of biological diversity, the sustainable use of its components and the fair and equitable sharing of the benefits arising out of the utilization of genetic resources' (Article 1). These objectives may be given more meaning through the recognition of the various movements from which the various parts of the biodiversity convention derived; these movements included: the 'parks and protected areas' movement (pursuing protected national parks systems); the 'sustainable utilisation' movement (pursuing controlled wildlife utilisation systems); and the 'plant genetic resources movement' (pursuing the managed maintenance of plant genetic resources and the fair distribution of their benefits). These distinct movements have all come together for the first time in order to generate the various terms and obligations set forth within the Biodiversity Convention.

Within each movement there has been a growing recognition of the requirement that resource conservation must be built around the interests of the individuals, communities and governments most concerned. In every case this will be the local peoples living with the resource. Other people may have a legitimate interest in the resource, but it is the local people who will decide its fate. The importance of building incentives into conservation objectives has developed independently within each movement in order to align the incentives of local decision makers with the objectives of the movement. For example, the parks movement has witnessed the development of programmes to involve local communities in the benefits and management of park systems (commencing with the CAMPFIRE community utilisation programme in Zimbabwe) while the plant genetic resources for agriculture movement has developed the international recognition of 'Farmers' Rights' within the International Undertaking for Plant Genetic Resources. The similar movement concerning plant genetic resources for general usage (largely pharmaceutical) has seen the creation of bilateral 'prospecting agreements' (commencing with the Merck/INBio agreement in Costa Rica). All of these developments constitute the recognition of the necessity of engaging the interests of the states, communities and individuals necessary for resource conservation; they are the initial attempts at introducing economic incentives into the international conservation of diverse resources.

The Biodiversity Convention itself represents an opportunity to integrate and extend these initial steps toward the rationalisation of these conservation movements. The Convention as written represents little more than a codification of the existing 'state of play' in the various strands of these international conservation movements; there appears to be no novel perspective on the problem incorporated within the terms of the convention, nor very many wholly new obligations distinct from those inhering in already-existing programmes and agreements (such as the International Undertaking on Plant Genetic Resources or the various conservation treaties such as the World Heritage Convention or RAMSAR). The Biodiversity Convention is of the nature of a so-called 'framework convention': it provides a framework for the ongoing negotiation of explicit obligations and responsibilities for the Parties to the Convention.

The Biodiversity Convention is best understood as the confluence of these major conservation movements: a 'snapshot' of the state of these negotiations at the time of the Rio conference. The implementation of the Biodiversity Convention constitutes an opportunity to integrate these concerns and to meet the problems that have arisen in the pursuit of their objectives. Therefore, at present, the Convention represents more of an opportunity than a set of obligations for the contracting states. This opportunity should be used to develop a coherent and efficient policy framework for addressing the fundamental problems that lie at the core of the problem of biodiversity decline, as they have been identified in the course of the discussions within the previous movements.

The Parks and Protected Areas Movement (Article 8)

The modern parks and protected areas movement was initiated in 1962 with the First World Parks Congress in Seattle, USA, and it has been spearheaded by the International Union for Conservation of Nature and Natural Resources (IUCN) since then. Prior to that time there were about 1 million square kilometres of protected areas, nearly all of it in North America and colonial Africa. Since that time the number and area of protected areas has increased approximately eightfold to 7.9 million square kilometres (MacNeely, Harrison and Dingwall, 1995). The practice of designating areas as protected under the IUCN system is now universal, with nearly 37,000 such sites so designated. This represents about 4 per cent of the remaining unconverted habitats globally.

Many of the long-standing objectives of the protected areas movement are listed within Article 8 of the Convention. This article concerns 'in situ conservation' and it is one of the backbones to the Convention. It requires in part that each Party establish a system of parks and protected areas (Article 8(a)) and also that each Party must generally promote development policies in, around and outside of protected areas that will contribute to the conservation of biological diversity.

What remains to be done now that these systems of conservation commitments are in place? Of course these commitments, if taken and implemented literally, would in themselves be sufficient to resolve many of the problems of biodiversity conservation. Their true import lies in understanding the incentives which countries have in creating and maintaining land use policies consistent with the conservation of biodiversity, whether inside of protected areas or not. Countries may take very different views of the extent to which these provisions require implementation within their own borders. This much is predictable because countries, in making these decisions, will be considering the domestic benefits that such protected areas will render and counterbalancing them with the costs that they will incur. Since biodiversity is a resource that renders benefits to many countries other than the host country, there will of necessity be inadequate consideration of the external benefits when making these decisions.

This is one of the fundamental problems of biodiversity conservation, i.e. how to cause countries to make their decisions about their own domestic resources taking into account the benefits rendered to other countries. Countries will need to see some form of flow of benefits to balance the costs they incur before they will undertake the commitments required to conserve biodiversity at an adequate level. In the contexts of parks and protected areas, the problem is that each country will provide land use planning and restrictions in accord with its own needs, rather than those of the global community.

The protected areas system fails to fulfil its promise when countries do not have the incentives to fully comply with their conservation commitments. This gives rise to the problem of 'paper parks'. Despite the existence of large numbers of protected areas in all parts of the world, there is very little real protection being afforded to many of these habitats and to their resident species. This is because protected 'status' alone is insufficient to guarantee the conservation of the resources within the designated area; it is essential to back up such commitments on paper with real, and costly, efforts on the ground. For example, the US budget for the management of its national protected areas exceeds US$2 billion (for 98 million hectares) or a mere US$20 per hectare, in one of the richest countries on Earth where there is little pressure for further conversions. Few other states with substantial protected areas are able to make such expenditures, and they are subject to much greater pressures on their lands. For example, Indonesia has had 20 million hectares under protected status with a *ten-year* budget of only US$45 million, or US$2 per hectare for the decade (Swanson, 1992a). As a general rule, management budgets for parks and protected areas across the world are closely associated with national incomes, with the developing countries only able to afford to spend a fraction of that being spent in the developed (James, 1995).

Why does low management spending result in loss of real parks and protected areas? Management spending is closely associated with real protection for the resources within these areas. For example, one study analysed the relationship between protected area budgets and rhinoceros poaching throughout eastern and southern Africa, and a close correlation was found between the amounts spent and the rate of change in rhino populations (Leader-Williams and Albon, 1988). Another example, cited previously, concerns the change in elephant populations in various African states in the 1980s; almost half of the continental elephant population was lost in four owner-states whose budgets ranged between US$5 and US$15 per square kilometre (as compared with those states with stable populations – South Africa and Zimbabwe – whose budgets were US$4300 and US$475 per sq km, respectively) (Swanson, 1993). Therefore, real protected status requires real resources, and many of the existing protected areas lacking such resources have constituted little more than 'parks on paper'.

Paper parks exist because countries find it virtually costless to designate certain areas as protected so long as they do not need to commit real resources to accompany that determination. An unreinforced designation may be adequate to solicit the international response that is desired, but it is clearly inadequate for the conservation of biodiversity. This is evident not only in levels of spending, but in much more basic ways as well. For example, recent protected areas reviews of one developing country's protected area network indicated that 60 per cent of the national parks and 92 per cent of the sanctuaries had not even achieved an adequate legal basis within that country; virtually nothing had been accomplished beyond its listing with the IUCN (WCMC, 1992).

This is indicative of the striking asymmetry between the levels of international display and the actual domestic implementation of conservation commitments. Many countries possess the best of intentions and goodwill on this count, but clearly lack the resources to give effect to their aspirations. The future problem for the protected areas movement lies within the conundrum that the major remaining sites for conservation lie primarily within those countries least able to invest the resources required for their conservation.

How has the protected areas movement dealt with the problem of creating incentives for the establishment of truly protected areas in countries with limited resources? A very basic method which has evolved for inducing other countries to designate parks and protected areas is reciprocity in kind, i.e. the establishment of a mutual commitment to the maintenance of natural habitat by listings on a common 'notice board'. The 1971 Convention on Wetlands of International Importance, known as the RAMSAR Convention, was the prototype of this genre. Under RAMSAR, each country designates certain of its lands as protected wetlands, often for the use of common waterfowl species, and receives the designations by other countries in turn. This makes a lot sense in the case of waterfowl, which are often shared across a large number of disparate countries.

Listing has been used in a number of other contexts as well. Probably the most extensive set of listings has derived from the UNESCO Man and Biosphere programme, initiated in 1976. This programme has focused on the conservation of important biomes, rather than specific species or habitats. There are also listing arrangements developed under numerous regional conventions: the Western Hemisphere Convention, the Berne Convention (for Europe), and the ASEAN Convention (for Southeast Asia). This listing approach to natural habitat conservation is very effective for certain shared regional resources, e.g. a shared lake, river or wetland, or shared species, e.g. the waterfowl managed under RAMSAR. It operates by providing that each of the states with an interest in the common resource should provide an express commitment to its conservation by listing a preservation site. All states have an interest to take part in order to encourage the others to do likewise; the listing operates as a form of barter mechanism – each state compensates the others in kind for their respective listings.

Such an approach is very effective for truly common resources, where equal access allows for equal sacrifices to be made. It is not very useful in the case of resources which are distributed very unevenly, as are biodiversity assets. In this case, there is little that the fully converted North has to offer the unconverted countries of the South in the way of in kind compensation. The converted countries must compensate the unconverted with some asset other than biodiversity. This asymmetry in endowments renders the simplest international conservation strategies infeasible; it will be necessary to create mechanisms that can be applied on a non-reciprocal basis.

This is where the protected areas movement begins to intersect with the funding mechanisms movement, discussed in the next section. The problem lies in creating incentive mechanisms which induce developing countries to provide more than a simple designation in respect to their biodiversity-rich areas. Real protection requires carefully constructed mechanisms for inducing the expenditure of the financial resources required to ensure that protection. This is why the protected areas movement has come to blend into the funding mechanism movement. Although the movement has been very successful in soliciting the designation of protected areas within most states across the globe, it has had less success in generating the funding levels required to sustain these areas. One important role for the Biodiversity Convention must be to secure a basis for the funding of the existing protected areas.

Finally, it is important to distinguish the biodiversity problem from the problem of regulating truly global resources. Many people might see the 'international park' concept developed around the Antarctic Treaty System as a role model for the development of future habitat protection. It is important to emphasise the difference between globally important resources such as the Antarctic and biodiversity. Biodiversity generates many values that are of the nature of global public goods but this does not render the resources from which they derive global in nature; they are almost always domestically managed resources with global significance. On the other hand, the Antarctic generates global services primarily because it is a global (rather than a domestic) resource. The difference is that the vast majority of biodiversity resources lie within the boundaries of sovereign states and have been in use in most cases for many centuries. A strategy based on non-use works in the case of Antarctica simply because a certain level of reciprocity is involved; the absence of a sovereign state or user community means that non-use has identical implications for almost every nation-state. Non-use of a given habitat or species usually has profoundly different implications where the resource lies within sovereign territory. Therefore, an international parks strategy is not a viable strategy in the case of biodiversity, where the source resources are domestic in nature.

The protected areas movement has been the core of the international commitment to conservation. Its weaknesses have given rise to new movements to redress these problems, e.g. trust fund movements and sustainable use movements. These new movements have arisen out of the need to provide incentives for establishing alternative land use policies in a real and effective sense. Thus the protected areas movement has developed down many different branches in response to these various problems, and the Biodiversity Convention records this diversity of approaches both within its text on in situ conservation and elsewhere within the convention. (Compare Article 8(c) on sustainable use and Article 10.)

Funding Mechanisms Movement (Articles 20, 21)

This book is less concerned with the issue of raising funding for biodiversity conservation than it is with the problem of how to apply it. The latter is the more fundamental question. This is because the theory of the biodiversity problem advanced here (i.e. one of a global public good) indicates that if the funds are properly applied they will generate their own replenishment. So long as funding generates biodiversity (and biodiversity is a recognised global public good), then it will (in theory) become self-perpetuating. The problem is to provide the instrument by which the users are able to compensate the suppliers for the flows of diverse services that they receive. This is the 'missing markets' approach to solving environmental problems: the belief that the solution lies in the creation of mechanisms that enable people to pay for the sort of world that they would like to live within. A funding mechanism is defined as the instrument which makes this solution possible.

What is the difference between 'funding' and a 'funding mechanism'? This is a difference with real meaning and importance for the conservation of biodiversity. A funding mechanism for biodiversity conservation would take the form of an instrument through which people are assured that additional funds translate into additional biodiversity conservation. The need for funding is a critical component of conservation; as noted above, protected areas cannot survive in the absence of adequate funding for their protection. However, the generation of international funding mechanisms is the more fundamental problem, for without it all funding and hence all conservation will ultimately cease. It is important to examine how the international funding of conservation has occurred in the past, what is required to make a funding mechanism successful, and how this aspect has been incorporated into the biodiversity convention.

One of the first international conventions in this arena – the World Heritage Convention – is still one of the best examples of a true funding mechanism and provides a good case study in the distinction between mere funding and a funding mechanism. The Convention Concerning the Protection of the World Cultural and Natural Heritage was adopted within the General Conference of UNESCO in 1972, making it one of the first international environmental laws in place (Lyster, 1985). Its fundamental importance lies in laying the groundwork for the development of an internationally recognised interest in the management of domestic resources. It applied the doctrine of the 'common heritage of mankind' to not just unowned resources, such as the sea or space, but to some of those which were clearly the property of individual states.

Previously, the import of international law was that domestic resource management was the sole concern of the state concerned. For the majority of resources, this makes good sense in an economic framework; secure ownership rights encourage investment in resources. However, it also makes perfect sense economically to speak of all resources as being the common heritage of mankind. That is, in an economic framework, all ownership (or sovereignty) is only an artifice by which the individual (or state) is given the correct incentives for the proper management of the owned resources for the benefit of all society (or societies). Ownership (or sovereignty) is not a licence to degrade or destroy, but, hopefully, an incentive system to encourage stewardship and investment in resources. It is a property rights-based mechanism for creating incentives for investment.

Applying the common heritage of mankind doctrine to domestic resources in the context of the World Heritage Convention serves two important purposes. It recognises this ultimate, overriding interest of global society in domestic resources; that is, domestic resources are only domestic because it serves the entire *world's* interest that they should be so. Secondly, it recognises that situations exist in which the assignment of certain resources to exclusively domestic management can break down as a management system, and then the global interest in managing those resources must be reasserted.

The existence of trans-boundary pollution was one of the first instances in which the overriding international interest in domestic management was asserted. The World Heritage Convention probably represents the second context in which international interests were deemed pre-eminent, and this time it was asserted in order to address the public good problem discussed above. Essentially, the world community was asserting its interest in various cultural (e.g. the pyramids, the Taj Mahal) and natural resources, and recognising the responsibility then incumbent upon it to participate in the payment for the management of these resources. Article 6(1) of the

> While fully respecting the sovereignty of the States on whose territory the cultural and natural heritage ... is situated, and without prejudice to the property rights provided by national legislation, the States Parties to this Convention recognise that such heritage constitutes a world heritage for whose protection it is the duty of the international community as a whole to cooperate

World Heritage Convention provides that:

This is an example of a shared management system, whereby the domestic regime undertakes the responsibility for management of the resource at the level that its global values recommend, while the global community undertakes the responsibility for funding this incremental management.

The World Heritage Convention operates as a funding mechanism through the workings of the World Heritage List (Art. 11) and the World Heritage Fund (Art. 15). The World Heritage List has been developed by a committee of delegates from 21 of the states party to the Convention (elected at each meeting of the conference of the Parties). It is composed of various areas submitted by their host states as potential World Heritage Sites, and, if accepted by the committee, they are then eligible for funding from the World Heritage Fund.

The World Heritage Fund has been established by making compulsory donations of 1 per cent of the member states' UNESCO contribution. Since UNESCO contributions are derived from a general United Nations' formula based upon ability-to-pay, the Fund is similar to an income tax on the states that join the Convention.

Table 5.1 Funding available under the World
Heritage Convention (1000 US$)

Type	1983	1984–85	1986–87	1988–89	1990–91
Voluntary	2278	805	1082	1260	633
Mandatory	1842	1842	931	1442	2110
Total	4120	2647	2013	2702	2743

Source: Data supplied directly by the Secretariat of the World Heritage Commission

The World Heritage Convention broke much new ground. Besides developing the first income tax system for assisting countries in the management of domestic resources for the global good, it also created express obligations for states to do just that (Article 4 of the Convention obligates the parties to do 'all that it can ... to the utmost of its resources' to conserve listed sites) and it provided the incentive system – the Fund – for the enforcement of those obligations. In meeting the model of the sort of funding mechanism required for the supply of international public goods, it fits very well.

Its limitations are attributable to small and short-term thinking. The amount of funding – about US$2 million per annum – provided for the purposes of this Convention is minuscule. As a result, the World Heritage List represents only a very small portion of the world's natural and cultural capital. More importantly, there is no provision within the scheme, or within the budget, for any manner of dynamic interaction. The funding available is insufficient to provide the basis for long-term commitments for all of the important sites. Hence, most sites are funded on a one-time project basis, which provides little incentive for the long term conservation of the area.

With the specific limitations noted, the World Heritage Convention remains an excellent example of funding mechanism-based conservation. It is now being replicated to an extent by the development of International Trust Funds within the context of other international regimes. For example, the RAMSAR Convention has now established a Trust Fund for the compensation of wetland sites listed in developing countries. The difference between a funding mechanism and simple funding is the presence of a system of incentives which directs that funding into the supply of public goods. The World Heritage Convention accomplishes this object through its List and Fund, and thus qualifies as a funding mechanism for the supply of global public goods. Aid without incentives relies more upon a state's good intentions, and is distinct from a mechanism for supplying global public goods. Much of the international development assistance that flows to the developing world does so without a dynamic framework of incentives, and therefore does not provide much incentive for long-term investments in international resources which primarily benefit global welfare. The pursuit of an alternative development path requires the creation of stable institutions promising long-term flows of funding to these investments, and a funding mechanism for biodiversity conservation must take this form.

An example of funding without a funding mechanism was the Tropical Forestry Action Plan, initiated by the World Resources Institute and then joined by the World Bank, FAO and the United Nations Development Programme (UNDP) in 1985. This commendable effort attracted substantial funding from the developed world; about US$180 million was committed in 1990, with a further US$140 million pledged. In total it has been estimated that about US$1 billion per annum was being spent on development assistance for tropical forestry projects. Although these are substantial sums of money, relative to the World Heritage Convention budgets for example, the programme did not have the structure to channel these funds into the long term provision of international public goods. It awarded funds to countries that submitted research proposals regarding forestry policy and evaluation, but it did little to recognise the need for funding to flow to these countries on a continuing basis in recognition of their provision of global goods. It was directed to the funding of worthwhile projects rather than alternative development paths.

Another project-based mechanism for funding biodiversity conservation is the Global Environmental Facility (GEF) initiated at the World Bank. This fund has been established by World Bank donors in order to allow a programme in globally important environmental projects to be considered. The facility initially consisted of Bank Special Drawing Rights in the amount of US$1.2 billion, of which approximately US$500 million was allocated to biodiversity conservation projects. Once the Biodiversity Convention was signed, the GEF was designated as the funding mechanism for the Convention on a temporary basis. Since that time it has passed through several additional funding phases, but it has not developed many of the characteristics of a true funding mechanism.

The basis on which the GEF funds biodiversity contains some of the elements of an efficient funding mechanism; however, once again there is no provision for a permanent dynamic incentive structure within the system of projects that it funds. The breakthrough in the case of the GEF occurred in that the terms on which the funds are allocated expressly recognise the importance of allowing compensation to countries for externally supplied benefits. That is, the GEF charter provides that the funds are to be allotted to projects where the domestic benefits would not warrant the project, but the inclusion of benefits flowing to other countries would provide a reasonable return to the investment. Clearly then this allows for the payment of compensation to countries which devise projects which contain public goods as a significant component of their product.

However, the GEF funds biodiversity chiefly on the same basis as any other World Bank project, with the exception of the global benefit clause. There is no provision for ongoing compensation for these public goods, and so there is no incentive to provide for their existence beyond the time horizon of the funded project. This means that the GEF focuses on projects rather than development paths. In a traditional development banking context, this approach to funding would be advisable, since the objective would usually be to put into place a new capital structure in the country that would then allow that country to continue operations on a sustainable basis. This is the manner in which development projects are usually funded, by financing the acquisition of capital that then becomes self-financing by virtue of its efficient implementation.

The need for a funding mechanism in the case of biodiversity is of a very different character. As was indicated in earlier chapters, the problem of biodiversity lies in the external uncompensated benefits that diverse resources render to the global community. No matter what values become appropriable by local communities, these external values will continue to exist, and it is necessary to re-channel these values to the local communities if the correct quantities of diversity are to be retained. The biodiversity problem is not an instance of assisting developing countries in the conversion to reliance upon new capital stocks, but it is instead the need to aid them in the development of their existing ones.

A funding mechanism for biodiversity must put into place a permanent fund that generates a flow of funding so long as certain forms of development are pursued. It cannot be based on the funding of alternative capital assets that generate their own returns, simply because the biodiversity problem emanates from the existence of natural capital that generates values that are not appropriable. The GEF project based lending may aid in the appropriation of certain values (such as tourism or extraction) but these are different problems. The fundamental task of a biodiversity funding mechanism is to provide long-term incentives for investments in the provision of the *non-appropriable* values of diversity; informational and insurance. For these values, a very different form of funding mechanism will be required.

Internationally Transferable Property Rights and Funding Mechanisms

One important question to ask is: When is it necessary to use a funding mechanism for biodiversity conservation and when is it possible to use a property rights-based regime instead? The object of a funding mechanism approach to biodiversity conservation is to encourage development of lands down certain pathways that are not based upon complete conversion. A funding mechanism could accomplish this purpose, for example, by means of a stream of payments for the acquisition of certain limited rights of use in specified lands, e.g. a commitment of rental payments for the rights to burn or clear an area of tropical forest. Then, so long as the land was not cleared, the funding mechanism would make a payment to the owners/managers. Why not accomplish this object through the use of a property rights regime instead? That is, why not simply acquire the full property rights in the land by becoming the owner, and then make use of the land only in ways consistent with the conservation objective?

In one sense the two approaches are equivalent. The total bundle of uses of the land is being divided between two different interest groups: the conservationist and the local communities. The only difference between the funding mechanism and the property rights approach is the identity of the owner: the party holding the residual rights to the development of the land. In the funding mechanism approach the local community holds the residual rights to development, while in the property rights approach the conservationist holds these rights. Although many interest groups may hold the residual development rights in land, it is illogical to give these rights to groups concerned with the non-conversion of those lands. There is too great a conflict of interest between the local communities' drive for development and the conservationists' interest in conservation. Instead, it has been learned that the property rights and hence the ultimate decision making power should remain with the locals, while conservationists should attempt to influence those choices through the creation of incentives and institutions.

This lesson was learned from the attempt to acquire title to certain lands and land uses in the less developed world, i.e. the so-called debt for nature movement. The motivating idea was to substitute holdings of land for the massive holdings of debt instruments in the North. These lands might then be given conservation area status. This has long been the approach of, for example, the Nature Conservancy in the US to the resolution of American conservation problems: buy it and bank it. The difference lies in the fact that the Nature Conservancy always made local subscription a major tenet of its land acquisition policy, while there were few, if any, locals able to put up funds to acquire lands in their own heavily indebted countries.

Nevertheless, the debt for nature movement was initiated on the belief that distant conservationists might be able to determine local land uses. It was seen at the time that one means by which people in developed countries might be able to invest in biodiversity would be to do so directly, i.e. to attempt to purchase natural habitats within the borders of other countries. In general, the notion of a property title in the territory of another state does not transfer easily across national boundaries. This is because property titles merely represent the state's promise to enforce the rights of a given individual to the use of the indicated resources, to the exclusion of all other individuals. As with all ownership, it is a mechanism which allows for the advancement of society's interest, by the use of incentives to correctly motivate the individual owner.

However, if a given owner's interest in the use of land comes to conflict with that of the society's, it is generally accepted that the state has the right to re-take some or all of the owner's rights in the property. This is precisely what happens in cases of planning, or eminent domain, in most countries; the state is asserting its pre-eminent right to dictate land use as against the owner's interests. In the usual context, this involves restricting the owner's rights of development when the owner's incentives are such that the property would be developed more intensively than the community would prefer. No person or interest group is able to hold absolute rights in land, in the sense that they are exercised in a manner that is contrary to prevailing national interests; a property right is only a creature of the domestic regime and it is subject to that regime's discretion.

International transfers of land rights for the conservation of biodiversity are necessarily in conflict with national interests. This is because the nature of biodiversity is such that many of its values must flow to foreigners. The developed nations would like to purchase 'development rights' in developing nations in excess of that which those countries see as being in their own interest to set aside. This tension between domestic and foreign interests renders the mechanism of an internationally transferable property right in residual development rights untenable, despite its immediate appeal.

Nevertheless a substantial part of the conservation community has attempted to implement some form of rights-based policy. Given existing rates of exchange and land prices, it was possible in theory to purchase titles in quite substantial chunks of developing world real estate. It was this perceived value for money that motivated the debt for nature swaps of recent years. Three hundred and fifty million US dollars' worth of debt for nature swaps were reported to be in process in 1990 (Dogse, 1991). However, debt for nature swaps never did exist in the form that they were often advertised, i.e. as purchases of protected areas within developing countries. Once it is recognised that property rights cannot be exercised in a fashion that clearly conflicts with state interests, then it also becomes clear that the strategy of transboundary transfers of property rights cannot have any real long-term impact on state decision making regarding resource development. In this sense, international 'title transfers' are essentially equivalent to one-time payments to countries in exchange for a promise not to develop a specified habitat. These sorts of mechanisms have no dynamic incentive structure to them and therefore they must fail over time as internal pressures for development increase.

Since real debt for nature swaps were infeasible, the alternative to international transfers of title has been the transfer of development rights to groups within the country concerned. These debt-for-nature exchanges have been organised around a local conservation group, which is then vested with the management or development rights regarding the real estates. Of course, national governments need not honour the property rights of internal groups any more than external when their rights clearly conflict with the social interest, but this now becomes a matter of national politics. In effect, the transfer of resources to a domestic conservation group builds a political power base within the country whose objectives are consonant with the global conservation interests. It is something akin to the development of an internal pressure group, and their empowerment with hard currency. It may be a very effective agent for change, but the direction of that movement is unclear and uncertain.

This approach to the establishment of conservation has continued to evolve with the establishment of many independent 'environmental trust funds' throughout much of the developing world. These funds are of interest in that many have been established on a quasi-permanent basis, through the establishment of a capital fund from which the income alone is to be used. Therefore, the need for a dynamic and permanent source of funding has been recognised and implemented; to this extent these trust funds represent the state of the art in the creation of effective funding mechanisms. They clearly do have the long term capability for affecting the investment paths of the countries in which they reside.

It is unclear how this power will be exercised. These trust funds exist outside of any particular international legal structure; as creatures of domestic law with representation from various external bodies. The National Environmental Fund movement has arisen out of the debt for nature movement, and it has institutionalised the features that characterised many of the previous swaps: the establishment of a local power base with objectives consonant with the conservation interests (IUCN, 1995). A random example indicates the structure of these funds. The Indonesian Biodiversity Foundation was established under Indonesian law on 28 February 1994. It was conceptualised and provided with start-up funding through US$5 million of the US Agency for International Development (USAID) monies, and it is to be capitalised at the level of US$40 million by virtue of a grant agreement between the governments of Japan, the US and Indonesia. The Board of Trustees will invest the proceeds of the fund into activities in furtherance of the Biodiversity Conservation Strategy and the National Biodiversity Action Plan. That Board is necessarily devoid of governmental representatives and is constituted of: NGOs (7); natural scientists (6); social scientists (3); private sector representatives (4); art organisations (1); and donor organisations (2).

The evolution of the environmental trust fund movement out of the debt for nature movement brings us back full circle. Even the attempts to develop property rights based approaches to habitat conservation have resulted in the creation of various forms of funding mechanisms. Despite the capacity of these domestic institutions to bring some global interests into the equation, it is clear that these institutions cannot displace the required international funding mechanism. The object of such a funding mechanism should be twofold:

- to induce domestic investments consonant with global conservation objectives (as in the case of the National Environmental Fund movement); and also
- to induce continued international investments in global biodiversity.

The funding mechanism must both generate funding and apply it effectively. The Biodiversity Convention recognises the need for an international funding mechanism for the funding of the global goods of biodiversity, and this funding mechanism must still be brought into being.

CITES and the Sustainable Utilisation Movement (Article 10)

One important subset of the values of diverse resources pertains to the use values of the resources themselves: forests for timber and firewood; plants for foods and medicines; wildlife for a range of products. An important subset of these use values is the value generated through the international trade in these products; tens of billions of dollars are generated each year by virtue of this trade in wildlife (Fernandez, Luxmoore and Swanson, 1996). This is a significant stream of funding, flowing largely from developed to developing countries, in return for a flow of goods and services derived from diverse habitats. The issue is whether this form of use might itself be turned into an instrument for long-term biodiversity conservation: Can sustainable wildlife utilisation be translated into biodiversity conservation? The sustainable use movement has grown out of the discussions and debates surrounding this controversial question.

The leading piece of international legislation concerning trade in wildlife is the Convention on International Trade in Endangered Species (CITES), signed in Washington, DC, in 1972, and convening a Conference of the Parties biennially since then. Of the large number of international environmental conventions, CITES has probably the single most detailed control structure. It was the first international wildlife treaty to provide for both express obligations and international monitoring. Therefore, CITES represents an important step along the road toward making substantive international law with concrete impacts (Lyster, 1985; Wijnstekers, 1988). The CITES based 'trade control movement' has played an important role in the development of one part of wildlife conservation policy.

However, CITES was drafted with little attention to the problems of the developing countries in maintaining their diverse resources. It focused instead on the identification of endangered species and the banning of the trade in the same. This might make sense from the perspective of persons resident in the North; however, for those who share their lands with the vast majority of the remaining wildlife, it is not a very constructive approach to conserving this biodiversity. There are many paths to extinction, and overuse is only one of them. Trade bans address this one source of endangerment but leave the same species even more vulnerable to the other, more fundamental, causes (conversions). What is required instead is a trade control mechanism: an instrument through which destructive trade is quashed and constructive trade is encouraged. The sustainable use movement has evolved out of the recognition that trade must be constructively channelled as well as controlled.

CITES itself functions as a potential trade control mechanism primarily through the operation of two Appendices, on which potentially endangered species are listed. Appendix I is intended as a list of those species which are currently threatened with extinction (Art. II(1)), while Appendix II is to contain a list of species for which there is some indication that they might become threatened (Art. II(2)). The Conference of the Parties to CITES makes these determinations at its biennial meetings.

Once a species is listed on either of the CITES Appendices, it becomes subject to the permit requirements of the Convention. An Appendix I species may not be shipped in the absence of the issuance of an export permit by the exporting state (Art. III(2)). And, this permit may not be issued, under the terms of the Convention, unless both the exporting state certifies that the export will not be detrimental to the species and the importing state certifies (by the issuance of an import permit) that the import will not be used for commercial purposes (Art. III(3)(c)). Therefore, an Appendix I listing acts as an effective ban on the trade in those species and, even if exporters wish to continue the trade, the importing states have the duty to deny all commercial imports.

An Appendix II listing, on the other hand, leaves the decision on trade control wholly to the discretion of the exporting state. That is, there is no role for the importing state other than to ensure that an export permit is issued for each specimen (Art. IV(4)). And, these permits are allowed to be issued so long as the exporting state itself certifies that the export will not be detrimental to the survival of the species within the exporting state (Art.

IV(2)). The other important responsibility of member states is to provide annual reports to the CITES Secretariat on the amounts of trade in listed species (Art.VIII(7)). The Secretariat also sometimes acts as the intermediary between exporting and importing states, in order to confirm the authenticity of trade documents for example.

This system of bans on commerce in endangered species is required of all parties to CITES. In addition, there is the requirement that the member states adopt internal legislation implementing the terms of the Convention. Many states, particularly developing countries, have implemented absolute bans on all wildlife exploitation. In many developing countries it is illegal to hunt, capture, trade or export any part of the wildlife resource. This is true for most of the states of South and Central America. For example, Brazil and Bolivia have total bans on all wildlife exports, as does Mexico. Many of their neighbours have partial or full bans in place (IUCN Environmental Law Centre, 1986). Also, in sub-Saharan Africa, there are half-a-dozen states with complete wildlife exploitation bans in place, and many others with severe use restrictions (IUCN Environmental Law Centre, 1985). Of course, all of these impediments to the development of diverse resources make it difficult to foster these as alternative development paths.

In short, the CITES convention was not drafted to provide incentives for the constructive use of diverse resources; it was instead focused on shutting down the trade when it was deemed to be out of control. It has not always been effective, even at this more limited goal. The history of the CITES convention has witnessed some species progress from Appendix II to Appendix I, as potentially unsustainable trade levels raise concerns about the viability of the species. This has occurred in many instances, the most well publicised case being that of the African elephant for which a 12-year listing on Appendix II ended in 1989 with its 'uplisting' by the Conference of the Parties.

Why might the listing of an endangered species be ineffective? Consider the implications of increasingly more serious listings. An Appendix II listing requires the exporting country to complete paperwork prior to the export of listed species, and to file an annual report on the number of such permits issued for all the listed species. There is no independent assessment of or assistance for the completion of these tasks. This leaves each range state operating independently, with no international assistance to perform the additional tasks or producer coordination to provide the incentives to undertake them. Therefore, an Appendix II listing provides only additional tasks, and no real incentive framework, for the control of the trade in a listed species. It is the equivalent of an internationally imposed tax (or burden) on the export of the listed species, with no attendant benefits corresponding to these burdens.

An Appendix I listing promises much more in the way of international cooperation; however, the international efforts are put to no constructive effect. If the regulated species completes the progression from virtually uncontrolled Appendix II species to endangered Appendix I species, the international community then initiates concerted action to ban all trade in the species. An Appendix I listing requires the issuance of an import as well as an export certificate for trade to occur, and it effectively ends the majority of the trade in the Appendix I species.

The primary drawback of the CITES Appendix I approach is the blanket nature of most of these trade bans: they apply equally to those countries investing and those countries not investing in the conservation of the specified species. This punishes the various producer states equally, despite the fact that their approaches to investment might vary widely. Thus, both Zimbabwe and Zaire were equally punished by the ivory trade ban, despite the fact that the former was investing at a rate approximately a hundred times greater than the latter in elephant management. Such a blanket approach to trade control provides dangerously inappropriate signals to those states investing in their diverse resources.

Recently, the Conference of the Parties to CITES has been taking steps toward a more constructive approach, with the attempted development of various sorts of constructive utilisation systems. Although these are still in their formative stages, they represent the recognition of the developing countries' perspective on the problem. At various times, important but not always effective steps toward the construction of a rationalised international control structure have been taken. These are all part of the sustainable utilisation movement for biodiversity conservation.

As early as 1979, the delegates from developing countries brought the anomaly of 'indirect extinction in lieu of direct overexploitation' to the attention of the Conference of the Parties. In San Jose, Costa Rica, they argued that there must be an economic benefit from the controlled species if they were to be able to justify protecting their habitats from development. These concerns gave rise to the first step towards the reform of CITES, with the adoption of Conference Resolution 3.15 at the New Delhi Conference of the Parties in 1981. This resolution provides for the downlisting of certain Appendix I populations for the purposes of sustainable resource management. The criteria which specify how Appendix I species may be utilised in order to procure compensation for their habitat are known as the 'ranching criteria', and each Conference of the Parties usually sees a large number of such proposals for review and possible acceptance. The first ranching proposal accepted involved the transfer of the Zimbabwean population of Nile crocodile to Appendix II in 1983 (Wijnstekers, 1988).

Ranching proposals tend to be focused on a particular state, or operation, and do not constitute mechanisms for the constructive control of the entire trade. In essence, they continue the ban in effect while allowing very limited, individual operations to recommence. They indicate the direction for change but they do not constitute attempts at harnessing the value of an entire species for its own conservation. In 1983, a species-based approach to trade management was first adopted with regard to the exploitation of the African leopard. Although listed on Appendix I, it was recognised in Conference Resolution 4.13 that specimens of the leopard could be killed 'to enhance the survival of the species'. With this, the Conference of the Parties approved an annual quota of 460 specimens, and allocated these between the range states. In 1985 this quota was then increased to 1140 animals, and in 1987 to 1830.

This approach to trade management was then generalised in 1985 with Resolution 5.21, which provided for the systematic downlisting of populations where the countries of origin agree a quota system which is sufficiently safe so as to not endanger the species. Under this Resolution, five different species have been subject to quota systems: three African crocodiles, one Asian crocodile, and the Asian bonytongue for which the Indonesians were allowed a quota of 1250 specimens (the last being a fish much admired by the Japanese as a wall hanging). None of these ranching systems went any further than the development of a species-based quota. In particular, no external control structure was ever implemented, this being left to the discretion of producer states. Thus, predictably, these quotas can be abused. For example, Indonesia is believed to have issued permits for about 140 per cent of its first year's quota of bonytongues.

At the Seventh Conference of the Parties, in Resolution 7.14, this scheme for developing quota systems was made time limited so that no quota system could continue beyond two Conferences of the Parties. The argument there was that CITES should encourage a movement away from general quota systems, and toward specific ranching regimes. This, however, is closely linked to the 'captive breeding' movement: a movement inspired by the belief that the endorsement of farming operations for wildlife will reduce pressures on the same wildlife species in natural habitats. It is important to emphasise that it is not only the farmers who benefit from farming what was formerly wildlife; conservation benefits accrue when harvests occur in the wilds, thus rendering wildlife use an instrument for habitat conservation (Luxmoore and Swanson, 1992).

The third avenue of innovation under CITES, and the most concentrated effort thus far at the development of an international control structure within the system, was the creation of a Management Quota System (MQS) for the African elephant populations under Resolution 5.12. This system was founded upon the ideas of management-based controls with consumer-based enforcement. Annual quotas were to be constructed at the outset of each year, and producer states were then to issue permits not exceeding these quotas. Then consumer states were to disallow all imports unless accompanied by a Management Quota System permit.

This did not result in an effective control system for one very important reason. The Management Quota System provided no external checks on the discretion of the producer states in the issuance of permits. The determination of annual quotas and the issuance of MQS permits was within their unsupervised discretion. Specifically, there was no mechanism for ensuring that these permits were issued in accordance with a sustainable management system. Consumers purchasing ivory under MQS permits had no assurance whatsoever of the meaning of that permit. In fact, most states based their annual management quotas of ivory on the expected confiscations from poachers, implying little or no effective investment in elephant management. In addition, there were also no disincentives or cross-border exploitation, since consumer states were allowed to import ivory unquestioningly from any exporter issuing permits. Thus, Burundi, with one elephant, became the single largest exporter of ivory in Africa under this control regime (Swanson, 1989a and 1989b).

The Management Quota System failed as a consequence of these clear inadequacies, resulting in a collapse of public confidence in the capacity for trade controls to work (Barbier et al., 1990). These control system failures are not costless. It is essential that an effective trade mechanism is developed and implemented before all consumer confidence is permanently lost in the potentially constructive capacity of wildlife trade to act as an instrument for biodiversity conservation.

In sum, with the increasing recognition that the criminalisation of consumptive values does not halt the general decline of wildlife species, the conservation movement has instead shifted to a model of sustainable utilisation (IUCN, 1995). This represents an attempt to encourage the transferral of values from North to South through the mechanism of the wildlife trade, so long as the producers use their wildlife sustainably. CITES has evolved to recognise this need by means of the creation of various forms of sustainable utilisation exceptions to its broad-based bans: 'ranching exemptions', species-based quotas, and the ill-fated African elephant Management Quota System. None of these regimes has involved a concerted attempt to target value on those investing in biodiversity conservation measures, but they do represent the recognition of the need to provide for sustainable utilisation within the international trading regime (Swanson, 1992c). A very important role for the Biodiversity Convention is the encouragement of this trend through appropriate international mechanisms. The obligation to undertake sustainable utilisation measures is codified in Article 10 of the Convention.

Plant Genetic Resources for Agriculture: Gene Banks and Farmers' Rights (Articles 9, 20 and 21)

The green revolution has generated significant increases in average yields in most countries adopting the methods of modern agriculture; between 1960 and 1983, world food production increased by almost 3 per cent per annum largely attributable to the adoption of such methods. One of the linked inputs in modern agricultural production is the specialised high yielding varieties developed for use in intensive agriculture. These varieties are developed by plant breeding industries by selective breeding techniques making use of the entire gene pool available through the gene bank networks and through screening the various landraces still in use. Therefore, in recent history, a fundamental input into the modern agricultural process has been the range of varieties still being used by the non-modern (traditional) sector of agriculture.

However, despite the need for the inputs from the traditional sector, there has been no return from modern agriculture invested in the traditional sector in order to maintain it for this purpose. Inevitably, farmers given the choice have converted their production methods to the modern high yielding varieties, resulting in the continued expansion of the modern agricultural frontier across the developing world. Therefore, the very success of the modern agricultural sector has resulted in the erosion of the traditional sector upon which it has depended for raw material. The continuing loss of plant genetic resources closely related to those in use in modern agriculture has become a widely recognised by-product of the green revolution.

This conservation problem was first addressed through the establishment of the gene bank system under the Consultative Group for International Agricultural Research (CGIAR) in 1971, and the development of 13 International Agricultural Research Centres (IARCs) for the assembly of germplasm collections. The 13 IARCs now manage 227 seed banks in 99 countries which hold 90 per cent of known landraces of such crops as wheat, corn, oats and potatoes. There are also many other gene banks of use in agriculture that are owned and managed by national governments or private concerns; however, the IARC network remains a very important source of agricultural germplasm.

For many years there have been discussions within the UN Food and Agricultural Organisation (FAO) concerning the appropriate policies for the management of the IARC network, and germplasm generally. The countries recently adopting the high yielding varieties developed by plant breeders from the IARC germplasm claimed that they were being charged high prices for commodities that were in part their own. This was because much of the material supplied to the gene bank network was derived from countries where traditional agriculture still flourished, and this tended to be the less developed countries. These countries, when converting to modern agriculture, were then charged high prices for modern varieties developed by plant breeders. This was possible because the plant breeders had registered 'plant breeders' rights' in the modern varieties under the so-called UPOV Convention.

This international agreement allows plant breeders to claim exclusive marketing rights in new uniform varieties developed (in the past) by means of crossing previously existing ones. Member states agree to recognise the exclusive marketing right claimed by the first registrant of a new modern variety. Meanwhile, the germplasm held within the IARC gene bank network was being managed under a 'free access' scheme that provided germplasm to any applicant requesting it for use in research and development. They were to be made available for access under mutually agreed terms (i.e. by means of bilateral agreements), but most gene banks made germplasm freely available for research purposes in the belief that this strategy was important for fostering agricultural research and development. This dichotomy between the treatment of raw germplasm from developing countries and improved germplasm from the developed caused great furore within the FAO general assembly.

In 1986 this controversy resulted in the adoption of the International Undertaking on Plant Genetic Resources (IUPGR), in which the developing world agreed to recognise the legitimacy of the concept of plant breeders' rights in return for the creation of a reciprocal concept termed 'Farmers' Rights'. The IUPGR (and its associated FAO General Assembly Resolution 5/89) has seen the further development of the concept of Farmers' Rights. These are rights granted in recognition of the contributions of farmers toward the conservation of genetic resources for use in the plant breeding and seed industries generally. Through these, the farmers are intended to participate fully in the benefits derived from the development of genetic resources. At this point in time these rights have been vested in the international community (as a sort of trustee) for the benefit of the world's farmers and farming communities.

There has been a lot of discussion of the mechanism by which Farmers' Rights might be implemented. The mechanism is currently described as an international fund managed by the FAO to support conservation activities particularly in the developing countries. This international fund remains to be implemented, and there is no agreement as to the scale or the source of the contributions that it should contain. Of course, this situation renders the concept of Farmers' Rights largely ineffective to date.

The Biodiversity Convention includes several references to the conservation movement pertaining to genetic resources for agriculture. Many facets of the FAO's resolutions on Farmers' Rights have been incorporated into the terms of the Convention (see Articles 9, 20 and 21 of the Biodiversity Convention). These provisions also mention the importance of exclusive and contracted rights of access to genetic resources, and the basis for agreements on the same. Therefore, the Convention promises to continue the debate on the terms for access and the basis for compensating the providers of plant genetic resources for agriculture; the movement for Farmers' Rights continues.

Plant Genetic Resources Generally: The Bio-Prospecting Movement (Articles 15 and 16)

A closely related movement concerns the use of natural habitats for general screening purposes in regard to genetic resources. These uses concern species not already in human use (unless it is restricted to locally-known usages) which are often screened for usage in the pharmaceutical industry. Such screening can occur on a purely random basis, through the collection of samples and their investigation in the laboratory, or by reference to local usage. A large number of currently marketed pharmaceuticals have been developed from such a starting point. One study estimated that 25 per cent of all US-marketed pharmaceuticals were plant derived (Farnsworth and Soejarto, 1985). So, once again, this is an industry in which an important factor of production is going uncompensated, and thus unconserved. Despite the historical importance of the biodiversity resource in providing necessary inputs into this production process, there has been no flow of value to the raw resource nor to its conservators, the local communities.

The property rights dispute in this case relates to the fact that courts in the US (and EC patent law) have provided that naturally occurring organisms are not subject to property rights regimes. Exclusive marketing rights may be claimed in living organisms but only those in which it is demonstrated that human intervention has produced an organism that was not previously existing in nature. Otherwise it is necessary to synthesise the useful products of natural systems, in order to claim rights in them. This means that a useful chemical within a naturally occurring plant may not receive a protected return, while its synthetic counterpart (the same chemical in the form of a little white pill) receives the full protection of the patent system.

This is an indicator of the manner in which institutions often follow capital endowments, and also of the importance of providing a diversity of institutions suited to a diversity of capital endowments. For example, the developed countries might be best described as those societies which are biased toward human and physical (human-made) forms of capital while the developing countries are more biased toward natural forms of capital. In the case of biodiversity's informational value, the existing international institutions are heavily biased in favour of the developed countries and their capital portfolios. The international legal systems are requiring the processing of nature's information by human and human-made capital before granting exclusive marketing rights in it.

This bias is captured in some rough indicators of patent protection. Much of the intangible value of biodiversity is represented by the specific chemical and genetic structures of the various varieties present there. Given that the vast majority of the world's natural genetic wealth exists in the developing world and this is an important input into biotechnical research, it might be expected that there would be some bias toward the granting of patent rights to citizens of these countries. However, nothing could be further from the truth. Although the bulk of the world's genetic wealth resides in the less developed countries, nearly the entirety of the world's biotechnology patent rights are held by the developed countries. An example is provided by examining the distribution of European versus Latin American biotechnology patents.

Table 5.2 The distribution of biotechnology property rights: citizenship of recipients

Europatents granted %		Latin American patents granted %	
United States	36	Developed Countries	89
EC States	32	Latin American Countries	11
Japan	23		
Rest of World	9		
Latin Americans	0		

Sources: Howard, 1991; Hobbelink,1991. Data are for the first quarter of 1990

This institutional bias is one of the primary contributing factors to the continuing depreciation of natural genetic capital. Since the holders of the natural capital stock are not vested with rights in the returns they generate, there is very little incentive to undertake substantial investment programmes to maintain that natural stock of capital. The rights in joint products of biology and technology are instead vested in those countries whose advantage lies in technology rather than biology. This bias exists on account of clearly drafted laws which discriminate against naturally occurring genetic capital in favour of human altered varieties. For example, Article 53(b) of the European Patent Convention states that no protection is available for 'plant or animal varieties or essentially biological processes for the production of plants or animals'. Similarly, in the landmark US decision, *Diamond v. Chakrabarty*, which established the first rights to patents in live organisms, plants and animals in 1980, the court stated that the basis for awarding a patent in a living organism was that: 'the patentee has produced a new bacterium with markedly different characteristics than any found in nature ... His discovery is not nature's handiwork, but his own; accordingly, it is patentable subject matter under patent law.' In the US extremely wide patents are being granted to living organisms, so long as they have been subject to some application of human technology, e.g. the famous onco-mouse patent and the infamous patent application on behalf of the Human Genome Project.

These selections provide an indication of the extent of the bias which exists in favour of rights in genetic structures when altered by human intervention, and against similar structures if developed by nature. In essence, the legal system has contrived to treat the informational products of nature as 'open access', and thus the only appropriable genetic information is that which results from human intervention. Again, such a bias actively discourages any investment in the maintenance of the stocks of natural genetic capital, instead encouraging the development of capital stocks that are compatible with the international property rights structure. This must be one of the reasons why developing countries want 'technology transferred'; it is only by virtue of acquiring technology that compensation for already existing natural capital services may be acquired. This bias within the property rights system is a fundamental factor in the continuing conversion, and hence decline, of the natural genetic capital stock.

Recently there has been a movement to develop a mechanism for compensating for this use of plant genetic resources. It has been based on the idea of making payments for prospecting rights, and it has been advocated by the World Resources Institute (and other NGOs) and suggested by an agreement between Merck, Inc. and INBio in Costa Rica. The idea of a bio-prospecting agreement is to make an exclusive arrangement for plant screening concerning a certain geographical area on terms agreed between the two parties involved (Reid et al, 1993). This agreement can provide for up-front prospecting fees or use-based royalties or both. The fundamental idea is to base compensation upon bilateral negotiations between the supplier and the user of the (basic) plant screening services. There is an important role for the Biodiversity Convention in supplying the foundations for efficient international property rights and the contracting that would occur within such a system. The Biodiversity Convention provides for this role in Articles 15 and 16.

Conclusion

The Biodiversity Convention is a true meeting place for all of the various facets of this global problem. This chapter has outlined some, but not all, of the major movements associated with the various components of the

Convention. If the Biodiversity Convention is to have a real and substantial impact on the international management of biodiversity, then it will have to give fruition to these various movements – in the form of real substantive international law created to instil incentives for the conservation of biodiversity. One important role for the Biodiversity Convention to play is as a meeting place for the continued development of the ideas and solution concepts that have been fermenting within each of the conservation movements: parks and protected areas; funding mechanisms; wildlife utilisation; farmers' rights; and property rights for genetic resources generally.

At base each of these movements involves the recognition of the mutual interest of the material-rich states and the biodiversity-rich ones in respect to the appropriate path for the development and conservation of the remaining biological diversity. New institutions are required if the diversity-rich states are to be encouraged to pursue alternative development paths. These alternative paths will be based upon the diversity-rich states' investment in and development of their diverse resources rather than their conversion to reliance upon others. At present international institutions encourage development, and they encourage it down the same path as those that went before, i.e. the conversion of natural capital stocks to other, preferred forms of capital holdings. The international community's responsibility under the Biodiversity Convention must be to recognise that all of these movements at base require the development of new, diverse international institutions capable of rewarding investments in natural forms of capital. Development institutions must not continue to discriminate against such diversity. The Biodiversity Convention also affords an opportunity for a meeting of the minds on this issue.

The Biodiversity Convention is therefore a very important international meeting place, with an already long history of movement. The importance of this meeting place lies however not in its past but with its capacity to determine the future. This opportunity must be seized to shape future international institutions and, most importantly, to shape the development choices of those countries with the greatest capacity to determine what will remain of global biodiversity. It is to these questions that the remainder of this volume now turns.

6

THE INSTITUTIONS REQUIRED FOR EFFECTIVE BIODIVERSITY CONSERVATION: THE GENERAL PRINCIPLES UNDERLYING EFFECTIVE CONSERVATION

Institutions for Solutions: Where Do We Stand?

This is the midpoint of this volume, and the starting point for the discussion of the solutions required to address the problems outlined within the first part of the text. The first half of the volume presented the 'existing state of play': the point at which we stand in terms of nature, development and international institutions. It is now possible to commence bringing together the various parts of the previous sections into a single framework for discussing the necessary mechanisms for optimal biodiversity conservation. Chapters 2 and 3 indicated the nature of the economic forces at work shaping the biosphere into a more homogeneous set of assets; without the forces for conversion used for the betterment of human societies, there would be no threat to diversity. Chapter 4 discussed the reasons why these conversions represent a cost as well as a benefit to human societies. Diversity performs services of value to society just as does uniformity, but diversity is disappearing because the values of diversity are systematically underappropriated by those deciding whether to undertake conversions. The conservation of the optimal amount of diversity will require the correction of this in-built bias toward conversion within the human development process.

Chapter 5 charted where we stood at the time of the Biodiversity Convention with regard to the regulation of this process. Over the past few decades several distinct movements have grown up to address the problem of unmanaged development and its impacts on the biological world. Several of these movements have focused on particular policy issues and instruments (such as agricultural genetic resources or national parks), and many of them progressed with little knowledge of each other, but all were concerned with the same general underlying problem: the management of the forces within development that endanger biological diversity.

The remaining chapters discuss the integration of these various concerns and pursuits into a single international management structure devised to manage optimally the development process as it affects this global resource. This chapter categorises all of the various approaches to conservation under two analytical headings, and discusses when each approach might best be used. Then the subsequent chapters develop these various mechanisms in more detail, explaining how they should be used and how they should be institutionalised into an international regulatory structure.

The remainder of this volume argues that effective international regulation of global biodiversity will require the development of three protocols to the Biodiversity Convention, which will give effect to the ideas of the various movements that caused this convention to come into being. These protocols need to establish international regulatory mechanisms for:

- a global planning authority;
- a global certification system; and
- a global property rights registration system.

This chapter will discuss the nature of these regulatory mechanisms very generally; the next three chapters will discuss them successively in much greater detail.

The Need for Protocols

Why is it necessary to proceed to the development of protocols to an already lengthy convention? The Convention on Biological Diversity is of the nature of a so-called framework convention. This is an agreement that represents more of a beginning than an end to the negotiations between the countries concerned. The basic framework for the agreement is apparent. It is represented in those Articles of the Convention in which the Parties undertake to conserve and sustainably use biodiversity. It is also present in those Articles in which the developed countries promise to provide the financial resources to make the performance of these commitments a possibility. Together, these Articles provide the framework for a workable solution to the biodiversity problem.

The problem remains to put some flesh on the bones of this agreement. Clearly it will not simply be enough to have financial resources expended by the developed world in the name of biodiversity conservation; they must be spent in a carefully structured fashion if the objective of real and substantial conservation is to be attained. The object must be the creation of instruments for change, not simply one-time investments in conservation.

This is the role of the protocols to the Convention. They should provide the mechanisms through which the investments of the developed world are able to generate increased investments in biodiversity in the developing world. This is not a simple task, but it is one that must be accomplished if the hopes and aspirations set forth in the Convention are to be realised.

The protocols must give details of how the financial resources of the developed world are to be channelled in a structured fashion. These structured channels for the flow of funds between the material-rich and the biodiversity-rich are the new international institutions that must be established to support biodiversity-compatible development. In sum, the object of these protocols must be the establishment of new international institutions that will provide the incentives to develop down new pathways – ones that are compatible with their diverse biological resources. The international community must recognise that a diversity of international institutions is required in order to support a diversity of development paths. The protocols to the Biodiversity Convention are the route to the registration and institutionalisation of this recognition.

International Land Use Planning and Financial Mechanisms

One structured approach to the channelling of resources for biodiversity conservation would be via a stream of international payments intended to compensate a state for any specific development obligations it undertakes for the purpose of conserving biodiversity. This system of payments would necessarily be made conditional upon the host state's application of them to the conservation of some specified part of its diverse resources. An effective 'contract' for the supply of biodiversity would have to have both of these facets: specific forms of development obligations plus a stream of rental payments. The idea is to influence the state's choice of development path via the establishment of an assured flow of benefits conditional on specific development choices.

These development obligations would be of the nature of the land use restrictions common in so many countries. In effect the object would be to implement some types of land use restrictions (e.g. clearance restrictions, burning restrictions) in certain important zones for biodiversity conservation. How much would a country need to be compensated for undertaking these development restraints? One of the most important determinants of the amount of the payments required for effective conservation would be the rental value of the affected lands, with and without the development restraint.

A crucial feature of any effective international contract will be its necessarily dynamic nature. The stream of payments to the supplier state must be based on conditionality. That is, it is only possible to restructure the owner-state's decision making process if the payment is offered at the end of each period that the state takes the specified action (Swanson, 1992a). This allows the rental payment to be used as the enforcement mechanism for the contract, which is much more cost-effective and otherwise virtually non-existent at the international level.

This is, in essence, an enforceable version of the transferable development rights approach to diverse resource conservation. To the extent that the international community wishes to reduce the development intensity away from the local optimum (of high intensity conversion and use), then it must be willing to provide a stream of *ex post facto* payments to compensate for the forgone development and to pay for the additional factors required (management, land, stocks).

The simplest example of such a transferable development rights agreement would be the designation of some parcel of land as a 'reserve' under an international trust fund agreement. A reserve in this context means the dedication of a given land area to a very restricted set of uses consistent with the maintenance of its diverse resource base, such as a restriction to use only for plant prospecting. In effect, such a trust fund agreement would have as its objective the acquisition of the rights to virtually all uses. The trust fund would be established to provide the flow of compensation to the state in an amount necessary to compensate for all of the forgone uses.

This is, in general, a problematic approach on account of its overbroad targeting of its objective. First, this agreement, to be effective, would require the payment of a substantial periodic compensation fee (corresponding to each of the 'factors' required for the conservation of the diverse resources, i.e. land, management, diverse resource stocks). Secondly, such an agreement is an extreme approach to resource conservation that denies local communities the use of their local resources. This approach is costly for both global and local communities, entailing higher management costliness and greater-than-necessary intervention within the rights of sovereign states and local communities. Such an extreme approach to conservation should be reserved only for extreme situations. Much of the motivation for the sustainable use movement has been derived from the witnessing of the excessive costliness of the implementation of these overbroad approaches to conservation.

What is required is a mechanism that will acquire from the local community the smallest number of uses necessary for the preservation of the diverse resource base. The conservation of diverse resources will often be compatible with a wide range of forms of resource utilisation. It is possible to allow many of these uses to continue while restricting a few in order to protect particular values of biodiversity. This is because an 'absolute property right' in a tract of land represents a 'bundle' of many distinct rights and uses. The function of most zoning laws under national legislation is to allocate the various rights of use regarding a piece of land between a number of competing individuals and groups. The purpose of an international agreement would be to create a self-enforceable mechanism to accomplish the same thing at the international level.

International zoning should be conducted within the framework of an international institution established for the purpose of establishing and implementing a global land use plan: a global land use planning authority. The principles motivating the establishment of such an institution mirror exactly those which underlie the establishment of domestic institutions for the same purpose. The idea is to determine the range of land uses that must be retained, and hence the development that must be constrained, from a global rather than a local perspective. This planning authority is then able to address the problem of determining the range of habitats, systems and species to conserve from a global perspective, and it is able to choose between the various potential providers of these services from the range of potential suppliers.

The planning authority would have the capacity to generate the greatest level of global diversity with the minimum level of intrusion upon local communities' rights of development. Given that the rights to engage in various uses with regard to a particular piece of land are separable, this means that land uses may be divided between the global and the local communities in ways other than 'all or nothing'. Then the international community may intervene selectively to acquire only designated rights of use in particular tracts of land, while leaving the residual to the local community. The role of the planning authority is to ensure that these development constraints aggregate to provide the greatest amount of global diversity at the least amount of expense and burden.

Generally, an efficient contract between the planning authority and the host state would be of the form of an *international franchise agreement* (Swanson, 1994b). This is a three-way agreement (between owner-state, planning authority and franchisee) in which the authority provides a stream of rental payments to the owner-state in return for its agreement to zone a piece of land for use only for restricted purposes (as specified within the international franchise agreement). That is, the land would be franchised for use to individuals or groups within the local community franchisees, but only for those uses consistent with the agreement between the national government and the planning authority.

The franchising mechanism allows for the efficient allocation of land uses between the global and local communities. If the global community wishes to restrict certain local land uses, then it must be willing to pay the full rental value of those uses. Similarly, the uses that remain for the franchisee are likewise charged at their full rental rate. Then these rental rates are determined in a limited auction (e.g. the global community could make bids for the same limited rights of use in a number of different tracts of land across the world) and only those states which wish to accept the international bid are bound by the conditions of agreement. In this way the 'incremental burdens' of diversity conservation (through use restrictions) are only undertaken voluntarily, and only if the price paid by the global community is sufficient to induce agreement.

At the same time, an international franchise agreement also creates an enforcement mechanism for the channelling of these funds into diversity conservation. By paying a periodic rental rate, the international community is assured of receiving a stream of conservation benefits in return for its payments because, if the use restrictions are not enforced, the international community retains the right to withhold payment of future rents. In this fashion, the agreement is rendered 'dynamically consistent': each party has the capacity to withhold performance in each period until it sees the other fully perform its own obligation, and thus each party is capable of self-enforcing the agreement.

A franchise agreement is simply an economically efficient form of contracting to provide certain services; here the services to be rendered are those of the diverse resource stocks. The crucial components of such a contract are the efficient allocation of the various uses of a tract of land between global and local communities – in the context of a self-enforcing agreement. The approach of selective intervention has the twin advantages of decreasing the required global funding while increasing the benefits flowing to local communities from local resources.

The Biodiversity Convention must have a component within it to provide for efficient contracting for the supply of diverse natural habitats and systems. The sort of international institution which could fulfil this role is an international planning authority, which performs the same sort of function at the global level that is necessary at the national or local level. In order to effectuate its plans, this institution will need to enter into dynamic forms of agreement, something like the franchise agreements seen in the domestic context. The first protocol of the Biodiversity Convention should be addressed to the establishment of an international funding mechanism for these purposes. (Chapter 7 provides further detail about the mechanism.)

Certification of Sustainable Use Regimes

There are two basic approaches to the installation of incentives for biodiversity conservation: development constraint compensation and diversity-based development appropriation. The logical alternative to the subsidisation of the costliness of the development constraints is the enhancement of the returns derived from diverse resource production. The former option effectively reduces the costliness of making the decision not to convert diverse resources; the latter option (analysed here) effectively increases the benefits from investing in diverse resource systems. Therefore, the impact of either approach is the same on the host state's decision making regarding land use conversion.

Enhanced appropriation is based more upon intervention within markets (in order to influence incentives) rather than attempts to construct incentive systems more directly. Market regulation is a policy based on ensuring that the host state receives an enhanced value from the marketing of its diverse resources. At present, this is the opposite of what is occurring with respect to most diverse resources. African countries had been capturing about 5 per cent of the value of their raw ivory exports during the height of the ivory trade (Barbier et al., 1990). Tropical bird harvesters around the world acquire between 1 and 5 per cent of the wholesale value of the animals (Swanson, 1994). This is even true with regard to many exports of tropical forest products (Repetto, 1988). The host states of diverse resources do not place much effort into the appropriation of the benefits of diverse resources, choosing to encourage conversions instead. Market regulation reforms are intended to redress this balance.

The crucial element to a market-based approach is the creation of a price differential for diverse resources that is available only to those host states conserving their diverse resource stocks. The choice of alternative development paths requires investments in diverse resource stocks, and it is these choices and these investments that must be subsidised. Hence it is not the mere supply of diverse resources to the markets that must be subsidised; instead, it is the demonstration that these supplies derive from well managed stocks.

It is the difference between the prices received by subsidised and non-subsidised producers that creates the constructive incentives within the mechanism. The price differential creates the capacity for some manner of dynamic conditionality, as is required in an effective agreement. The prospect of receiving the price differential constitutes the inducement to meet the conditions required to be entitled to the differential, and the receipt of this entitlement (combined with period inspections) constitutes the incentive to continue satisfying these conditions.

The suppliers to receive the price differential would have to be certified as 'sustainable producers'. The conditions that would need to be satisfied in order to receive this entitlement would be both stock-related and flow-related, i.e. they would specify the levels of the conservation of lands or stocks of diverse resources required to be included within the regime as well as the supplies that may be taken sustainably from these stocks. The stock constraints could take the form of a number of hectares of specified diverse stocks or diverse production methods or even hectares dedicated to restricted uses. The flow constraints would consist of maximum quotas that might be derived from the listed stocks on a sustainable basis.

The price differential is effectuated via market regulation in the consumer states. The simplest form of such an agreement would be a restriction on all purchasers to acquire the diverse resource only from the listed suppliers. Such 'exclusive purchasing agreements' will always create a premium for the favoured suppliers and a penalty for the disfavoured. The key to the success of such agreements is investment by the consumer states into the discrimination between the two sets of imports; to the extent that consumers invest each period in barring imports from non-certified producers, an enhanced price will be available to the certified suppliers.

The importance of a truly international (i.e. multilateral) mechanism is made clear in this context. The extent of the price differential will depend entirely upon international enforcement of the ban on unlisted producers; otherwise, a single non-compliant state may act as a conduit for unlisted suppliers, mixing the two sources and exporting both as high price commodities. In the final analysis the extent of such piracy determines the ultimate price differential achievable by sustainable producers, because it is capable of flooding the market with competing supplies. Therefore, the development of mechanisms to minimise the impacts of such pirates is essential to the success of a rent appropriation mechanism.

A bilateral agreement is also an inadequate means for appropriating these values. A bilateral agreement may assure a particular market to a particular supplier, but the highest price that the consumer state will be willing to pay will be dependent upon the exclusivity of its rights in the subject resources (otherwise it owns nothing). Since the producer state cannot guarantee exclusivity (because of other potential producers and potential leakages to other consumers), the value of its resources is much enhanced if a simultaneous agreement is reached with all other significant consumer states to recognise the exclusivity of its rights in the goods traded with other consumer states. Then these consumer states receive these exclusive rights in the transaction, and their willingness to pay is determined by their belief in the assurances of the other consumer states. The distinction between an international and a bilateral agreement for purposes of value appropriation is the creation of this assurance of exclusivity and the value that it represents.

Enhanced value appropriation is therefore dependent upon the efforts of all consumer states to enforce the discrimination between sustainable and non-sustainable producers of diverse resources. The extent of international cooperation and individual (consumer state) investments will determine the prevailing price differential. The differential rents available to sustainable producers may be further enhanced by virtue of management of the quantities traded between suppliers and consumer states. The maximum rental available may then be determined, and the maximum produced quantity that this implies would be allocated between the various host states, developing a form of cartel-based pricing system for the resource.

Why would the global community wish to participate in such a price-enhancing scheme? The important point to remember is that this enhanced value is being paid not only for the good in trade, but also for the global services that its manner of production implies. So, if the sale of a particular commodity (such as Brazil nuts) that is produced within a sustainable production system implies the retention of the habitat from which it derives, then this strategy implies the retention of all of the other services the system generates. Then a subsidy to Brazil nuts is only an instrument for cross-subsidising all of these other unpaid goods and services. The incentive to conserve both arises out of the fact that the production method (combined with the use restrictions) generates both the tangible and the intangible goods and services.

An example of this cross-subsidisation approach has been attempted in Sub-Saharan Africa. After the ban on the ivory trade in 1989, several of the sustainable producers of elephants grouped together to form an 'Ivory Exchange', based in Malawi. The idea of the Southern African Centre for Ivory Marketing (SACIM) is to provide a verifiable conduit for ivory flowing from managed elephant stocks, and thus to provide a mechanism for consumer states to ensure their purchases come from sustainable producers. The enhanced rental value that would result would subsidise not only sustainable elephant populations but also all of the other wildlife and systems that live on the lands dedicated to these populations (Swanson and Pearce, 1989).

In summary, the idea of such exclusive market agreements is to allocate the consumer markets only to those owner states investing in their diverse resources. The owner states that choose to mine their diverse resources will otherwise drive down the prices, and rents, available to all states providing diverse resource flows. An agreement to restrict consumer markets to those owner-states that invest in their diverse resources (and the systems from which they derive) creates a price differential: a price premium target to all sustainable producers and a price penalty target to all non-sustainable producers. Such a mechanism might be used in a wide variety of circumstances, where the stock-related investments are directly linked to the final product.

The second protocol to the Biodiversity Convention should be developed for the purpose of creating an international institution for the certification of sustainable producers within diverse natural habitats. This institution should audit these producers and the consumer states to ensure that the conditions for certification are continually met, and that the price differential is being sustained through exclusive purchasing. This protocol is further discussed and developed in Chapter 8.

The Use of Property Right Regimes

Another example of an exclusive purchasing scheme would be any form of an internationally recognised *property right regime*. Such a regime also allots specific markets in consumer states to specific producers in order to compensate for socially important investments, but the connection between the market and the investment may be less direct as compared with the case of the certification of sustainable wildlife producers. That is, the idea remains to enhance the value of certain products via exclusive purchasing but the link between the habitat and the products marketed may become much more indirect.

Intellectual property rights provide an example of mechanisms that operate in this fashion. The role of any form of intellectual property rights regime is to provide a basis for compensating investments in stocks that do not generate directly compensatory flows; specifically, intellectual property regimes reward inappropriable investments in ideas with rights in discrete product markets. It has transpired in modern societies that investments in human forms of capital (e.g. education and training) have become very important for production and growth; however, the outputs from these investments are usually intangible and nonappropriable, e.g. ideas and insights (Romer, 1990a, 1990b).

If there were no protection for the ideas and innovations generated by reason of human capital, then the pirates of the world would simply watch for innovations and then copy these inventions and market them to the consumer states themselves. International agreements recognising property rights in such ideas usually take the form of exclusive purchasing agreements in specific products of those ideas. These exclusive purchasing agreements give the products enhanced value because they provide consumer states with the assurance that their purchase of a product based on a widely known idea or innovation will be assured of its exclusivity, and therefore they are able to pay the producers of such innovations a differential price in accordance with this exclusivity. The extent of the universality of these agreements and the extent of individual states' efforts to enforce them determines the values that flow to human capital investments.

In essence, the states generating ideas and innovations are analogous to the sustainable producers of ideas; these are the states that are producing ideas by investing in humans. The pirates in the markets are analogous to the non-sustainable producers; they are not investing in humans and only supply innovations to the extent that others invest. If the price to both groups were the same, then there would be no incentive to invest in human forms of capital. Intellectual property laws provide the price differential for those states able to demonstrate such investments, and thus they maintain the incentives for continuing investments in the production of these intangible forms of services.

The characteristic that distinguishes an intellectual property right from other exclusive purchasing agreements is the extent to which the property is carefully defined in an individual tribunal award. For example, a patent carefully describes a specific exclusive consumer market that is offered as a reward for a general idea. The idea is then released to the global community for general and widespread use, while the specified consumer market operates as an international exclusive purchasing agreement to create the award for the innovator.

Property right mechanisms are mechanisms by which socially valued investments are rewarded. Since it may be very difficult to draw specific lines around things as abstract as ideas or traits, intellectual property rights sometimes introduce a dichotomy between the valued investment and the awarded market. A concrete example of this dichotomy between the investment and the award is the innovation of the optimal sized racquet head, developed from a more general formula that determined the optimal trade-off between wind resistance (too large a head) and required accuracy (too small a head). The inventor of the 'oversized' tennis racquet determined that a racquet of 117.5 square centimetres was optimal for tennis. In fact, this represented an investment in the creation of a pure idea that would not have been appropriable through marketing of tennis racquets (because other sellers would have immediately entered the market with the same head). In addition, the value of the idea was also far more general than the specific application of tennis, as the same formula could be applied in many other sporting contexts.

However, the intellectual property rights regime awarded this inventor with a protected market right in all racquet head sizes between 100 (the original size of a tennis racquet head) and 135 square centimetres. All consumer states then, effectively, entered into an exclusive purchasing agreement with this innovator for these sizes of racquets. This protected market then acted as compensation for the investment in information-creation made by this inventor.

The important point about the nature of the intellectual property regime is that the exclusive rights in the tangible good did not match up very well with the actual idea being awarded. The innovator's idea was more specific than the range of tangible goods allocated, but this product market area was what was required in order to compensate the idea adequately. Similarly, the innovator's idea was also far more general than simply this one application would indicate; however, the patent allowed the more general uses of the idea to flow into the public sector while allotting a range of more specific uses to the inventor. Therefore, the tangible good acts as an award for the provision of intangible services, but it does not need to match up with the intangible services as well, as in the case of the market mechanisms mentioned previously.

It is equally possible to link protected markets to investments in diverse resources stocks, because these stocks also feed into various industries in an indirect and usually inappropriable fashion. Just as investments in human capital will generate information (ideas and innovations), investments in human capital also generate informational values. The problems are virtually identical: How is it possible to encourage societies to invest in forms of capital that generate inappropriable but important goods and services?

For example, many pharmaceutical innovations are developed from a starting point of knowledge derived from the biological activities of natural organisms. When a new start is required, it is often initiated by returning to the uncharted areas of biological activity (unknown plants and insects), but after the long process of product development and introduction, there is no compensation for the role played by the diverse resource in initiating the process. The informational input supplied from the diverse resource system goes unpaid for, and this means that there will be no incentive to invest in the natural capital that generates this information.

A *sui generis* property right system could be constructed that would be analogous to an intellectual property right system. There would not be anything in this that would conflict with existing regimes; it would simply represent an extension of this idea for compensating intangible services into realms other than those deriving from human-capital investments. To a large extent, the extension of intellectual property regimes to include natural resource-generated information simply levels the playing field between those societies which are more heavily endowed with human capital and those which are more heavily endowed with natural forms of capital.

The third protocol to the Biodiversity Convention should be one that establishes an international rights registration authority for the purpose of awarding property rights in useful characteristics or traits deriving from natural resources. This rights registration authority would serve the same function as a national patent office, and its registered rights would be accorded the same respect by the various national legal systems. The distinguishing feature of this authority would be its requirement of a given level of investment in the retention of diverse habitats and systems for the purpose of prospecting, before any rights could be awarded under the system. The protocol is further developed and described in Chapter 9.

Conclusion

This chapter has presented a quick overview of the developments foreseen for the Biodiversity Convention. Recent history has demonstrated that the basic nature of the problem of biodiversity conservation is appreciated by a wide range of movements, and the Biodiversity Convention has codified the basic framework for a workable agreement. The problem remains to give some flesh to the bones of this Convention, and it is the object of this volume to set out the direction for the future development of the Convention and the reasons for the choice of these options.

This chapter has outlined the basic nature of the protocols that are required for the implementation of the Convention in a real and substantive fashion. In sum, it is necessary to invest in a diversity of international institutions that will support development down a diversity of paths that are based upon a diversity of resources. Otherwise, global development will continue to erode the diversity that once resided on Earth: institutional, social and biological. The three layers of diversity are all built one upon the other.

The protocols to the Convention must establish a layer of international institutional diversity which will support diverse development paths and hence diverse resource bases. The protocols selected for presentation here are those which establish international institutions which absolutely necessitate universal acceptance for their success. The continuing negotiations under the Convention should be focused upon those roles that cannot be assumed by any other forum, and it is this criterion that recommends these specific protocols.

7

CONTRACTING FOR BIODIVERSITY: TRANSFERRING DEVELOPMENT RIGHTS ACROSS INTERNATIONAL BOUNDARIES

Introduction: Contracting for Biodiversity

This chapter addresses the general nature of the contract form that would be required for the effective conservation of biodiversity in those countries which host it. That is, this chapter enquires as to how the global willingness to pay for biodiversity might be translated into biodiversity supplies in the most direct fashion. This is not a simple question from the incentives standpoint. It is not a straightforward matter of simply transferring funds from demander to provider; it is instead necessary to transfer those funds in a structured fashion so that incentives to conserve biodiversity are instilled. As has been discussed here and elsewhere, the creation of instruments that have real and substantial impacts on incentives to conserve biodiversity is difficult to achieve (Munasinghe and McNeely, 1994).

The nature of the necessary form of contract is indicated by reference to a hypothetical world in which rights in biodiversity services could be fully marketable. In such a world, broader communities (local, national and global) could then bargain with local land owners in order to acquire the right to these services. In the context of biodiversity, this would entail the acquisition of the rights to particular land uses that are especially detrimental to the supply of biodiversity. For example, there have been suggestions that the supply of biodiversity from the Amazon could be ensured if only the 'burning rights' were acquired from local users (Schneider, 1992). Hence, a contract for the transfer of all the rights to clear and burn the lands in the Amazon basin would be adequate to supply the biodiversity demanded from that region.

Why would land owners agree to the transfer of any of the rights to develop land in any manner? The theory is that the land owner could be induced through agreements to transfer such rights in return for payments for those rights. If such rights were freely transferable, then it would be anticipated that the optimal distribution of land uses would result. The broader community would continue to acquire any particular land use rights (burning, clearing, ranching, timber extraction) so long as the value of the services obtained from denying such uses was higher than the value of that use to the land owner. When exchanges stopped, the land owner would continue to hold all uses that were not expressly transferred, and would have been compensated for all of those that were. So long as all of the uses of a given area are valued, the property rights approach allows for the allocation of land uses between the various competing users (Pearce, 1991).

This is the theory behind the *transferable development rights* approach to biodiversity conservation. In short, when it is possible to unbundle the various services flowing from the ownership of a parcel of land, it would be possible in theory to use a form of property rights to efficiently allocate the various rights of land use between the interested parties. If it were possible to do this in the case of biodiversity's services, then there would be no biodiversity problem. The people who wanted biodiversity would simply acquire the rights from those who are able to supply it. This is the motivating idea for looking at property rights/contracting forms of solutions to the biodiversity problem.

The practice of transferring development rights differs quite considerably from the theory. The closest approximations in real life involve the debt for nature and the environmental trust fund movements. However, neither of these come close to creating an explicit international bifurcation of specific rights in real property. They have instead concentrated on creating funds for the general implementation of domestic strategies concerning the conservation of parks, protected areas and biodiversity. These are also important roles to fulfil and useful mechanisms, but they do not constitute a solution to the underlying problem of necessary international institutional development.

What is required is a new multilateral international institution on a global scale that will provide a dynamic and perpetual mechanism for transferring the values given to biodiversity's services from the global community to the host states. This mechanism will generate future funding by effecting current contracted-for results. It will effectively allow for the introduction of some modicum of global land use planning (by determining and effecting a minimum level of diversity retention) without any derogations of national sovereignty. It will not so much transfer development rights as enable alternative development paths. The purpose of this chapter is to demonstrate how both the theory and the practice of transferring development rights need to evolve in order to most effectively conserve global biodiversity.

The chapter proceeds by initially describing how property rights institutions operate in the domestic context to solve problems similar to the biodiversity problem, and then why they do not operate in the international context. The section on alternative international financial mechanisms critically summarises the current practice in these institutions, and indicates what is missing from these approaches. The following section specifies the particular constituents of the institution required to address this facet of the biodiversity problem, while the section on efficient international financial mechanisms indicates what shape the institution will take for maximum effectiveness. The workings of the suggested institution are then described.

The biodiversity problem represents a challenge for the international community to create institutions that reward very different forms of development than have gone on before. One type of institution required is a regime that will look at land use from a global perspective, and then enable the representation of the global community's preferences at the ground level. Local peoples will then consider these preferences for biodiversity's services in their decisions concerning land uses because they are backed up with funding, just as they consider global preferences for more standard commodities such as beef, tea or timber. All that is required is the willingness to invest in the international institution that will make such exchanges possible.

The Efficient Management of Land Use in the Domestic Context

The first point to make concerns the use of property rights institutions in the domestic context to resolve land use conflicts. If there is a particularly interesting parcel of land with multiple land uses (e.g. residential vs. parkland), then there is always the question of how to determine the use(s) that are to be effected. One possibility is for society to allow absolute property rights to a particular individual, and allow that person to make all determinations concerning all aspects of the property's use. There are very few societies where this all or nothing approach is the exclusive option; in most countries, there is always the possibility of dividing the various uses of the property between various constituencies (neighbours, industries, city citizens) with the residual of the rights in the property redounding to the owner.

In short, it is always possible to unbundle many of the various services that flow from a parcel of land and give these as rights to various individuals or groups. In the context of private transactions, this is precisely what occurs in the case of the use of various forms of easements, servitudes, rights of way, sub-surface rights and leases. It is possible to separate out many of the various uses of a piece of land from the residual rights, and to convey them separately. This has been done with regard to particular rights of use (e.g. a servitude not to develop the land for commercial use or not to alter its appearance) and with regard to the total rights of use (e.g. a fixed term lease). In the domestic context it is possible to unbundle the various rights in real property and to engage in a transaction in regard to any manner of right of use or development.

Sometimes there are interests in land uses that are communal rather than individual in nature. For example, in the development of a city, it may be in the community interest to restrict building intensity and building height in order to preserve light and air quality. Any individual within the community would like to develop his or her property to the fullest, but all recognise the community interest in a joint restriction on aggregate development intensity. Similarly, it is often important to take an overarching perspective regarding the range of land uses that will be allowed and where to allocate them. This ensures that all forms of activities have a place in the community and that the positive and negative externalities between them are taken into account in determining how much land to allocate to particular uses. Hence, many communities recognise the importance of providing for green belts or parks within their boundaries in order to provide the land uses that these designations afford.

These collective forms of land use allocation are accomplished by means of legal devices known as *land use planning* or *zoning*. This occurs either when all parcels of land in the same vicinity undertake the same restriction on use (e.g. no commercial development in a residential community) or when certain parcels are designated for very restricted uses for the benefit of the entire community (e.g. greenbelt designated properties). The former case requires no compensation to be effected, while the latter usually does. This is because the former is equivalent to a conveyance of specific limited rights to the community, in return for the receipt of all other land owners' conveyances of the same rights. There is a form of reciprocity involved in the mechanism. In the latter case where the community wishes to acquire most of the rights of use to a particular parcel of land, then some form of compensation device is required. This is not problematic in the domestic context, as the state is usually considered to be the fundamental arbiter of property rights within most societies. In this role, it may exercise the so-called power of *eminent domain*: the right to determine unilaterally the fair price for the rights it wishes to acquire. By means of the exercise of its powers of zoning and eminent domain, the community is able to implement a community-wide land use plan.

Land Uses involved in Transfer:

	TOTAL	PARTIAL
PARTIES: Private to Private	CONVEYANCE	EASEMENT
Private to Public	EMINENT DOMAIN	ZONING & REGULATION

Figure 7.1 Transfers of Land Use Rights – The Domestic Context

Figure 7.1 demonstrates the various bundlings of land uses which have been developed within the domestic context in order to allow the transferral of partial rights of use. This unbundling of all of the uses of a particular parcel of land allows for the division of its uses between a large number of competing interests. In this way, the allocation of the rights of use in a land parcel may proceed on an efficient basis, enabling the transfer of particular uses while retaining the residual.

In short, pure property rights institutions have been very effective in the domestic context for the solution of problems similar to the biodiversity problem. Communities have been able to create joint restrictions on development that preserve the common goods and services from restricted development, e.g. the preservation of light and air quality in certain densely populated areas. They also have been able to create community plans which guarantee the existence of a wide range of land uses, sometimes incorporating very broad restrictions on the rights to development. Most cities have used this approach to guarantee the presence of some green areas or belts within their boundaries which would not otherwise exist. These institutions have already existed for 100 years in the domestic context; the question at hand concerns the capacity to translate such institutions to the global context for the preservation of large 'green belts' for biodiversity conservation.

The Inapplicability of Domestic Property Rights Institutions: Revisited

The global problem of biodiversity conservation is analogous to the problem of land use allocation that occurs within the domestic context. What is required is a global land use plan that shows the range of land uses that should be preserved in the global interest, and also some means of implementing this plan. As in the domestic context, one facet of implementation will involve reciprocity; this is the approach taken under those international treaties which work on a 'listing' basis. For example, the RAMSAR Convention concerning the preservation of wetlands operates by means of an internationally published list of RAMSAR wetland sites; this list allows each country to view the efforts of others in the conservation of such sites, and affords each the opportunity to publish its own efforts in the hopes of affecting others' determinations. Such lists operate as international zoning schemes in that they allow countries to demonstrate their development restrictions on a reciprocal basis (WCMC, 1992; Swanson and Barbier, 1992).

The difficult facet of the global biodiversity problem arises in those instances where reciprocity is unavailable. This is the case for example in those situations where the systems or species to be preserved are relatively restricted or unique, e.g. the tropical rainforests or certain endangered species. Since the majority of biodiversity is often asserted to fall within the borders of a small number of 'mega-diversity' states (Brazil, Zaire, Indonesia), and the vast majority falls within the developing world, reciprocity is unlikely to be an instrument capable of resolving the problem (Swanson, 1994). In the domestic context, this problem is overcome by recourse to the instrument of eminent domain (because it is recognised that property rights values may be unilaterally determined by the purchaser/state); however, this instrument is unavailable here because the property rights' values are determined by the supplier in the context of biodiversity rather than the purchaser. This means that some form of mechanism must be put into place that will enable the land use planning authority to agree the value of the rights with the host state.

The biodiversity problem lies in the fact that the global community is interested in acquiring a set of land uses in particular habitats from individual states, because these land uses (e.g. modern agriculture, burning and clearing) are incompatible with the provision of biodiversity's services. The global community would like to develop a mechanism that allows the unbundling of land use rights in certain parcels of land, and the acquisition of certain of these rights from the supplier state. The problem lies in the recognition that it is the supplier that has the power to determine its own valuation of those rights and the power to enforce the property rights distribution.

An efficient financial mechanism for biodiversity conservation would perform the role of efficiently allocating these land uses between land owners and the global community. It would do so by enabling the transfer of the rights to develop particular land uses from owners to the global community – in those circumstances when the relative valuations induced such an exchange. That is, an efficient financial mechanism would fill this missing market.

The translation of the domestic institutions set out in Figure 7.1 to the global context has been proposed by various authors (Panayotou, 1992). Panayotou proposes that an institution similar to a conservation district be translated to the developing world. In this instance, the developing country would allow certain districts of their country to be zoned for conservation, with foreign entities eligible to acquire the development rights within these districts. He cites the Merck Pharmaceuticals payment of US$1 million to Costa Rica as an example.

The problem with the idea of translating the domestic concept directly to the international level is that property rights institutions do not exist across national boundaries. Rights in land flow from the sovereign, and so they may be allocated and enforced as the sovereign sees fit. Property rights are allocated efficiently by the sovereign when they are given with certainty and full transferability. However, this assumes that the holder of these rights puts them to use for purposes consonant with the national objectives. If the holder instead puts them to use toward other objects (here, the global objective of biodiversity conservation), then there is an inherent conflict between the global and national objectives. Since the nation is the source of all property rights, it is able to resolve the conflict by redefining the prior conveyance.

This is the paradox of the biodiversity problem. At present biodiversity's services are uncompensated and so they are underprovided by their owner states. All parties would be better off if a transfer of land uses occurred which compensated those states for providing biodiversity services. However, if such a transfer occurred, it would immediately be voidable by the owner state that had just been compensated. Hence, the transfer will not occur and the efficiency gain will not be acquired. The absence of the appropriate institution guarantees the continued loss of biodiversity. The biodiversity problem is a problem of the non-transferability of real property rights for these purposes beyond national boundaries; that is, it is a problem precisely because this instrument does not exist at the international level. The only property rights that are transferred in such an exchange are those which the owner state is willing to enforce *ex post facto*. If the state has already received the entirety (or even the majority) of the compensation that it anticipates receiving, then the state will not be willing to enforce an allocation of land use rights that are, by definition, against its own interests. A pure property rights approach of the domestic variety cannot resolve the biodiversity problem, simply because property rights (the whole bundle or mere parts) cannot be transferred across national boundaries in a straightforward manner. This much is a given, and it is the ultimate source of the biodiversity problem from a property rights perspective.

Alternative International Financial Mechanisms for Transferring Land Use Rights

Many people and organisations have previously recognised the non-transferability of real property rights within the international context and they have proposed alternative institutions. (Hansen, 1989; Katzman and Cale, 1990; Schneider, 1992). All of these institutions are based on the idea of establishing some form of indigenous representation of the preferences for conservation. Recently some of these institutions have even come into being, in the form of the environmental trust fund movement. It is important to analyse both the evolution of the theory, and the initial practical steps in this direction, in order to understand what sort of institution is required for the resolution of the global biodiversity problem.

The underlying research indicates the basic nature of these institutions. Katzman and Cale (1990) proposed the initiation of a tripartite foundation within the state's boundaries, consisting of representatives of the state, donor groups and multilateral organisations. This foundation would then have the right to purchase 'conservation easements' within that state. Schneider (1992) proposed the development of indigenous legislation to foster a 'transferable burning rights' system. These rights would be acquired by intra-state organisations with, presumably, extra-state resources. Hansen (1989) discussed the model on which these newer institutions are loosely based, i.e. the debt for nature swap. In these contracts, indigenous foundations were endowed with external purchasing power to acquire rights of land use for conservation purposes.

The problem with these proposals and the institutions they have spawned is that these mechanisms fail to include the crucial ingredient for cost-effective conservation, i.e. a dynamic and conditional contract carefully specifying the flows between the international community and the owner state. Instead, they all operate through a 'black box' termed an indigenous foundation.

For example, the Indonesian Biodiversity Foundation was established under Indonesian law on 28 February 1994. It was conceptualised and provided with start-up funding through US$5 million of USAID monies, and it is to be capitalised at the level of US$40 million by virtue of a grant agreement between the governments of Japan, the US and Indonesia. The Board of Trustees will invest the proceeds of the fund into activities in furtherance of the Biodiversity Conservation Strategy and the National Biodiversity Action Plan. That Board is necessarily devoid of governmental representatives and is constituted of: NGOs (7); natural scientists (6); social scientists (3); private sector representatives (4); art organisations (1); and donor organisations (2) (IUCN, 1995).

Why are the unconditional commitments (represented by the establishment of this foundation under the auspices of the national Conservation Strategy and Action Plan) inadequate to the task of generating the efficient level of finance for the conservation of Indonesia's biodiversity? As indicated previously, the fundamental problem of biodiversity is the efficient registration of the preferences of the global community with land holders making crucial land use decisions. References to 'indigenous foundations' leave this mechanism unspecified; that is, the establishment of such a foundation does not indicate precisely how the preferences of the global community are to be translated into flows of biodiversity. Such a mechanism would instead provide the means for the global community to provide a flow of compensation conditional on the receipt of an ongoing flow of biodiversity's services.

The various debt for nature and environmental trust fund movements suffer from the failure to establish this form of contractual conditionality. On account of this these mechanisms do not provide an institution for transferring rights across borders. In order to accomplish this, there will be the need to establish some form of dynamic conditionality, where one party provides a service and the other provides payment for that service followed by another period's services, etc.

This is essential because the inclusion of a dynamic sort of conditionality is required to address the problem of 'demand revelation': the extraction of the maximum amount of compensation for biodiversity's services. The global community will only be willing to transfer the full amount that they are willing to pay for the conservation of biodiversity if they are able to see that these payments will be effective in accomplishing their objectives. If the real and effective acquisition of further development rights is not clearly seen to be related to the expenditure of each additional dollar, then the mechanism will be inadequate in capturing the full amount that the North is willing to pay for biodiversity conservation.

The Required Form of Institution for Global Biodiversity Contracting

What is the nature of the institution that is required to establish this level of credibility? The nature of the optimal financial mechanism is not a property rights institution, but a three-party contract between Global Community, Owner State, and the Land Holder. The contract must allocate the rights of use in the land between the global community and the land holder. It must also provide a mechanism for enforcing this allocation. Finally, it must provide inducements for the owner state to continue within the agreement (Cervigni, 1993; Swanson, 1994).

Box 7.1 Elements of an optimal financial mechanism

The necessary elements of an effective international financial mechanism are:

- contract between global community and owner state;
- allocation of land uses between global community and land holder;
- conditional system of rental payments.

The contract form must be between the global community and the owner state, because the object is to transfer land use rights between the two. The owner state is required to be a party as it is the source of all enforcement authority for all property rights within its territory. The contract must then allocate land uses between the global community and the land holder, by allowing the global community to purchase those restrictions for which it is willing to outbid the land holder. The form of compensation must be a stream of rental payments paid to the owner state contingent upon its enforcement of the agreed allocation of land uses in prior periods.

Therefore, an international financial mechanism for the transfer of land use rights will take the form of a contracted stream of payments paid over time to the owner state for the enforcement of its agreed allocation of rights. This is the form that the mechanism must take in order for it to be effective, because it specifies the necessary parties and their necessary roles.

Efficient International Financial Mechanisms

In order for the financial mechanism to be cost-effective, there must be methods for determining and implementing the agreed allocation of land use rights at least cost. The specific mechanism employed for this purpose is known as a *franchise agreement*. Its implementation in this case is complicated only by the fact that it has never before been attempted within the public sector at the international level. There are numerous examples of franchise agreements in both private and public sectors, but they are found only within the private sector at the international level (Klein and Saft, 1988).

In the public sector, franchise agreements are utilised to contract out to private operators limited term monopoly rights in the provision of various public services, such as transport, communications or electricity (Vickers and Yarrow, 1988; Williamson, 1976, 1985). In general, a franchise agreement operates through the state's claim to a natural monopoly right in the provision of a particular good or service. Then the state holds an auction to allocate this right, and the winning bidder receives a limited term franchise in return for an annual rental payment.

A franchise agreement differs from a standard two-party rental agreement in that (at the domestic level) it implicitly includes a third party. In the domestic context, the third party is the public interest, and this interest is used to justify a wide variety of constraints and restrictions on the use of the franchise (e.g. price restrictions, universal service requirements, etc.). These restrictions are not viewed as burdensome by the party receiving the franchise (the *franchisee*) because they were part of the franchise when the franchisee made its bid. Therefore, a domestic franchise agreement is an implicit division of rights between franchisee and third party (the public interest).

An international form of franchise agreement would be a more simple version of its domestic counterpart. It would be based on the *explicit* allocation of rights between the franchisee and the third party, and *both parties* would be required to tender explicit rental payments for their allocations. This would make perfectly clear what rights are being offered to each party, and it would allow for the creation of 'markets' (auctions) for these rights. If these rights are auctioned in a non-collusive environment, then the incentives for their subsequent enforcement are created with their transfer.

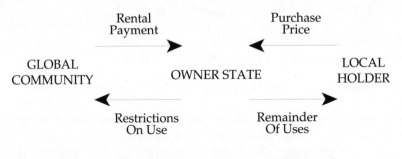

Figure 7.2 Optimal international mechanism for allocating land use rights

In terms of Figure 7.2 the owner state uses an international form of franchise agreement as the method for determining the allocation of land use rights in a parcel of land. It may auction the rights to certain land use restrictions within designated zones of its territories to the global community (represented through a multilateral organisation). The rights that are auctioned may be purchased by either the global community or some local developer, depending on the bidding. The bid and the payment for these rights is in the form of a stream of conditional rental payments. If the owner state fails to enforce the agreed allocation in any one period, then the remainder of the payment stream is forfeited.

In this way, the allocation of rights between global community and local land holders may be accomplished cost-effectively. Each party has the incentives to participate within the agreement only to the extent that the proposed allocation is first-best. If a party enters into the agreement willingly, then it has the incentives to perform its undertakings.

How Would Contracting for Biodiversity Work in Practice?

The fundamental need is for a global land use planning authority that has the responsibility for devising a plan to ensure that a diversity of land uses continues to exist across the globe, and the resources to ensure that its plan is given effect. The important point to make in the context of this meeting however is that the effective implementation of such a plan should in turn generate the resources to keep that plan in effect. Once the financial mechanism is shown to be a credible instrument for translating global preferences into prevailing land uses, this should in itself go a long way toward attracting the funding that it requires.

How would the initial institution be developed in order to establish this credibility? It would work something like as follows:

Development of Global Land Use Plan
The first step would seem to be the creation of a global land use planning authority, whose charge it is to develop some sort of a plan incorporating the range of land uses that should be retained and in what approximate proportions. This plan must at the outset be general enough to allow for a number of different avenues for its implementation; that is, it should stop at the level of generality of general systems such as tropical and temperate forests, wetlands etc. The object of such a plan is to create a generally agreed direction for conservation, not a specific plan for particular land areas. It would be based on scientific recommendations, but include inputs from all portions of the geo-political community. The plan does not constitute a required agenda for action, but a general statement of the range of land uses to be conserved.

Specification of Restrictions and Conditions
The second step toward the creation of the financial mechanism is the first step in the implementation of the land use plan. An institution must be established for the purpose of channelling available funding into the enactment of the plan (call this the Land Use Agency (LUA)). The LUA selects one of the land uses that it deems most threatened (e.g. tropical forests) and constructs a package of land use restrictions which it proposes

to acquire (a Restricted Land Use Agreement (RLUA)). For example, the LUA could develop a thirty-year agreement for the acquisition of all rights to clearing and burning in a 100,000 hectare area of tropical forest. This contract would then detail all of the conditions that must be satisfied (by certification of the LUA standards committee) at the end of each year of the term of the agreement. If the conditions of the RLUA are fully satisfied over the entire territory, then the full agreed rental rate is paid and the contract continues. If only partially fulfilled, then the rental rate is paid on a per hectare basis, and the remainder of the contract is terminable by the LUA.

Tender of Restricted Land Use Contract

The contract for these land use restrictions is then put out to international tender. It is advertised in the international press, with the full terms of the contract available to all interested parties. The tender announcement states a date and time by which any interested party must make its bid for the contract. Bids should usually be made by the host state, or by a private individual with the support of the host state. The bid should specify:

- willingness to accept the terms of the RLUA;
- the territory to be subject to the terms of the agreement (indicated on a fully specified map); and
- the per hectare annual rental payment required by the host state (and/or owner) for the acceptance of the agreed restrictions.

Designation of Agreed Restricted Territories and Certification of Status

Once the bids are received the LUA then must ascertain the number of the bids to accept, ranging from all to none. Once accepted, the LUA's responsibility is to undertake inspections to ensure compliance with the restrictions within the agreement. The payments for the restricted land uses flow to the contracting party (usually the host state), which then enforces the division of land uses between the LUA and the local communities by whichever means it deems fit. When the LUA certifies the status of its zoned territories and distributes its funding between them, it simultaneously announces its list of desired acquisitions in a call for additional funding from all sources. This additional funding is then guaranteed to flow to the acquisition of additional restricted lands.

Summary

The global land use authority would generate a very general global land use plan and a very specific map of the territories in which it ensures the application of particular land use restrictions. The certification and publication of these two lists on an annual basis would generate the credibility that is required for the resolution of the global biodiversity

Box 7.2 The issue of land use allocations

Potential Allocations of Rights in Biodiversity Conservation Region (The Range of Possible Divisions of Land Use Rights)			
Development Rights primarily allocated to:			
Global Community			Franchisee
Title for Zone:			
International wilderness	International park	Extraction reserve	Non-burning area
Allowed Uses:			
Limited tourism Indigenous peoples	Tourism	All extraction	All uses but burning

problem, since contributors could then view precisely how additional funding has already translated into additional conservation zones. All future flows of finance are channelled directly to the maintenance of existing, and the acquisition of additional, conservation zones. The only institutional investment required is that to maintain the staffing at a level sufficient to undertake the tasks of: plan formulation and interpretation; bid construction and implementation; and, zone certification and documentation. For this investment in a diverse international institution, the global community receives an instrument capable of allocating land uses between the global and local community in accordance with the perceived values of the various uses of that land.

Conclusion: A protocol for a planning authority

Contracting for biodiversity conservation is something that has occurred in many different contexts to date. There have been debt for nature swaps, environmental trust funds, and project-based lending by the Global Environmental Facility. All of these various movements have made some impact in the area and the approach to effective conservation has evolved considerably over this time, but there remains the need for the creation of a framework that ensures effective conservation for funds expended.

This is not simply necessary from the economic perspective; it is also necessary to ensure that future funds are forthcoming. The problem of global biodiversity may be seen as the need for a credible financial mechanism that will channel non-domestic values into effective biodiversity conservation. An international institution established under the Biodiversity Convention would be a significant step in the direction of consolidating the gains achieved and signalling the priority given to this problem.

What sorts of characteristics must this international institution have in order to be effective? The most important characteristic it must demonstrate is a dynamic structure, i.e. a structure that channels international funding only toward those states that are conserving biodiversity effectively. Another important characteristic is cost-effectiveness. The value of the land use rights obtained should be acquired at the least cost to the global community, for the purpose of obtaining the largest amount of diversity for a given budget. The fulfilment of these objectives will endow the mechanism with the credibility that it requires in order to generate a long-term flow of funding for biodiversity conservation.

Therefore, a protocol to the Convention should be adopted which establishes a single land use planning authority for these purposes. This authority would have the task of both preparing and implementing a plan for the global conservation of land use diversity. The most efficient framework within which it might work for these purposes would be that utilised in the domestic context for the franchising of specific tasks between potential suppliers. If constructed and conducted efficiently, this institution should be able to perform many of the tasks that are required for the channelling of funds between the material-rich and the biodiversity-rich.

8

INTERNATIONAL REGULATION OF THE WILDLIFE TRADE: RENT APPROPRIATION AND BIODIVERSITY CONSERVATION

International Intervention and the 'External' Regulation of Domestic Resources

Ultimately, state investments into the management of diverse resources will be constrained by the benefits that such investments are able to generate. International intervention that is based upon the direct inducement of further state investments in diverse resources will be similarly constrained. However, there are instances in which *external regulation* of the resource (i.e. in its product markets rather than its place of production) will yield greater returns per unit of investment. In that case, it may be optimal for the global community to utilise the instrument of external market regulation, generating supplier-state benefits through such intervention in consumer-state markets.

The regulation of the trade in the tangible goods of diverse resources (the wildlife trade) is a case in point. Although these resources are sourced, by definition, in the world's last refuges of diversity, the consumers of these products are often situated in the states with little diversity remaining. Turning once again to the African elephant for illustrative purposes, although the thirty host states reside within sub-Saharan Africa, the vast majority (about 80 per cent) of the tangible products from the African elephant have found their way to final consumers in the North: the US, Europe and Japan (Barbier et al., 1990). Since the flow of the wildlife trade through this 'pipeline'from South to North is fairly common for most diverse resources, this affords the possibility for Northern-based regulation of this exclusively Southern resource (Oldfield, 1984). When it is both more cost-effective and rent-productive to base regulation in the North, then an external method of intervention is the instrument of choice.

All of the necessary conditions for the construction of an effective international agreement apply equally here. In particular, this manner of global intervention must remain dynamically consistent through conditionality on state management spending. That is, the global community must invest each period to maintain the *external regulation mechanism*, in response to the supply state's management spending. This external mechanism must then automatically confer the enhanced benefits upon the investing supplier states. However, there is another role that an external regulatory mechanism must fulfil. The creation of enhanced benefits from trading the tangible goods and services of natural habitats will not necessarily generate increased investments in those habitats. This is because the enhanced benefits of wildlife trade will also generate increased pressure on the natural habitats, and thus increase the costliness of managing natural habitat production. The rents from diverse resource flows are equal to the gap between revenues received and the costs incurred per unit of production, and it is very likely that both revenues and costs will move together in the context of natural habitat management.

A constructive wildlife trade regime must be developed in order to fulfil this dual role: the creation of incentives for investment (through rent maximisation) and the minimisation of the costliness of diverse resource management. To some extent, these two objectives are in conflict; however, the optimal institution for regulating wildlife trade will take both into consideration.

This chapter considers the institutional detail of the solution to this problem. These are the institutions put into place under the Convention on International Trade in Endangered Species (CITES). This chapter constitutes a comparative case study of both the nature of the institution that would satisfy the requirements of a constructive trade control mechanism and the institution that currently exists, i.e. CITES.

The International Regulation of Wildlife Utilisation – An Economic Framework

A strategy of wildlife utilisation often has much to commend itself as a conservationist tool. It generates revenues for conservation and (in some cases) it creates incentives for the application of these revenues to that purpose. The latter objective is equally as important as the first. This has become apparent with the large number of conservation failures such as the establishment of 'paper parks' (i.e. established, but unmanaged national parks). It is the fact that it has the potential to combine these capacities, i.e. fund raising and incentives generating, that makes a strategy of wildlife utilisation so appealing. However, it is also apparent that a simple strategy of unregulated wildlife utilisation is not capable of generating these incentives in and of itself. Thus, wildlife exploitation remains a significant threat to many species. This happens whenever wildlife utilisation generates revenues but not rents. The difference is crucial, as revenues are simply returns that result from the labour expended in an activity (such as the hunting of wildlife) while rents result from the creation of a return to resource ownership. Where there are revenues to be earned from resource utilisation, but not rents, the incentives are to exploit but not conserve the resource.

Therefore, the object of a constructive *wildlife trade regulation mechanism* (in the sense of the creation of incentives to wildlife conservation) must be the creation of *rents* in the wildlife resource. What are the predictable difficulties that arise in the attempt at installing such a system? This chapter considers both 'sides' to the problem (demand and supply) and discusses the nature of the international environmental agreement required to address them.

First, the demand-side problems of wildlife utilisation will be considered. Here, the primary limitation of a utilisation strategy is its inapplicability to species which have low 'consumptive' use values. That is, some species happen to have developed prior usefulness and thus have a means of paying their way; others, however, have not. It is problematic that a strategy of wildlife utilisation extends expressly only to the conservation of the former and not to the latter.

The greater part of this chapter will focus, however, on the supply-side difficulties with wildlife utilisation. This is because it is often the case that the management of natural habitat utilisation is both difficult and costly to control, and this is one of the primary reasons why overexploitation has so often occurred in the context of natural habitats. Some of these difficulties are relatively easily remedied, for example by devolving the habitat from state to local community control (Swanson and Barbier, 1992). However, these problems can remain costly on account of the less intensive techniques used for control (e.g. lack of fences); and, in some instances, the conversion of natural habitats to more intensive forms of production (e.g. ranching or farming) will occur simply on account of these cost considerations.

A 'constructive' approach to wildlife utilisation must take these two factors into consideration and develop mechanisms which address both. The demand-side considerations (concerning the non-consumptive values of certain species) can be addressed through rent creation policies involving the construction of a *quota system* or its equivalent. The supply-side considerations (concerning the costliness of natural habitat control systems) can be addressed through selective purchasing policies involving the invocation of *conditionality* in consumer purchasing systems. Together, an effective constructive wildlife regulation system is capable of creating rents and channelling them to the conservation of species (Swanson, 1989).

Demand-Side Management of Tradable Wildlife Resources

The point of demand-side management is simply the maximisation of the rents potentially appropriable by the owners of the resource. All species have value, and much of this value resides in the northern developed countries. One facet of this value is consumptive in nature, i.e. individuals are willing to pay for the species' existence for the purpose of direct use of its characteristics. In order for the maximum number of any species to exist, the full extent of each type of value must be appropriated by its (and its habitat's) managers. This is the process of maximising the rents to the owners.

Revenue maximisation is a precondition to rent maximisation, and it is achieved through the control of the price at which the tangible products from natural habitats are sold. All goods have a certain price at which revenue maximisation occurs, and if there are not good substitutes for them, that price can often be quite a bit higher than that which exists in the market. The fact that natural habitat is becoming more scarce, and is expected to become even more so, contributes to the relative scarcity of its products, and this makes its revenue maximising prices (and the total revenues potentially appropriable from them) even higher (Krutilla, 1967). In short, one of the consequences of centuries of conversions of natural habitat to more specialised production systems is to increase the inelasticity of the flow of goods from the former (as supplies of these goods and their closest substitutes become more restricted) and to decrease the elasticities of the goods from the latter (as their supplies flood the market) (Swanson, 1991a).

This is the basis for the expectation that the demand for the tangible products of increasingly scarce natural habitats will usually be inelastic. This was found to be the case in a recent study of the demand for African elephant ivory, where it was found that an increase of 100 per cent in the price of ivory in Japan would result in a fall in quantities of only 70 per cent, thereby resulting in an overall increase of 30 per cent in the total revenues flowing to its suppliers (Barbier et al., 1990). Therefore, there is both a theoretical and an empirical basis for the expectation that revenues from the sale of the products of natural habitats might be enhanced through carefully orchestrated price controls.

The maximisation of the revenues from the consumptive use of wildlife resources is important precisely because it is representative of so much value that is *non-consumptive* in nature. That is, the regulation of the wildlife trade should be considered to be simply the regulation of those few bits and pieces of biological diversity that are valued on the market.

The maximisation of wildlife utilisation revenues provides the means of indirectly compensating for these inappropriable values. When it is clear that there are important positive, inappropriable, external values closely associated with the provision of a tangible good, there is good reason for society to increase the reward to the tangible good in order to provide an implicit return to the intangible one. That is, when these products come jointly (tangible/intangible) but it is only possible to price one of the two goods (because the other is of the nature of a public good), then it can be the optimal second best policy to provide price supports to the tangible good in order to foster the incentives to invest sufficiently in the habitat which supplies both.

In essence, in this framework, all of the species inhabiting a given parcel of natural habitat are being viewed jointly. While all of these species have value (in the sense that we would like to see them continue to exist), some of them have consumptive values and others do not. Since it is very hard to require payment of 'existence values' to the owners of the natural habitat, an alternative means of acquiring additional value is to instead increase the amount of the 'consumptive value' appropriated. To some extent, the surplus consumptive values captured by the landowners with respect to a few species replace the inappropriable non-consumptive values of many other species, and restore the correct incentives for investing in unaltered habitat. The parcel of natural habitat is kept for the use of all of its resident species, and paid for by the price supports on the consumption of a very few of them. This is the rationale for encouraging the creation of mechanisms for rent appropriation in wildlife utilisation.

The Nature of Rent Appropriation Mechanisms

One of the most substantial obstacles to increased investments in diverse resources is the generally low rate of resource rent appropriation in the supply states. That is, very frequently, diverse resources are sold in product markets at or near the cost of harvesting them (labour costs, capital costs); there is often no value received in these markets that is attributable to the natural resource itself (Swanson, 1991b).

It is clear that an open access management system will produce this result. With no coordination of the harvesting sector, the harvesters (if there are enough of them) will harvest until the price is driven down to the costs of access, i.e. zero natural resource rent (Gordon, 1954; Clark, 1976). If there were sufficient returns available to the management of this commons, it is predictable that the state would invest in altering the prevailing management regime. However, it is very often the case that the supply state does not invest in its diverse resources.

One reason for this is that there are in fact two layers of commons involved in the production and marketing of the resource, and the individual supplier state only has control over one. There are limited returns available to expenditures on management when they only reach a part of the management problem. On the demand side of management, the problem is that there are many different potential suppliers of the same wildlife resources in most cases, and hence each individual supplier sees little incentive to manage its resources particularly well. Even if one supplier manages its resources well, the other suppliers will dominate the market with their lax management and ill-managed supplies. Therefore, even if a diverse resource is potentially profitable, if production is properly managed, there may still be a disincentive to investments in domestic management by reason of non-coordination with other producer states.

This indicates the nature of the route for intervention by the global community. In short, recall that the driving motivation for state management spending is likely to be the increased state benefits received through increased unit resource rents. External regulation should be used to do this when it is more cost-effective than internal. The precise form that this manner of international regulation takes mirrors the problem that must be solved in respect to any commons. The objective is to invest sufficient resources to remove some producer states from the international market place. Such a mechanism creates an incentive to invest (in order to get into the mechanism) and then sustains that incentive (through increased benefits from internal management expenditures).

In principle, it is possible for the global community to generate the maximum resource rental value, as there is no reason why there need be more than one supplier to the international market. All that is required is that the consumer states agree to make all purchases from a single point of supply, which then acts as a conduit for all supplier states. At this point in the market, coordination of all states' production occurs in order to maximise aggregate rents. In essence, the maximum unit rental value is available to each of the states supplying this conduit, and the incentives for managing the resource are based around this value.

Supply-Side Management of Wildlife Resources

The international community has the ability to use its power (as the consumers of wildlife products in international trade) to create rents in wildlife products. Difficult problems are created simultaneously, however, because the creation of rents will simultaneously create a group of opportunists who will seek to capture these rents to the detriment of the range states and the wildlife resources.

Therefore, it is necessary for the international community to create a system for the careful discrimination between different groups of suppliers of the wildlife product; otherwise, it is predictable that a rent-creation strategy must fail. The cost of producing wildlife sustainably will always be greater than the cost of open access exploitation (because the latter includes an implicit rent to the resource). Without an effective mechanism for discriminating between the two types of suppliers, the unsustainable producers will drive the sustainable from the market (Akerlof, 1974).

The remainder of this chapter is an analysis of the necessary components of an international regime for the discrimination between producers, and a comparison of the existing regime to investigate how it performs as a constructive trade control mechanism.

Stock Conditionality

The international community wishes to confer the enhanced benefits from demand management only upon those states that generate global benefits from their diverse resources. This implies that there must be some conditionality on the assignment of enhanced benefits, and this conditionality must relate to owner-state investment in the maintenance and management of diverse resources. The requirement that diverse natural habitats be conserved for low-intensity uses will be termed *stock conditionality*. The essence of supply-side management is to create a system that effectively discriminates between the flow of wildlife goods from investors in diverse resource stocks, and the flows of such goods from all others.

Certification is the process that enforces stock conditionality. Suppliers would be certified on the basis of their demonstrated management of the natural habitat and wildlife resources for which they are responsible. Specific criteria indicative of the sustainable management of natural habitat (regarding the nature and extent of development in the species' habitat) would need to be included within the trade control regime in order to provide the basis for differentiation between certifiable and non-certifiable suppliers.

This system of indicators must be applied periodically to determine whether a state is to be given certified status, and also to determine whether that status is to be retained. In this way, consumer state purchasing is made conditional on diverse resource stocks in each and every period. Such a tailored control regime fosters an international system of incentives toward sustainability, as potential suppliers pursue certified status and the already certified strive to retain it.

To this point, there is little to differentiate the analysis of this chapter from that of Chapter 7, other than the attachment of the global premium to the wildlife product. The remainder of this chapter however examines the particular costliness of this manner of benefit enhancement, i.e. the costliness that comes from attempting to segregate between products that have been sustainably and non-sustainably produced.

An International Mechanism for Controlling Access to Natural Habitat within National Borders

A primary objective of an effective supply-side policy is to reduce the costliness (or to increase the cost-effectiveness) of owner-state management of designated natural habitats. This is because there are always two factors placing pressure on natural habitats: the costliness of its management in low intensity uses and the opportunity costs of its development for high intensity uses. In addition, attempts to combat the latter (via a wildlife rent creation strategy) will consequently increase the costliness of the former (by increasing pressure on the habitat). Therefore, the effectiveness of an international regime to create rents depends upon the capacity of that regime to reduce the costliness of managing the pressures that it creates internally.

This problem is complicated by the fact that it is not desirable to move toward simple, intensive management of the habitat. In general, it is inconsistent to speak of intensive controls in connection with natural habitat. One of the primary attributes of such habitat is its unregimented nature; this is what allows diversity to flourish. Therefore, one of the requisites of an effective supply-side policy will be its capacity to control supplies without intervening drastically within the habitat (by the use of fences, massive patrolling etc.).

A policy of selective purchasing solves the problem of management costliness in theory. A consumer-enforced commitment to purchase only from the designated supplier accomplishes this. In short, there is no incentive to engage in unauthorised harvesting if there is no market for the produce.

However, there are always black markets which undermine such controls. The extent of an illegal market is largely determined by the method of implementation and the consistency between the objectives of the controller and those being controlled. With regard to the latter, the vast majority of the *ultimate* consumers of many wildlife products reside in developed countries, where there is a widely expressed demand for more effective controls over natural habitat production. These persons can be expected to support a more effective system of trade controls.

This has been demonstrated in the case of the recent ivory trade controls implemented by the primary consumer states (the EC, the US and Japan) where the end consumers have effectively shut down the trade by refusing to purchase ivory products. Prices of ivory products have fallen precipitously in the US and EC end markets, while remaining fairly stable in the Asian. Therefore, unlike consumer state controls on the import of substances widely demanded by the citizenry of those states (e.g. various narcotic substances), the objectives of the end consumers of wildlife products are often fully consistent with the reduced flows of those products. When this is the case, it is possible to implement low-cost regulation based upon selective purchasing agreements.

Even assuming that the objectives of wildlife producers (the investors in diverse resource stocks) and wildlife consumers (the consumers of the end products) are broadly consistent, there remain other, intermediate groups whose interests are conflicting. An international trade mechanism must still deal with the problems raised by entities that come in between a direct producer-consumer exchange.

The Problem of Cross-Border Incursions

Even with a designated supplier system, there still remain incentives for the excessive exploitation of natural habitat. This is because each supplier has no incentive to restrict flows derived from natural habitats other than its own. In essence, conditionality which is based upon the status of a state's own diverse resource stocks provides no incentives to care for the resources of other states. Therefore, a system of conditionality with a narrow focus (on only the stocks of own-state resources) can encourage cross-border incursions as suppliers are willing to trade in any wildlife that does not visibly affect its own stocks.

The solution to this dilemma is for consumers to adopt *flow conditionality* as well. This would restrict the purchasing of quantities from a designated supplier to an amount that would correspond approximately to the quantities which could feasibly issue from the sustainable management of that supplier's own diverse resource stocks. The conditionality of certification must then be based on both the state of the diverse resource stocks *and* the maximum sustainable flows from those stocks. A consumer-enforced system of individual owner state quotas is the result of the second requirement. Given individual quotas, the owner state has absolutely no incentive to look elsewhere for supplies, as the correct management of its own diverse resource stocks will satisfy its quota (and correct management is a prerequisite to the retention of its certified status). In addition, given that the same system is applied across all other certified owner states, there is no longer any incentive for any of them to pursue others' supplies. Each supplier's habitat is secured because the size of its market is secured; cross-boundary excursions cannot increase the size of that market and so there is no longer any incentive to undertake them.

Such a system could be effectively implemented through a number of different mechanisms. Individual quotas – based on the anticipated sustainable flow of products from the correct management of designated natural habitat – could be established by a technical committee. These quotas could then be enforced through the issuance of 'coupons' or the construction of an 'exchange'. Coupons essentially take the place of the regulated commodity in the market. Once a given number are printed, then the consumer states enforce the regulatory system by refusing to admit the regulated good without a coupon. When the coupons are distributed to the designated suppliers, the task of controlling access to the species becomes one of controlling access to the coupons instead, which is usually a far less costly proposition (Swanson, 1989a, 1989b).

Alternatively, the consumer states could construct an 'exchange', which is a mechanism for assuring that goods on the market are 'exchanged' only between consumers and designated suppliers. An exchange operates by allowing certified trade to occur only within its walls, while consumers enforce the exchange mechanism by refusing entrance to any goods other than those traded through the exchange. Again, the exchange would have to establish and enforce individual quotas for each designated supplier, disallowing sales within the exchange beyond the annual quota (Swanson and Pearce, 1989).

The Problem of Manufacturer States

Both of the above options hinge upon the satisfaction of one of two conditions for their effective implementation: *either* all existing and potential consumer states agree to enforce the quota (this implies the full cooperation of all states as 'consumer state' must be defined to include all consumers of the worked and the *unworked* natural product, and the latter has been demonstrably mobile in the past); *or* all final consumers must agree to enforce the quota, and there is no allowed re-export of worked or unworked natural product (which implies the full cooperation of only the primary consumers: the US, the EC and Japan).

The first option above is a pipe dream, and its pursuit has brought international trade regulation into ill repute. It cannot work for two reasons. First, any given state in the world can be a possible manufacturing state. That is, although the raw material and the final consumers are relatively fixed, the labour necessary to work raw materials is very fluid. Therefore, a regime based on regulating the manufacturers (rather than the final consumers) of natural habitat materials must necessarily have the active cooperation of all the states of the world. This is not possible. There are too many states, and there is also a positive return to be had from breaking the system. Controls based on this mode of operation will only redirect, not restrict, the trade (Swanson, 1992a). Secondly, although the incentive to 'free ride' exists (in favour of deviating from the system) irrespective of whether the state is manufacturer or a consumer of the raw material, there is little countervailing incentive in favour of conservation in the manufacturing state. In the consumer state, however, the raw material is valued for its final use, and there will be an interest in its long-term conservation. For the manufacturer, raw material is more of an object with which to mix labour prior to sale; usually, there is a good prospect for moving to another, different material if the first comes into short supply. The manufacturer is, in essence, selling its skills more so than the raw materials (for which it is paying the full value to the producer states).

Therefore, in most instances, only the latter option exists, i.e. restricting all re-exporting of the natural materials. Initially, this sounds more harsh than it is in actuality, as its only implication is that the manufacturing sector must move its facilities to the consumer markets and import the raw material there for working and final sale. Given the demonstrated fluidity of most of these manufacturing industries (in both wildlife trade and other industries) this should not ordinarily be a major problem if the manufacturer is truly interested in the commodity.

Layers of Selective Purchasing Programmes

In the event that a problem with the relocation of the manufacturing sector does arise, there is an alternative, but it is generally too costly and cumbersome to be effective. This alternative allows the manufacturing sector to remain within one state while exporting to another, but only on the condition of consumer state enforcement of the control system as against the manufacturing states. Again the system hinges on consumers' rather than manufacturers' support – but this time the consumers' threat to withdraw custom applies to non-viable manufacturers, not to the producers of the raw materials. It requires the manufacturers to conform to the selective purchasing system (with regard to raw material purchasers) through a final consumer-based system of selective purchasing that is applied to the manufacturers.

This could operate through a 'restricted marking' system, whereby each final product for sale in a consumer state is provided with a numbered mark corresponding to the licence or permit under which it was imported into the manufacturing state. It would fall to the consumer states to maintain full records on their own imports of manufactured materials as well as the manufacturers' imports of raw materials *and* then to perform the complicated task of matching up manufactured quantities with licensed imports. This is a much more complex and costly system, and so its costliness will often dictate a policy of prohibited re-export instead. However, it demonstrates that the conservationist interests of final consumers can always be brought into use in trade regulation, but sometimes in a multiple-layered regime.

Demand- and Supply-Side Management Combined

Therefore, just as there are a number of demand-side options for controlling the international trade in wildlife products, there are a number of supply-side options as well. For each industry (constituted of range states/manufacturers/consumers) there will be a first-best system of controls which will combine some manner of demand-side controls with the best supply-side controls for that situation.

The combined system has as its objective the creation of *rents* in the wildlife resource and the channelling of those rents to the local managers through a system of *conditionality*. The key to the entire system is the enforceability of this conditionality in the context of natural habitat production. The system must create rents for the flows from diverse resource stocks by focusing on the simultaneous support of prices and reduction of management costliness (but only for the certified producers). The system commences with the commitment of funds by all of the *consumer* states to the system's enforcement of the conditionality of purchasing. These funds are the means by which rents are created and allocated, and hence they generate the enhanced benefits from diverse resource management.

The system is only as effective, in general, as is the weakest significant consumer's enforcement efforts. For this reason, the restriction of the necessary consumers to the smallest number possible, and to the group whose objectives are most consistent with diverse resource conservation, is important. Diverse resource conservation through wildlife utilisation is very likely an objective shared by producer states and end consumers. The regulatory problem often comes down to the elimination of intermediaries, whose interests are not similarly aligned.

One means by which the system can be made operable is through the elimination of intermediaries. A restriction on re-exporting accomplishes this. This creates the possibility for a direct purchasing agreement between owner state and final consumer. Therefore, an optimal wildlife utilisation regulatory system should move toward consumer-enforced 'commodity cartels', where the consumer states act to enforce the price supports adopted by the producers' association *on the condition that production occurs on a sustainable basis*. This will increase the returns to particular consumptive goods of natural habitat (and implicitly compensate investments in the supply of related non-consumptive goods as well) plus it will also decrease the costliness of natural habitat production.

An Example of a Rent Appropriation Mechanism – Natural Resource Exchanges

An example of this sort of mechanism would be a 'resource exchange'. Such an exchange would be the agreed supplier for all consumer states (group North), and the Northern states would then maintain the mechanism through continuous monitoring (expenditures) to prevent imports other than from the exchange. The exchange would purchase its supplies in an amount maximising aggregate rents. The aggregate quota would be allocated to participating states, and each would receive an enhanced unit rental value.

In consideration of the continued support by the Northern states for the exchange mechanism, the supplier states would allocate the exchange quota to sustainable producers of the resource, i.e. states investing in the management of their resource stocks and habitat. These producers would then receive an exchange-determined resource rental value, while other supplier states would receive an effective price near zero (depending upon the level of Northern funding invested in supporting the exchange mechanism). This would create incentives for other states to invest in diverse resources in order to join the exchange. To the extent that an exchange requires start-up costs, such as physical site and equipment, these would represent the asset-specific sunk costs required to institutionalise the mechanism. Such institutionalisation creates the assurance that is necessary for international regulation.

Existing and Optimal Trade Control Mechanisms

As indicated in Chapter 5, CITES is not at present structured in the form of a constructive trade control mechanism. In general, an Appendix II listing does little or nothing to supply incentives to control the trade; it is more of a monitoring mechanism. An Appendix I listing acts to withdraw demand from all suppliers of a species, the sustainable as well as the non-sustainable.

There is a fundamental need to understand the nature of the forces involved in a market, before there is any prospect for the development of constructive controls. CITES, despite the best of declared intentions, has failed structurally to provide these. Without constructive trade controls, there is an enhanced risk of species decline on account of both direct causes (overexploitation) and indirect (loss of habitat). All of the proximate forces for extinction are closely linked to the quantities of efforts and resources put into the management and conservation of the species and its habitat. Overexploitation pressures must be met with well-financed management operations. Development pressures must be met with land acquisition operations. The presence of both of these forces throughout the developing world requires the development of a trade control mechanism which *constructively* addresses both forces; one alone is insufficient. The failure of existing controls, domestic and international, to create and to constructively channel rents from wildlife resources to their management and to habitat conservation is at the heart of both forms of extinction threats, direct and indirect. It is for this reason that CITES must evolve to address these needs.

A constructive trade control mechanism should consist of the following:

- Optimal demand-side policies – These consist of price support policies which maximise the per individual value of a species, thereby enhancing the prospects of the species in the competition for scarce resources, and hence in the competition for survival.
- Optimal supply-side policies – These consist of trade control policies which structure trade to make it conditional on demonstrated sustainable utilisation of the producer state's natural habitat and the wildlife which it sustains.

The Direction for Change

Natural resource trade control mechanisms should evolve in the direction of constructive trade control mechanisms in order to address the joint threats of overexploitation and habitat losses as causes of species extinctions. In accordance with the analysis set forth earlier in this chapter, this will imply the need for the development of a regime of conditionality, where developed consumer states withhold purchases from developing supplier states unless:

- Stock conditionality – the supplier makes and enforces a commitment to conserve specified habitat for the species concerned; *and*
- Flow conditionality – the supplier's total annual product conforms to an externally determined quota which is linked to the total sustainable off take achievable from the designated habitat.

For many diverse natural resources, this form of regime would imply the creation of quotas in the range states – only to the extent that 'Wildlife Management Areas' were designated as available for the species and then only in quantities which might flow from that habitat. If any of these states were not to designate areas as protected habitat, then they would not achieve certified supplier status. When that status was conferred, it would only be for a quota that the designated area could sustainably generate. If activities incompatible with either designated habitat status or the allotted quota occurred, then the certified supplier status would be withdrawn for a small number of years. This system would provide incentives for non-certified range states to work toward sustainability, and for certified states to maintain it.

Then, it is the responsibility of the developed consumer states to enforce these quotas for the producers, creating and returning the rents from the resource to the managers of the resource. This would be done by the development of a rent maximising joint quota, which is then divided between the certified producers in proportion to their sustainable quotas. As with most wildlife resources, almost the entirety flows to the developed countries: the US, the EC and Japan. These states would have the responsibility of investing substantial amounts of resources to the monitoring of imports, in order to assure that only certificated diverse resources enter their borders.

Since it is very difficult to monitor for many diverse resources once they have been rendered into finished products, there are good reasons to simply disallow the re-export of manufactured goods made from these diverse resources. So long as manufactured goods are allowed to be exported, there is the possibility of disjunction between the manufacturer and the final consumer, and the former generally has less interest in the long-term survival of the resource. The disallowance of re-exporting may seem harsh, but it only implies that the manufacturer must move facilities towards the final markets. In this era of fairly fluid capital markets, it is not very unusual for manufacturers to do this.

Alternatively, there is also the option of direct green labelling of products. Final consumer states would then match up labels with the quotas purchased by that manufacturer. This would require a good centralised data handling centre, and very substantial commitments by consumer states to monitoring (of both retailers and ports). It is a hugely expensive alternative that cannot operate effectively in the absence of substantial commitments of funding, but it is the only option unless re-exporting is disallowed. However, this alternative might also be preferred for another reason. The use of green labelling at the individual consumer level would provide the consuming public with the important message that there are two kinds of wildlife products – those which are sustainably produced and those which are not. The former are pro-conservation and the latter are anti-conservation. At present, most consumers do not understand that such a separation is necessary; this has resulted in the withdrawal of substantial value from wild species, thus further threatening their existence.

The essence of a constructive trade control mechanism is to provide the means of making this distinction – between sustainable and unsustainable utilisation. The development of an option which recruited broad-based consumer support for such a mechanism would be a positive step. For this reason, the expensive step of multiple levels of screening might be pursued with regard to some wildlife resources.

Conclusion: A Protocol for Sustainable Use Certification

The Biodiversity Convention should be developed in the direction of creating mechanisms for discriminating between those suppliers which meet some criterion of sustainability and those which do not. At base what is required is an international institution that develops both the set of conditions required for certification as a sustainable producer, and the auditing mechanisms for implementing these certifications. It is no longer possible to employ blanket bans and expect them to have beneficial results for the diverse resource and its habitat; there is too much pressure on both species and habitats for a less-than-comprehensive approach to be successful. The potentially constructive effect of wildlife use and trade must be constructively channelled into biodiversity conservation. This raises many difficult issues concerning enforcement and implementation. It would make sense for the international community to embrace the concept of green labelling, and place its financial resources into an institution which is able to create and enforce producer standards. This chapter has outlined the conceptual basis for the development of such an institution (Fernandez et al., 1996).

9

BIODIVERSITY CONSERVATION AND INTELLECTUAL PROPERTY RIGHTS: CAPTURING INFORMATION'S VALUES

A Property Rights Approach to the Conservation of Biodiversity?

The problem of appropriating international flows of wholly intangible services has been recognised and addressed for over 100 years. The very first international convention, the Paris Patent Union, was on precisely this subject; it attempted to create in 1868 an international mechanism for repatriating compensation to those who invested to generate information. Since that time a very substantial body of national and international law has developed around the idea of generating flows of compensation to those individuals who invest in the creation of practical ideas. These laws are known collectively as intellectual property rights (IPR).

As will be demonstrated in this chapter, however, there is little in common between IPR and traditional property rights mechanisms. The latter deal mainly with tangible commodities capable of exclusive possession and clear delineation. IPR deal almost exclusively with informational services which are intangible and amorphous; they are not readily susceptible to either possession or delineation. An IPR regime deals with this difference through the mechanism of 'surrogate rights', i.e. monopoly rights delineated in a dimension that is tangible in lieu of rights in a dimension that is not. The one acts as a surrogate for the other, in order to encourage investments in the intangible resource.

It is this surrogate rights form of mechanism that might be applied in contexts other than human-created information. It would never be literally correct to discuss the use of intellectual property rights in the context of naturally generated forms of information; the intellect is the source of information deriving from investments in *human capital*. Human capital is the term used by economists to describe all of the various types of skills that humans are able to generate by virtue of investments in themselves through education, training and experience. When human capital is created, one of the ways that it manifests itself is in the intellect, and this is then a source of information. An intellectual property right is a form of property rights mechanism that has been created to ensure that investments in human capital will be rewarded (and hence that such investments will be made).

It should be clear from earlier chapters that there are sources of useful information other than the human intellect. The diversity that exists within nature is an important and useful source of information that feeds into our industries and into our lives. This diversity and the information that it generates will not continue to exist unless there are investments in the *natural capital* from which it derives. An analogous form of institution is required to safeguard these investments as already exists to safeguard investments in human capital. Since it is inaccurate to refer to such a regime as an intellectual property right, it is more appropriate to recognise that it is a *sui generis* (free standing) property rights institution that is required. The role of property rights mechanisms is simply to compensate valuable investments, and this is one means of addressing the problem of the inefficient conversion of global biodiversity.

Failures in Property Right Regimes – Unchannelled Benefits

A generalised statement of the purpose of decentralised management regimes is the encouragement of investments at the most efficient level of society, i.e. by those individuals who have the information and capability to invest most effectively in a particular asset (Hart and Moore, 1990). A very general statement of the nature of a decentralised management regime is a mechanism that targets individuals making socially beneficial investments with awards approximately equal to the benefits generated.

This is the nature of a property rights regime, i.e. it is a mechanism for channelling benefits in a concentrated form through the hands of investors. It accomplishes this through the monopoly right known as a property right, which is a carefully delineated monopoly in the flow of goods and services from some specific asset. With the institutionalisation of the monopoly (and thus the assurance of the expectation that the state will invest to channel the asset's flow of benefits initially through the 'owner'), the individual is given the identical incentive framework as society's, i.e. the 'owner' will invest in the asset until the marginal benefit equates with the marginal cost (which will produce a globally efficient result so long as there are sufficient numbers of competing producers in the same product markets).

For these reasons, property right regimes are very useful mechanisms for inducing efficient levels of investments in various assets. However, some forms of assets are not amenable to the application of property right institutions because their benefits are not readily channelled. In general, property right institutions operate well if the flow of goods and services is densely concentrated in at least one 'dimension' at one point in that flow. Then it is possible to delineate and segregate the investor's flow from others', and hence to channel that flow. For example, most of the benefits from standard agricultural production (i.e. the produced commodities) are appropriable by the demarcation of exclusive rights in the land; the individual associated with a particular parcel of land (the owner) has the exclusive right then to the entire flow of benefits (produce) from that parcel. In this instance, there is a close correspondence between the total benefits generated and the benefits individually appropriated at one point in the process (i.e. at the point where the commodities are being produced on the land).

Many assets are not of this nature. Some have the characteristic that their benefits are instantaneously diffusive, so that investments in the asset generate benefits throughout a wide area. Others are of the character that their benefits diffuse rapidly and it is costly to segregate between beneficiaries and non-beneficiaries of the flow. This is the general nature of assets that are not easily subjected to property rights institutions: the flow that they generate is too disorganised to be readily channelled. It is not easy to discern the point at which the award of a monopoly right will capture a significant part of the flow of benefits.

Consider again the first example of a globally recognised public good, i.e. the information developed for industrial applications that was the subject of the Paris Patent Union. Investments in such information are not readily generated in the context of a property rights regime, and so industry lobbied for novel forms of institutions (although confusing the issue by use of the same name). Information is a global public good for two reasons. First, information as a product has an innate capacity for diffusion, as remarked upon in Arrow's Fundamental Paradox of Information. The paradox states that information is not marketable until revealed (because its value is unknowable prior to revelation), while the consumer's willingness to pay can be concealed after revelation of the information (because the transfer has already occurred). In addition, information is often revealed on the mere inspection of a tangible product within which it is embedded. Therefore, the mere act of marketing of a product created from useful information often releases that information to the world, rendering it far less valuable.

Secondly, it is extremely difficult to segregate between information flows. This is because all information is built upon a common base (the common understanding that makes up all knowledge and language) and there are a multitude of potential pathways leading to the same conclusion. Therefore, an attempt to segregate between the path leading to one piece of information and the entirety of the remaining body of knowledge is an unlikely task, because it implies an attempt to untangle all ideas back to the common starting point.

For example, consider the innovation of heat resistant, resilient plastics sometime during the past 50 years. Most people site this innovation with the US space programme, where these substances were introduced in order to serve various purposes on the exteriors of space craft. However, on the use and observance of this information (i.e. the idea of durable uses for synthetic polymers), this idea diffused throughout the world economy. Soon, durable plastics appeared in the entire range of products from automobiles to pots and pans. Even assuming that all of the consumer benefits from the use of these new products derived from the innovation at NASA, it would be very difficult to delineate clearly between the various uses (of a wide range of different polymers) or to trace their diffusion from the single point. The nearly instantaneous diffusion of this idea throughout the economy demonstrates the difficulty of using property right regimes to induce investments in a global public good, such as information. The benefits are never concentrated enough at one point in time to be channelled through the hands of an individual investor because they diffuse so quickly and completely. For these reasons, other mechanisms than property right regimes must be used to encourage investments in assets that generate these types of flows.

The Role of Surrogate Right Regimes (and IPR Regimes)

An alternative to a property right regime is a *surrogate right regime*. Such a regime operates by channelling benefits to an investor from a monopoly right in a tangible good, as a reward for effective investments in an asset generating a non-tangible flow. In short, the surrogate right regime sidesteps the problem of non-appropriability by substituting a surrogate monopoly right (in a dimension that is suitably appropriable) for the impracticable property right in information. This is the nature of an IPR regime: it substitutes an appropriable flow for an inappropriable one in rewarding information-generating investments.

In order to understand how an IPR regime operates, consider again the example of the innovation of durable polymers. An IPR regime does not attempt to protect the investment of the agent who generated this fundamental idea; this would be impracticable for the reasons mentioned above. Instead, the IPR regime allows the agent to stake a claim in a carefully specified area of 'product space' where the idea is to be introduced. That is, the laws of patent do not offer rights in the idea itself (durable synthetic polymers) nor to the entire range of products to which this abstract idea is subsequently applied (all uses of resilient plastics from pots and pans to automobiles). Instead, the applicant for a patent right must select a reasonable range of specific products that will make good use of the idea, and claim monopoly rights in the marketing of these. The inventor patenting the use of resilient synthetic polymers in pots and pans would not necessarily have any claim to a monopoly over their use in any other consumer goods, such as automobiles.

These benefit systems are not of the nature of property right systems, but instead constitute a type of hybrid system for making awards to investors in information generation (inventors). The general problem that the state must solve is how to create a cost-effective 'prize system' that will target efficient inventors accurately (in terms of identity and size of award) when the basic product is of such a nature that a pure property rights system is impracticable. It is not at all clear *a priori* that a surrogate rights regime is the most efficient institution for addressing this problem, but it is an interesting and internationally important example of a method for flow appropriation. However, there are several trade-offs involved in this particular solution to the problem, but initially the nature of a surrogate right regime will be detailed.

The Theory of Surrogate Property Rights

The problem of creating incentive mechanisms for the production of information is a very general one. The same problem has been analysed in regard to regulating the generation of information at different levels of a firm or distribution network. This analogue will be used in order to provide a private sector benchmark against which to compare the need for public sector institution-building (Matthewson and Winter, 1986).

Consider, for a concrete example, the problem of a manufacturer of a sophisticated consumer product (such as a personal computer) that wishes to market this product efficiently. The maximum number of sales will occur only if substantial amounts of information are included with the sale, e.g. informal demonstrations, lessons and instructions provided to prospective purchasers. For maximum effectiveness, this information must be provided on a decentralised basis (i.e. at the retail level) where the interface with the consumer is direct (in order to tailor the demonstration to the needs of that customer). However, these optimal investments will not occur on a decentralised basis on account of the inappropriability of retailer-generated information. That is, retailers who invest in the provision of these informational services (training of sales personnel, provision of demonstration rooms and equipment) will not be able to compete with those who do not make these investments, because consumers will have the incentive to acquire the (unpriced) information at one retailer and make their purchase at the other. Manufacturers need to construct mechanisms that channel the benefits from informational investments through the hands of their investing distributors, the identical decentralised investment-in-intangibles problem faced by the state in a more general context.

The private sector institution used to address this problem is the 'exclusive territory' regime incorporated within vertical distribution agreements. Such a regime, established by the manufacturer, provides that no other retailer shall be allowed to market the manufacturer's products within a carefully defined territory (from 50th to 195th street, say). This territorial monopoly right provides a local captive market from which to recoup the retailer's investments in informational services. Note that the desired investments are in a wholly inappropriable dimension – information – while the monopoly is allowed in an easily demarcated and segregated dimension – physical territory. The problems of inappropriability in the former dimension are addressed by allowing surrogate rights in the latter.

Analogously, the state needs to supply concrete rights in a dimension that can be demarcated, and product space serves this purpose. In the case of an IPR regime, a market is allocated by the specification of a concrete boundary in product space (as opposed to geographical space in vertical distribution agreements). An IPR regime acts to remedy this distortion in information generation by granting monopolies in certain territories in product space. That is, in recognition of the impracticability of allowing monopolies in information, this regime instead allows monopolies in a range of products which incorporate this information. This supplies a remedy for the first problem of inappropriability (diffusion within industry) while supplying a premium to compensate the firm for the second problem of inappropriability (diffusion across industries).

An example of this is provided by the patent allowed to the innovator of the oversized tennis racquet. The actual innovation involved in that case was the idea that sports equipment sizes and shapes might be optimised; however, this concept (although widely implemented) is too abstract to be appropriable. Instead, the patent allotted to the innovator allowed exclusive marketing rights for all tennis racquets with head size between 95 and 130 sq cm in area. The tennis racquet actually marketed was of a single size that fell in the middle of this territory, however the entire territory was allotted in order to create the monopoly rent.

Therefore, the idea of giving 'exclusive territories' as incentive systems for investment in certain assets may be applied even when there is a complete disjunction between the territory given and the asset requiring investment. The inducement of efficient investments requires institutionalised award mechanisms, and all institutions have their own forms of costliness. Surrogate property rights are clearly second-best types of solutions, but this is true of all institutions. The idea that a property right accomplishes a perfect match between asset and territory is illusory in every instance, giving rise to the prevalence of externalities. To advocate well-defined property rights is equivalent to advocating perfect competition. It is important to recognise all property rights for nothing more than what they are: institutionalised incentive mechanisms for making awards (imperfectly) to investors. Surrogate property rights are substantively indistinguishable from all other property rights; they are all exclusive territories operating as award mechanisms for beneficial investments. The difference is quantitative, in the quantity of externalities prevailing under the institution.

The Application of Intellectual Property Rights Regimes to Biodiversity Conservation

The entirety of the theory developed in this chapter applies directly to the problem of biodiversity conservation. This is because investments in stocks of diverse resources (species and habitats) generate not only tangible goods and services, but also intangible ones (specifically, insurance and information). On account of the diffusiveness and non-segregability of these services, it is not possible (under existing institutions) to channel these global benefits initially through the hands of individuals living within their host states. However, this flow of information is only maintained by way of investments in diverse stocks by individuals in the host states. If these diverse assets are not included within state portfolios, then the flow of these services will cease. It is equally important to reward investments in natural capital that generate informational services as it is to reward investments in human capital-generated information. The base problems are identical, only the physical character of the asset involved is changed.

The only element to add to the theory of surrogate property rights is the potential production of valuable information from inputs other than human capital. As has been indicated at several points in this book, this is the essential value of biological diversity – its informational content. It must be recognised that human capital alone may not be capable of producing all important and valuable information. There is also a base biological dimension which generates information.

This biological dimension is the evolutionary process which through biological interaction and the process of selection, generates communities of life forms that contain substantial amounts of accumulated information. Because the competition for niches is constant and pervasive (occurring at all levels), the naturally evolved life forms contain biological materials which act upon many of the species with which they share the community. A community that has co-evolved over millions of years contains an encapsulated history of information that cannot be synthesised.

Supplanting a naturally evolved habitat and slate of species with a human-chosen slate may confer tangible productivity gains, but it also removes the information that was available from that community. The information from co-evolution, the product of the evolutionary process, is lost with the conversion.

Therefore, the conservation of the last remaining unconverted natural habitats equates with the retention of this evolutionary product, i.e. the information generated by co-evolution. The mere existence of this habitat represents information production, in the sense of the retention of an otherwise irreplaceable asset. Valuable information may be produced by investments in natural capital as well as through investments in human capital.

Consider how the global community can use a surrogate rights regime in order to conserve optimal biological diversity. The global community is faced with the same regulatory problem as in the case of regulating intellectually-produced information but with slightly different dimensions involved. If natural capital-based surrogate rights were introduced, the benefits to supplier states would flow primarily from allocations of exclusive markets in consumer states, while the benefits to consumer states would flow primarily from the retention of natural habitats in supplier states. This is analogous to the object in the case of IPR; the problem is to invest in institutions to maximise the aggregate benefits from informational production for both consumers and suppliers. In essence, the global community is allocating territories in Northern product markets in exchange for the conservation of designated territories in Southern natural habitats. These rights constitute *ex post facto* awards for past effective investments, but also *ex ante* awards to encourage investigations for further useful information in those territories. Such awards function in precisely the same way as intellectual property rights in encouraging investment, except that in this case the regime is focusing upon natural resource (rather than human resource) generated information.

The supplier states now have incentives to invest in their diverse resources. Host states have the incentive to maintain their resources and investigate them in order to be awarded product market territories, and these states have the incentive to continue to invest in their diverse resources in order to generate new information useful in respect to their market allocations. The extent of these incentives depends entirely upon the breadth and length of the awards. The breadth is determined by the extent of product market allocation and the length is determined by the duration of the allocation. Different critera should be used in determining breadth and length. Length should be determined primarily with regard to the costliness of the selection process. Breadth should then be used to establish the desired amount of the award.

As with any surrogate right, it is a more efficient instrument if it is able to capture a large proportion of the information's value in the product space allocated. However, by the definition of information (i.e. its diffusive nature), this is not generally possible. It must be recognised that the ultimate object of any surrogate right (intellectual property right) regime is to accurately target prizes to efficient investors in information generation, and that it is only institutional costliness that warrants the use of surrogate dimensions for this purpose. Therefore, intellectual property rights can be an effective instrument for the generation of a flow of value to states investing in the conservation of biological diversity. This instrument should be considered with the others as a potentially cost-efficient method for conservation.

An Example of *Sui Generis* Property Rights in Biodiversity Conservation – Informational Resource Rights

Many pharmaceutical innovations are developed from a starting point of knowledge derived from the biological activities of natural organisms. When a new start is required, it is often initiated by returning to the uncharted areas of biological activity (unknown plants and insects), but after the long process of product development and introduction there is no compensation for the role played by the diverse resource in initiating the process. The informational input supplied from the diverse resource system goes unpaid-for, and this means that there will be no incentive to invest in the natural capital that generates this information.

An 'informational resource right' system could be constructed that would be analogous to an intellectual property right system. There would not be anything in this that would conflict with existing regimes; it would simply represent an extension of this idea for compensating intangible services into realms other than those deriving from human-capital investments. To a large extent, the extension of intellectual property regimes to include natural resource-generated information simply levels the playing field between those societies which are more heavily endowed with human capital and those which are more heavily endowed with natural forms of capital. It is a very rational approach to the resolution of the biodiversity problem, just as the adoption of the Paris Patent Union 100 years ago was a rational approach to the problem of protecting investments in human innovations in industry.

An informational rights regime based on natural resource investments would allocate product market territories in response to effective natural habitat investments. The regime would then operate through central registration and private trading. Effectiveness would be demonstrated initially through the establishment of 'biodiversity reserves', restricted to uses compatible with biodiversity prospecting. A state's programme would qualify for inclusion within the regime by means of investing in biodiversity reserves and establishing prospecting programmes. Then any discoveries within these areas should be made subject to internationally recognised exclusive rights upon registration with some sort of centralised office (analogous to a patent office).

The registration office would then have the responsibility for determining the scope of the monopoly rights afforded by the registration. When such a programme is established, the potentially useful life forms need to be tendered to the registration office, together with a list of the range of chemical, genetic and other characteristics first identified within the species. The panel would then determine two issues: 1) whether an award should be made to the programme; and 2) what characteristics of the life form (chemical, genetic, entire organism) are to be subject to exclusive rights.

The determination of the first issue depends upon the believed usefulness of the natural habitat being conserved, the identified life form and its chemical characteristics. Issue two turns on the scope of the right that is required to generate a reasonable return to the investment. Of course, the length of the award is a separate, institutional issue determined uniformly by the costliness of the selection process.

If an award is made, then any subsequent development of a product that incorporates a chemical combination within the scope identified by the registration office must have a licence. In this fashion, a constant source of funding for natural habitat conservation could be maintained in a fashion that links funding to usefulness and also creates incentives to invest in the source habitat.

Conclusion: A Protocol for Registration of *Sui Generis* Rights in Natural Resource Information

It is clear that there is no distinction in substance between investments in information-generating natural capital (such as biodiversity) and other information-generating assets (such as other human capital-based research and development activities). Therefore, there is no logical reason why property right regimes should not be applied to the conservation of biological diversity. For example it can be no more difficult to value and assign rights in the services rendered by natural diversity than it is in regard to the 'look and feel' of a computer–user interface (patent granted to Apple Computers). The analogy is direct between the computer software industry and biodiversity conservation. Both 'industries' produce information – one in the variety of the code and one in the variety of the life forms. Both forms of diversity are useful – one in the operation of a computer and one in the operation of the biological production system. But the values from both forms of informational services are largely inappropriable (after first sale) unless governments make a concerted attempt to reward the producer.

The primary difference between the application of IPR regimes to software versus biodiversity is the identity of the rewarded producer; a biodiversity-related regime would produce largely North-to-South flows while the existing regime produces substantially North-to-North flows (and substantial South-to-North flows). Possibly for this reason, there are massive resources being spent on the reform of the international IPR laws concerning software protection, while there remains little interest in investments in the creation of IPR in natural resources.

However, if this is the case, then this myopic view of Northern self-interest concerning international IPR regimes completely misses the point. The rationale for an international institution should be the appropriation of the 'gains from cooperation', and in the case of biodiversity, the gains from cooperation are inherent when Northern states transfer funds to the South in return for the Southern states' conservation of diverse resource stocks. If properly calibrated, these transfers will be made in a fashion that will reward and induce compensating investments in diversity. For this reason, IPR regimes for natural resources should generate a net gain for Northern states, although the flow of funds under their auspices will be unidirectional North-to-South.

The solution to the global biodiversity problem requires the creation of some mechanism for appropriating the values of evolutionary-supplied information. If this is not put into effect, then we can continue to expect human societies to replace evolutionary product with their own selections across the face of the Earth, simply because the latter are more effective instruments for channelling the biosphere's flow of goods and services to local decision makers. For this reason it is necessary to expand the range of 'global services' that we reward individually beyond the narrow confines of intellectually-generated information. The conservation of diversity and diversity's values will require the creation of a diverse set of international institutions. For this reason, a protocol to develop a *sui generis* regime of property rights in natural resource-based information should be adopted.

10

THE CONCLUSION OF THE BIODIVERSITY CONVENTION: AND A FUTURE FOR BIODIVERSITY?

The Beginnings of the Biodiversity Convention

The UN Conference on Environment and Development and the acceptance of the text of the Convention on Biological Diversity signalled a beginning for the process of regulating global biological diversity. With the subsequent ratification of this Convention, the foundations are now in place for the establishment of a real and effective system of international regulation. / The international community has recognised the basic principles on which this system of regulation should be built within this text. These principles require that biodiversity be conserved through a combination of measures based on the sustainable use and protection of biodiversity, funded through the provision of resources by the developed countries and by the institution of mechanisms for the fair and equitable sharing of the benefits from the development of genetic resources./

Although these principles create a solid framework upon which to develop a global regulatory regime, they are too abstract to yield one by themselves. In order to give effect to these principles it is necessary to consider the nature of the biodiversity problem, and the nature of the specific regulatory actions that are required of the international community for its resolution. These actions must then be implemented in a real and concrete fashion in order to give effect to the underlying principles within the Convention. This is what is required for the conclusion of the Biodiversity Convention's objectives. At present the Biodiversity Convention represents a mere framework, only a beginning, not an ending.

The Overarching Objective of the Convention

It must be recognised that the overarching objective of the Convention is to intervene within the process of development as it is occurring across the face of the globe. This is one environmental problem for which the solution is not more of the same; further growth and development of the sort that has occurred in the past will not automatically generate a solution to the biodiversity problem. Instead, the general solution to the biodiversity problem calls for greater reliance upon a diversity of different land uses, agricultural practices and commodity utilisation. Intervention within the existing development system is necessary in order to ensure that development does not simply generate more of the same.

If it is accepted that all human societies have equal rights to development, then there is a unique solution to the suggested problem. This is the creation of international institutions capable of channelling the values of diverse resources to their host states. The creation of a diversity of international development institutions equates with the creation of a variety of different pathways to development. These alternative pathways to development maintain the important natural asset of diversity as well as the essential human right. It is the fostering of development compatible with diversity, by means of investments in international institutions, that should be the object of the Biodiversity Convention.

The Development of the Biodiversity Convention: The Necessary Protocols

Clearly, there are many other problems that might be included under a wide-ranging rubric such as biological diversity. The intent here is not to attempt the solutions of all problems relating to biological resource management, but rather to attempt the solution of one very specific problem with very important implications for this resource system: the management of the global conversion process. This is the problem of biodiversity losses discussed here, and the solutions concepts outlined here are directed to this one specific purpose.

The development of the Biodiversity Convention must be directed toward encouraging those less developed countries with substantial quantities of diverse resources to consider alternative pathways to development that do not require the conversion of their resources. This implies the development of policies for enhancing the benefits that these states receive when they invest in their diverse resources (as opposed to disinvesting in these resources). It will ultimately hinge upon the international community establishing institutions that support these diverse paths to development.

There are three methods available to the international community for the establishment of international institutions with the objective of conferring enhanced benefits upon those states pursuing development from a diverse resource base.

First, the international community might simply confer direct subsidies upon those states retaining stocks of diverse resources intact through low-intensity utilisation; the form of the international agreement that would divide the use of a diverse habitat between the international and the local communities would need to be regulated by an international mechanism instituted under the Biodiversity Convention. This mechanism would also need to ascertain the global needs for various forms of habitat conservation and ecosystem conservation, and allocate these needs across the various potential suppliers. In short, all of these tasks together mean that the mechanism would need to act and implement a global land use plan.

Secondly, the international community needs to intervene by means of regulating the trade in the tangible commodities that flow from diverse habitats in order to maximise appropriable rents. This would occur through reforms to the international wildlife trade regime. The need is for an institution that is capable of discriminating between those states supplying products from natural habitats on sustainable basis and those which are not. Such a mechanism would need to take the form of various types of certification mechanisms.

Thirdly, the international community needs to intervene by methods directed to reach the core of the problem of non-appropriable values, i.e. by the creation of mechanisms for the channelling of the currently inappropriable values of diversity (insurance and information) to the states that supply them. This would imply the development and institution of various property right registration regimes for purposes of diversity conservation.

In order to encourage the pursuit of diverse paths to development, the Biodiversity Convention needs to be developed down these three channels. This implies the creation of protocols under the Convention that will establish international institutions for each of these purposes. These three protocols are now reviewed and explained below.

A Proposal for a Land Use Planning Protocol

There is a need for the development of a global perspective on land use planning. If undertaken on a truly global basis, it would be the international equivalent to a zoning or planning process for the global development of land use patterns. That is, it would look at the globe as a whole and establish a plan for maintaining a real diversity of uses, habitats and systems.

The need for global zoning or land use planning is evident from the fact that such a mechanism would necessarily reach very different conclusions from domestic planning, in that global interests require a far greater amount of diversity in certain countries than any individual country has any interest in retaining. This is because in situ conservation involves the undertaking of domestic constraints on the development of certain lands; for example, the restriction of the range of land uses. Furthermore, it is not sufficient to simply zone a particular district for a particular land use. The land use classification will itself imply the expenditure of additional resources on the activities that classification requires: monitoring and protection of protected areas; cultivation of traditional landraces; prospecting activities in banking areas. These additional state investments must also be redirected toward the planning objective, otherwise the planning objective will not be met.

How would it be possible to implement such a plan, once established? The problem that must be addressed here is the creation of *both* an international mechanism for planning global land uses in accordance with the needs of the global community, *and* a mechanism that will generate the incentives for host states to retain and invest in their lands in conformity with the designated land use status.

If the international community wishes to acquire the 'development rights' of individual states with regard to particular diverse resources (habitats or systems), then it will be necessary to do so within the context of a dynamic international agreement. That is, there will have to be some overarching framework that provides for the systematic compensation of the owner state at the end of each period that the diverse resources remain unconverted. It is only through the creation of such a dynamically consistent scheme of payments that the agreement concerning development rights can be made enforceable.

In order to establish concrete incentives, this will imply the establishment of indefinite leases of particular land uses (e.g. burning or clearing rights) in designated parcels of land, with the annual rental rate determined by reference to the impact of these restrictions on the market value of the land. The lease will be between the planning authority and the host state. The host state is free to accept or decline the land use planning designation, and the compensation that goes with it, and so there is no compulsion involved in the exercise. The planning authority deals with several potential host countries simultaneously in its attempts to secure a particular form of habitat or species, and is thus able to secure the particular designation at least cost to the authority. The annual rent will be paid on an *ex post facto* basis, after the host state's enforcement of the planning restrictions has been audited by the independent international certificatory authority, ensuring that the land use restriction was obtained before the funds are released. With this sort of incentive-based financial mechanism, and the concrete results that it is intended to obtain, the funding level for the authority will be endogenous, i.e. funds will flow to the authority from states interested in securing diversity when its results are audited and certified by the independent body.

An international form of franchise agreement is the contract form that will allow for this system of governance. A franchise agreement is a contract that provides for a limited term of use by the holder of the franchise, subject to restrictions placed upon that use for the benefit of a third party. In this context the franchise agreement would divide the rights of use of a territory between the international community and the local community, with the owner state standing as the intermediary within the contract (i.e. the owner state is a party to the contract with the local community and with the global community). Both sides of this three-party agreement are made enforceable by means of the periodic payments made by both global and local communities in exchange for their partition of the rights of use; that is, the owner state has an incentive to enforce the agreed partition of rights in order to receive payments from both sets of users.

The international franchise agreement option is flexible enough to allow for virtually any manner of division of rights of use between local and global communities. If the global community is willing to outbid the local community for all rights of use, then the area may be effectively zoned as wilderness territory. If the global community bids a relatively small amount (compared to the area's use value), then the area may be zoned for all uses other than clearing and conversion. As mentioned above, whatever the partition between global and local communities, it is automatically enforceable because the partition is based upon an auction of the rights to use the land. The state must effectively enforce the agreed partition in order to receive payments from both sides to the franchise agreement.

The conference of the Parties should adopt a protocol to establish a global land use planning authority. This land use planning authority should undertake the task of setting out the basic global objectives in terms of habitat and system conservation, and then it should undertake the task of establishing the mechanism which would allow various countries to volunteer to enforce land use restrictions on offered habitats in return for a stream of periodic payments.

A Proposal for a Sustainable Use Certification Protocol

An alternative route to the subsidisation of alternative forms of development would be the payment of a premium to those states which produce goods and services in the context of unconverted habitats. The development of a premium attaching to specified diverse resources would be straightforward. This could be implemented through exclusive purchasing agreements between consumer states and producer state cooperatives. The members of the producer cooperative would then restrict production to the extent that maximises joint profits from their diverse resources.

A certification regime should operate in this fashion because it is essential that there be price discrimination between those supplier states which are investing and those which are not investing in their diverse resource bases. The formation of producer cooperatives consisting solely of the former creates a premium to that membership, and thus creates incentives for non-investing states to alter their investment strategies. It is the creation of the correct set of conditions for certification that will drive states down alternative development paths.

The complexities of a certification regime arise on account of the incentives that it creates for appropriating the premium without incurring the investment. Any state would have an incentive to attempt to sell diverse resources to the consumer states that were pirated from others. This implies the need for the construction of an elaborate set of certification and auditing conditions that ensure that certified products are derived only from properly managed habitats.

These conditions would primarily be comprised of individual supplier-state quotas based upon the natural habitats that they maintain and their capacity for production. Suppliers would have to indicate the nature of the land use restrictions that they were willing to enforce (e.g. non-burning, non-deforestation) and the area over which they would be enforced. The products to be derived from these areas would then be indicated and a proposal for a sustainable level of offtake submitted. It would be the responsibility of the international regime to certify that the proposed level of use is sustainable under normal conditions, and to audit the level of stocks and offtake in order to continue to ensure that this is the case.

This sort of mechanism must be established at the international level, for two reasons. First, the current system of incentives under CITES does not adequately discriminate between investing and non-investing states in regard to legitimate wildlife trade, and its blanket bans on endangered wildlife trade constitute a disproportionate punishment for the investing states (since they are then unable to acquire the returns on the investments they made). It bolsters the general impression throughout the developing world that diverse resources cannot be developed economically, and thus affirms the perception that conversion is the sole pathway to development.

Secondly, a protocol for the establishment of an international certification regime is necessary because the auditing of a producer's investments is an international function. This is because the enforcement of the certificate (through customs enforcement procedures) will be a national expense undertaken only if the receipt of reciprocal benefits is transparent. The benefits that must be afforded to the consumer states are those deriving from the auditing of the certified states' investment performance (i.e. the stocks of unconverted habitats retained). Therefore, the certification and auditing function must be implemented at the international level, not at the industrial or national level.

The enforcement of the certification status might be assisted through the organisation of the trade, where this is cost effective. For example, rather than requiring each individual customs service to maintain and enforce the certification procedure, an alternative approach would be to require all trade in specific commodities to flow through the international mechanism itself; this approach would be most effective where the resources concerned are best conserved on a centralised basis, as in the case of the agricultural gene banks. In these cases consumers would ensure that supplies were certified by means of exclusive purchasing from the certifying mechanism, and the customs authority would merely have to assure that all shipments of that commodity were coming directly from this central exchange.

The Conference of the Parties should adopt a protocol under which a range of certification regimes might be implemented. Certification is available to generate subsidies to sustainable habitat utilisation across a wide range of commodities including traditional wildlife utilisation, medicinal plant utilisation and even agricultural genetic resources. The conditions for certification need to be developed around the criterion of investment in diversity, as opposed to the conversion of habitats. A key component is the development of an international auditing mechanism to ensure that certification requirements are met on a continuing basis. Enforcement remains primarily a function employed by the consumer states, but this must also be audited. The development of such an international certification mechanism is a necessity if concrete incentives are to be implemented under the Convention.

A Proposal for a Rights Registration Protocol

The most direct approach to the regulation of extinction would be the creation of an international mechanism for rewarding investments in the generation of the inappropriable services of diverse resources. One of the most difficult forms of services to reward in the absence of governmental intervention is information. It was for this purpose that intellectual property rights mechanisms were developed, i.e. to generate compensation for the creation of human ideas and innovations.

Information can result from investments of various forms. Although it is easily seen to flow from investments in human capital (education and training) in the form of ideas, it is also one of the fundamental services known to flow from investments in the retention of diverse resources. This information also serves as an input into the creation of many useful products. Therefore, it is perfectly consistent to speak of developing property right regimes analogous to intellectual property rights regimes in order to generate rewards for naturally-generated information, as well as human-generated.

The creation of a rights registration mechanism would require the creation of an international agreement to award rights in product markets to those states successfully investing in the retention of diverse resource stocks for the purpose of information generation. Just as with patent competitions, states would have to compete for these awards by virtue of the demonstration of their conservation of natural habitats and their development of the capacities to effectively prospect within these habitats. They would demonstrate effective conservation by means of the listing of a particular area of habitat as a prospecting reserve, subject to the restrictions required by the registration board for such a reserve. For any natural organism discovered in the designated reserve, the applicant could then apply for exclusive rights to a range of chemical and/or genetic characteristics of the organism. In a periodic competition, the rights registration panel would make awards of certain ranges of characteristics to particular applicants in accordance with their demonstrated investments in the retention of habitats and investment in prospecting.

Then these property rights (in the specified chemical or genetic characteristics) could be licensed to various other users nearer to the product market for investigation and potential development into marketable products. The protocol would require national patent laws to recognise the validity of this panel's awards, and to amend patent legislation in order to make them more easily enforced. National patent courts would then be required to recognise and to enforce the decision of the international panel. Enforcement could be made more effective if all subsequent patent applications in these industries were required to trace their applications back to its source in either a public or private collection.

Since the values of these rights are wholly market-dependent, there is no value derived from the award of these rights unless the owner state has created that value in the discovery of the chemical combination. This is both equitable and efficient as it creates an explicit link between effective conservation and real compensation.

It also generates a clear alternative pathway to development for countries willing to invest in resource conservation. It should be noted that the idea of technology transfers is not an adequate substitute for the establishment of such a rights mechanism. Technology transfers are only perceived to be necessary because it is at the level of product development, rather than resource conservation, that rights to compensation are inherent. Hence, developing countries perceive the necessity to acquire technology before they are able to acquire the rights to the valuable genetic information that they produce. This is inequitable and strikingly inefficient. Since conservators and developers of genetic resources each generate value, both should have property rights to demand conservation.

In order to foster conservation, these rights must be established so that the conservators do not attempt to invest instead in becoming developers. One of the first principles of economics states that each part of the world should invest down the pathway of its own comparative advantage rather than transform its economic basis in the direction of enhanced appropriability. This is the philosophical basis which supports the idea of alternative pathways to development. At present, a developing country that wishes to capture the informational value of its diverse resources must become fully integrated vertically (from conservator through to developer) because the exclusive rights do not attach before the final consumer product is developed. The idea of establishing a new level for the registration of property rights in genetic resources is to allow developing countries to specialise in the conservation of genetic resources without the necessity of proceeding to the development of the final consumer product. This allows different parts of the world to specialise in the areas of their own comparative advantage, while not having to suffer from systematically biased terms of trade. This allows different countries to become developed through the pursuit of very different roles in the world economy.

The Conference of the Parties should adopt a protocol establishing an international rights registration regime. This regime should recognise a *sui generis* form of property right deriving from effective investments in the retention of natural habitats for prospecting purposes. The regime should do this through the establishment of an international panel for the award of rights in specified chemical and genetic traits deriving from organisms found within certified prospecting reserves. These rights will then generate their own market-determined rewards to conservation.

A Future for Biodiversity in Concluding the Biodiversity Convention?

The biological diversity that exists on Earth was generated over billions of years, but has become threatened in the space of a few thousand. The steamroller that is the human development process has continued to work its way across the face of the Earth leaving a sameness in the societies lying in its wake. Not only do these societies rely upon very similar tools, sciences and crafts for their industry, they increasingly rely upon the same base of natural resources. It is this worldwide convergence upon sameness that increasingly threatens the diversity that was previously resident.

Can the mere act of acceptance of the text of the Biodiversity Convention by 120 states of the global community do anything to halt this process? It is clear to all of those who have observed and fought the decline of the diversity in species, habitats and ecosystems over these past few decades that lofty language and non-committal commitments alone do nothing to solve these very real problems. What will be required is some substantive and enforceable commitments to real and concrete actions that impact at ground level. The Biodiversity Convention as it stands does not accomplish this object. It will be the role of the protocols of the Convention to take the lofty language and bring it down to earth.

The protocols described here are attempts at providing the templates upon which real and concrete institutions might be built. The need is for a diversity of international institutions that will provide developing countries with a diversity of pathways to pursue toward development. All countries should have an equal right to develop, but this does not require that each country must necessarily pursue precisely the same development path. A diversity of institutions will afford a diversity of pathways built upon a diversity of resource bases. The conclusion of the Biodiversity Convention awaits the conclusion of the negotiations concerning the protocols that will give it its final, concrete form. This is an important crossroads in the history of the biosphere. The future of biodiversity depends upon the successful conclusion of the Biodiversity Convention.

REFERENCES AND SELECTED LITERATURE

Akerlof, G (1974) 'The Market for Lemons', *Quarterly Journal of Economics*, 84(3):488

Alchian, A and Demsetz, H (1973) 'The Property Rights Paradigm', *Journal of Economic History*, 33:16-27

Anderson, J and Hazell, P (1989) *Variability in Grain Yields*, World Bank: Washington, DC

Aoki, M (1976) *Optimal Control and System Theory in Dynamic Economic Analysis*. North Holland:New York

Arrow, K (1962) 'The Economic Implications of Learning by Doing', *Review of Economic Studies*, 29:155-73

Arrow, K (1962) 'Economic Welfare and the Allocation of Resources for Invention', in R Nelson (ed.) *The Rate and Direction of Inventive Activity*, National Bureau of Economic Research, Princeton University Press

Arrow, K and Fisher, A (1974) 'Environmental Preservation, Uncertainty and Irreversibility', *Quarterly Journal of Economics*, 88:312-19

Arrow, K and Kurz, M (1970) *Public Investment, the Rate of Return and Optimal Fiscal Policy*, Johns Hopkins Press:Baltimore

Atkinson, I (1989) 'Introduced Animals and Extinctions', in Western, D and Pearl, M (eds) *Conservation for the Twenty-first Century*, Oxford University Press:Oxford

Barbier, E, Burgess, J, Swanson, T and Pearce, D (1990) *Elephants, Economics and Ivory*, Earthscan:London

Barrett, S (1994) 'On the Nature and Significance of International Environmental Agreements', *Oxford Economic Paper* 46:878-94

Barton, N (1988) 'Speciation' in Myers, A and Giller, P (eds) *Analytical Biogeography*, Chapman & Hall:London

Barzel, Y (1991) *Economic Analysis of Property Rights*, Cambridge University Press:Cambridge

Baumol, W and Oates, W (1990) *The Theory of Environmental Policy*, Cambridge University Press:Cambridge

Beckermann, W (1995) *Small is Stupid*, Duckworth Press:London

Bell, R and McShane-Caluzi, E (eds) (1984) *Conservation and Wildlife Management in Africa*, US Peace Corps:Washington, DC

Berck, R (1979) 'Open Access and Extinction', *Econometrica*, 47:877-82

Berkes, F (ed.) (1989) *Common Property Resources: Ecology and Community Based Sustainable Development*, Belhaven:London

Binswanger, H (1989) 'Brazilian Policies that Encourage Deforestation in the Amazon', World Bank, Environment Department, *Working Paper No. 16*, Washington, DC

Bjorndal, T and Conrad, J (1987) 'The Dynamics of an Open Access Fishery', *Canadian Journal of Economics*, 20(1):74–85

Boulding, K (1981) *Ecodynamics*, Sage:London

Boylan, E (1979) 'On the Avoidance of Extinction in One-Sector Growth Models', *Journal of Economic Theory*, 20(2):276–79

Brookshire, D S, Eubanks, L S and Randall, A (1983) 'Estimating Option Prices and Existence Values for Wildlife Resources', *Land Economics* 59: 1–15

Browder, J (1988) 'Public Policy and Deforestation in the Brazilian Amazon' in Repetto, R and Gillis, M (eds) *Public Policies and the Misuse of Forest Resources*, Cambridge University Press: Cambridge

Brown, G and Goldstein, J (1984) 'A Model for Valuing Endangered Species', *Journal of Environmental Economics and Management*, 11:303–9

Brown, J (1988) 'Species Diversity' in Myers, A and Giller, P (eds) *Analytical Biogeography*, Chapman & Hall:London

Brown, K, Pearce, D, Perrings, C and Swanson, T (1993) 'Economics and the Conservation of Global Biological Diversity', *Global Environment Facility Working Paper*, GEF:Washington

Caughley, G and Goddard, J (1975) 'Abundance and distribution of elephants in Luangwa Valley, Zambia', *African Journal of Ecology*, 26:323–7

Cervigni, R (1993) 'Conserving Biological Resources: Costs, Benefits and Incentives', Fondazione Eni Enrico Mattei, Working Paper 17–93

Cheung, S (1970) 'The Structure of a Contract and the Theory of a Non-Exclusive Resource', *Journal of Law and Economics*, 13(1):49–70

Cheung, S (1983) 'The Contractual Nature of the Firm', Journal of Law and Economics, 26(1): 1–21

CIAT (1981) *Report on the Fourth IRTP Conference in Latin America*, Cali, Colombia

Ciriacy-Wantrup, S and Bishop, R (1975) 'Common Property as a Concept in Natural Resources Policy', *Natural Resources*, 15:713–27

Clark, C (1973a) 'Profit Maximisation and the Extinction of Animal Species', *Journal of Political Economy*, 81(4):950–61

Clark, C (1973b) 'The Economics of Overexploitation', *Science* 181:630–4

Clark, C (1976) *Mathematical Bioeconomics: The Optimal Management of Renewable Resources*, John Wiley:New York

Clark, C and Munro, G (1978) 'Renewable Resources and Extinction: Note', *Journal of Environmental Economics and Management*, 5(2):23–9

Clark, C, Clarke, F and Munro, G (1979) 'The Optimal Exploitation of Renewable Resource Stocks: Problems of Irreversible Investment', *Econometrica*, 47:25–49

Conrad, J, (1980) 'Quasi-Option Value and the Expected Value of Information', *Quarterly Journal of Economics*, 94: 813–20

Conrad, J and Clark, C (1987) *Natural Resource Economics*, Cambridge University Press:Cambridge

Cox, C and Moore, P (1985) *Biogeography: An Ecological and Evolutionary Approach*, Blackwell: Oxford

Cropper, M (1988) 'A Note on the Extinction of Renewable Resources', *Journal of Environmental*

Economics and Management, 15(1):25–30

Cropper, M, Lee, D and Pannu, S (1979) 'The Optimal Extinction of a Renewable Natural Resource', *Journal of Environmental Economics and Management,* 6(4):49–55

Cumming, D, Du Toit, R and Stuart, S (1990) *African Elephants and Rhinos: Status Survey and Conservation Action Plan,* IUCN:Gland

Cyert, R, and DeGroot, M (1987) 'Sequential Investment Decisions', in R Cyert and M DeGroot, *Bayesian Analysis and Uncertainty in Economic Theory,* Chapman & Hall:London

Daly, H (ed.) (1992) *Toward a Steady-State Economy,* (2nd edn) Island Press:Washington, DC

Dandy, J (1981) 'Magnolias', in Hora, B (ed.) (1981) *The Oxford Encyclopedia of Trees of the World.* Oxford University Press:Oxford

Darmstadter, J (ed.) *Global Development and the Environment: Perspectives on Sustainability,* Resources for the Future:Washington, DC

Dasgupta, P (1969) 'On the Concept of Optimum Population', *Review of Economic Studies,* 36(3)(107):295–318

Dasgupta, P (1982) *The Control of Resources,* Blackwell:Oxford

Dasgupta, P and Heal, G (1974) 'The Optimal Depletion of Exhaustible Resources', *Review of Economic Studies,* Symposium Issue on Depletable Resources, 3–28

Dasgupta, P and Heal, G (1979) *Economic Theory and Exhaustible Resources,* Cambridge University Press:Cambridge

Dasgupta, P and Stiglitz, J (1988) 'Learning-By-Doing, Market Structure and Industrial and Trade Policies', *Oxford Economic Papers,* 40:246–68

Dasgupta, P and Weale, M (1992) 'On Measuring the Quality of Life', *World Development,* January

David, P (1985) 'Clio and the Economics of QWERTY', *American Economic Review,* Papers and Proceedings, 75:332–7

Davis, R (1985) 'Research Accomplishments and Prospects in Wildlife Economics', *Transaction of N American Wildlife and Natural Resource Conference,* 50:392–8

Davis, S (1982) 'The Taming of the Few', *New Scientist,* 95:697–700

Dawkins, R (1986) *The Blind Watchmaker,* Longman Scientific and Technical:Harlow

Demsetz, H (1967) 'Toward a Theory of Property Rights', *American Economic Review,* 57:34–48

Diamond, J (1984) 'Normal extinctions of isolated populations', in Nitecki, M (ed.) *Extinctions,* University of Chicago:Chicago

Diamond, J (1989) 'Overview of Recent Extinctions', in Western, D and Pearl, M (eds) *Conservation for the Twenty-first Century,* Oxford University Press:Oxford

Diamond, J and Case, T (eds) (1986) *Community Ecology,* Harper & Row:New York

Dixit, A (1992) 'Investment and Hysteresis', *The Journal of Economic Perspectives,* 6:107–32

Dogse, P (1991) 'Debt for Nature Exchanges and Biosphere Reserves', *Man and Biosphere Digest,* 6

Douglas-Hamilton, I (1989) 'Overview of Status and Trends of the African Elephant', in Cobb, S (ed.) *The Ivory Trade and the Future of the African Elephant,* Report of the Ivory Trade Review Group to the CITES Secretariat

Duvick, D (1989) 'Variability in U.S. Maize Yields', in Anderson, J and Hazell, P (eds) *Variability in Grain Yields*, World Bank:Washington, DC

Duvick, D N (1984) 'Genetic Diversity in Major Farm Crops on the Farm and in Reserve' *Economic Botany* 38:161–78

Duvick, D N (1986) 'Plant Breeding: Past Achievements and Expectations for the Future' *Economic Botany* 40:289–97

Ehrlich, P and Ehrlich, A (1981) *Extinction*, Random House:New York

Ehrlich, P (1988) 'The Loss of Diversity: Causes and Consequences', in Wilson, E O (ed.) Biodiversity, National Academy of Sciences:Washington, DC

Eltringham, S K (1984) *Wildlife Resources and Economic Development*, John Wiley: New York

Farnsworth, N (1988) 'Screening Plants for New Medicines', in Wilson, E O (ed.) *Biodiversity*, National Academy of Sciences:Washington, DC

Farnsworth, N and Soejarto, D (1985) 'Potential Consequences of Plant Extinction in the United States on the Current and Future Availability of Prescription Drugs'. *Economic Botany*, 39(3)

Fellows, L and Schofield, A (1995) 'Chemical diversity in Plants' in Swanson (1995b), cited below

Fernandez, J and Swanson, T (1997) *Economic Development and Wildlife Conservation*, Cambridge University Press:Cambridge

Findeisen, C (1991) *Natural Products Research and the Potential Role of the Pharmaceutical Industry in Tropical Forest Conservation*. Rainforest Alliance:New York

Fisher, A and Hanneman, W M (1985) 'Endangered Species: The Economics of Irreversible Damage', in Hall, D, Myers, N and Margaris, N (eds) *Economics of Ecosystem Management*, W Junk Publishers:Dordrecht

Fisher, A and Krutilla, J (1985) 'Economics of Nature Preservation', in Kneese, A and Sweeney, J (eds) *Handbook of Natural Resource and Energy Economics*, Elsevier:Amsterdam

Fisher, A, Krutilla, J and Cicchetti, C (1972a) 'Alternative Uses of Natural Environments: The Economics of Environmental Modification', in Krutilla, J (ed.) *Natural Environments: Studies in Theoretical and Empirical Analysis*, John Hopkins University Press:Baltimore

Fisher, A, Krutilla, J and Cicchetti, C (1972b) 'The Economics of Environmental Preservation: A Theoretical and Empirical Analysis', *American Economic Review*, 62:605–19

Fisher, A Krutilla, J and Cicchetti, C (1974) 'The Economics of Environmental Preservation: Further Discussion', *American Economic Review*, 64:1030–9

Flint, M E S (1990) 'Biodiversity: Economic Issues' unpublished paper for the Overseas Development Administration, London

Foy, G and Daly, H (1989) 'Allocation, Distribution and Scale as Determinants of Environmental Degradation: Case Studies of Haiti, El Salvador and Costa Rica', World Bank, Environment Department, *Working Paper No. 19*, Washington, DC

Freeman, A M (1984) 'The Quasi-Option Value of Irreversible Development', *Journal of Environmental Economics and Management*, 11:292–5

Futuyma, D (1986) *Evolutionary Biology*, Sinauer:Sunderland, MA

Gadgil, M and Iyer, P (1988) 'On the Diversification of Common Property Resource Use in Indian Society', in Berkes, F (ed.) *Common Property Resources: Ecology and Community Based Sustainable Development*, Belhaven:London

Gentry, A (1982) 'Patterns of Neotropical Plant Species Diversity', in Prance, G (ed.) *Biological Diversification in the Tropics*, Columbia University Press:New York

Gillis, M (1988) 'Indonesia: Public Policies, Resource Management, and the Tropical Forest', in Repetto, R and Gillis, M (eds) *Public Policies and the Misuse of Forest Resources*, Cambridge University Press:Cambridge

Godfrey, M (1985) 'Demand for Commodities', in Rose, T (ed.) *Crisis and Recovery in Sub-Saharan Africa*, OECD:Paris

Goldberg, V (1976) 'Regulation and Administered Contracts', *Bell Journal of Economics*, 7:426

Gordon, H S (1954) 'The economic theory of a common-property resource: the fishery', *Journal of Political Economy*, 62:124-42

Gould, J R (1972) 'Extinction of a Fishery by Commercial Exploitation: A Note', *Journal of Political Economy*, 80(5):1031-8

Grossman, S and Hart, O (1986) 'The Costs and Benefits of Ownership: A Theory of Vertical and Lateral Integration', *Journal of Political Economy*, 94(4):691

Grossman, S and Hart, O (1987) 'Vertical Integration and the Distribution of Property Rights', in Razin, A and Sadka, E (eds) *Economic Policy in Theory and Practice*, Macmillan:London

Hanemann, M (1989) 'Information and the Concept of Option Value', *Journal of Environmental Economics and Resource Management*, 16:23-37

Hanks, J (1972) 'Reproduction of elephants in the Luangwa Valley, Zambia', *Journal of Reproduction and Fertility*, 30:13-26

Hansen, S 1989 'Debt for Nature Swaps: Overview', *Ecological Economics*, 1:77

Hardin, G (1960) 'The Competitive Exclusion Principle', *Science*, 131:1292-7

Hardin, G (1968) 'The tragedy of the common', *Science*, 162:1243-8

Harrington, W and Fisher, A (1982) 'Endangered Species', in Portney, P (ed.) *Current Issues in Natural Resource Policy*, Resources for the Future:Washington, DC

Hart, O and Moore, J (1990) 'Property Rights and the Nature of the Firm', *Journal of Political Economy*, 98(6):1119-58

Hartwick, J (1977) 'Intergenerational Equity and the Investing of Rents from Exhaustible Resources', *American Economic Review*, 67(5):972-84

Hartwick, J (1978) 'Investing Returns from Depleting Renewable Resource Stocks and Intergenerational Equity', *Economic Letters*, 1:85-8

Hays, J, Imbrie, J and Shackleton, N (1976) 'Variations in the Earth's Orbit: Pacemaker of the Ice Ages', *Science*, 213:1095-6

Hazell, P (1984) 'Sources of Increased Instability in Indian and US Cereal Production', *American Journal of Agricultural Economics*, 66

Hazell, P B R (1985) 'The Impact of the Green Revolution and the Prospects for the Future', *Food Reviews International*, 1

Hazell, P (1989) 'Changing Patterns of variability in world ceareal production', in Anderson, J and Hazell, P (eds) *Variability in Grain Yields*, World Bank:Washington, DC

Hazell, P B R, Jaramillo, M and Williamson, A (1990) 'The Relationship Between World Price Instability and the prices Farmers Receive in Developing Countries' *Journal of Agricultural Economics*, 41(2)

Heal, G (1975) 'Economic Aspects of Natural Resource Depletion', in Pearce, D and Rose, J (eds) *The Economics of Depletion*, Macmillan:London

Henry, C (1974a) 'Investment Decisions Under Uncertainty: The Irreversibility Effect', *American Economic Review*, 64:1006–12

Henry, C (1974b) 'Option Values in the Economics of Irreplaceable Assets', *Review of Economic Studies*, Symposium Issue on Depletable Resources, 89–104

Heywood, V (ed.) (1995) *Global Biodiversity Assessment*, Cambridge University Press: Cambridge

Hobbelink, H (1991) *Biotechnology and the Future of World Agriculture*, Zed Books:London

Hoel, M (1990) 'Efficient International Agreements for Reducing Emissions of CO_2', mimeo, Department of Economics, University of Oslo

Holdgate, M, Kassas, M and White, G (eds) (1982) *The World Environment 1972–1982*, United Nations Environment Programme:Nairobi

Honneger, R (1981) 'List of Amphibians and Reptiles either Known or Thought to have Become Extinct since 1600' *Biological Conservation*, 19: 141–58

Hotelling, H (1931) 'The economics of exhaustible resources', *Journal of Political Economy*, 39:137–75

Howard, N (1991) 'Legal Protection of Biotechnology within the European Community with Reference to Environmental Protection', unpublished dissertation, University of London

Iltis, H (1988) 'Serendipity in the Exploration of Biodiversity', in Wilson, E O (ed.) *Biodiversity*, National Academy of Sciences:Washington, DC

International Institute for Environment and Development (IIED) and World Resources Institute (1989) *World Resources 1988–89*, Basic Books:New York

International Monetary Fund (1988) *World Economic Outlook 1988*, Washington

IUCN (1995) *National Environmental Fund Movement*, IUCN:Gland

IUCN Environmental Law Centre (1985) *African Wildlife Laws*, IUCN:Gland

IUCN Environmental Law Centre (1986) *Latin American Wildlife Laws*, IUCN:Gland

Ivory Trade Review Group (ITRG) (1989) 'The Ivory Trade and the Future of the African Elephant', report to the Conference of the Parties to CITES, Lausanne

James, A (1995) 'Analysis of Park and Protected Area Spending', report prepared under contract to the World Conservation Monitoring Centre, Cambridge (UK)

Johansson, P-O (1987) *The Economic Theory and Measurement of Environmental Benefits*, Cambridge University Press:Cambridge

Jones, S (1994) *The Language of Genes*, Oxford University Press:Oxford

Juma, C (1989) *The Gene Hunters*, Zed Books:London

Kahn, A (1988) *The Economics of Regulation*, MIT Press:Cambridge

Kaldor, N and Mirlees, J (1962) 'A New Model of Economic Growth', *Review of Economic Studies*, 29:174–92

Katzman, M and Cale, W (1990) 'Tropical Forest Preservation Using Economic Incentives', *Bioscience*, 40(11):827

Kiss, A (ed.) (1990) 'Living With Wildlife', draft report of World Bank Environment Division, World Bank:Washington, DC

Klein, B and Saft, L (1985) 'The Law and Economics of Franchise Tying Contracts', *Journal of Law and Economics*, 28:435

Krautkramer, J (1985) 'Optimal Growth, Resource Amenities and the Preservation of Natural Environments', *Review of Economic Studies*, 52:153–70

Krugman, P (1979) 'A Model of Innovation, Technology Transfer and the World Distribution of Income', *Journal of Political Economy*, 79:253–66

Krutilla, J V (1967) 'Conservation Reconsidered' *American Economic Review* 57:777–86

Krutilla, J V and Fisher, A (1975) *The Economics of Natural Environments*, Johns Hopkins University Press:Baltimore

Leader-Williams, N and Albon, S (1988) 'Allocation of resources for conservation', *Nature*, 336: 533–5

Ledec, G, Goodland, R, Kirchener, J and Drake, J (1985) 'Carrying Capacity, Population Growth and Sustainable Development' in Mahar, D (ed.) *Rapid Population Growth and Human Carrying Capacity*, World Bank Working Paper 690, World Bank:Washington, DC

Lee, R (1991) 'Comment: The Second Tragedy of the Commons', in Davis, K and Bernstam, M (eds.) *Resources, Environment and Population: Present Knowledge and Future Options*, Princeton University Press:Princeton

Leith, H and Whittaker, R (1975) *Primary Productivity of the Biosphere*, Springer-Verlag:New York

Lewin, R (1983) 'What Killed the Giant Land Mammals?', *Science*, 221:1269–71

Libecap, G (1990) *Contracting for Property Rights*, Cambridge University Press:Cambridge

Lovejoy, T (1980) 'A Projection of Species Extinctions' in Barney, G (ed) *The Global 2000 Report to the President*, Council on Environmental Quality:Washington, DC

Lucas, R (1988) 'On the Mechanics of Economic Development', *Journal of Monetary Economics*, 22:3–22

Lugo, A (1986) 'Estimating Reductions in the Diversity of Tropical Forest Species', in Wilson, E O (ed.) *Biodiversity*, National Academy of Sciences:Washington, DC

Luxmoore, R, Caldwell, J and Hithersay, L (1989) 'The Volume of Raw Ivory Entering International Trade from African Producing Countries from 1979 to 1988', in Cobb, S (ed.) (1989) *The Ivory Trade and the Future of the African Elephant*, Report of the Ivory Trade Review Group to the CITES Secretariat

Luxmore, R and Swanson, T (1992) 'Wildlife and Wildland Utilization and Conservation', in Swanson, T and Barbier, E (eds) *Economics for the Wilds*, Earthscan:London

Lynch, J (1988) 'Refugia', in Myers, A and Giller, P (eds) *Analytical Biogeography*, Chapman and Hall:London

Lyster, S (1985) *International Wildlife Law*, Grotius:London

Mabberley, D (1992) 'Coexistence and Coevolution' in *Tropical Forest Ecology*, Chapman & Hall: New York

MacArthur, R and Wilson, E (1967) *The Theory of Island Biogeography*, Princeton University Press:Princeton

Mahar, D (1989) *Government Policies and Deforestation in Brazil's Amazon Region*, World Bank: Washington, DC

Marks, S (1985) *The Imperial Lion: Human Dimensions of Wildlife Management in Africa*, Colorado:Westview Press

Marshall, L (1988) 'Extinction', in Myers, A and Giller, P (eds.) *Analytical Biogeography*, Chapman and Hall:London

Mathewson, F and Winter, R (1986) 'The Economics of Vertical Restraints in Distribution', in Mathewson, F and Stiglitz, J (eds) *New Developments in the Analysis of Market Structure*, MIT Press:Boston

McKelvey, R (1987) 'Fur Seal and Blue Whale: The Bioeconomics of Extinction', in Cohen, Y (ed.) *Applications of Control Theory in Ecology*, Lecture Notes in Biomathematics Series, No. 73: New York

McNeely, J A (1988) *Economics and Biological Diversity: Developing and Using Economic Incentives to Conserve Biological Resources*. IUCN:Gland

McNeely, J A (1992) 'The Sinking Ark: pollution and the worldwide loss of biodiversity', *Biodiversity and Conservation*, 1:2–18

Mc Neely, J A (1996) 'Economic Incentives for Conserving Biodiversity', in Szaro, R and Johnston, D (eds) *Biodiversity in Managed Landscapes*, Oxford University Press:New York

McNeely, J, Harrison, J, and Dingwall, M (1995) *Parks And Protected Areas*, IUCN:Gland

McNeely, J, Miller, K, Reid, W, Mittermeier, R, and Werner, T, (1990) *Conserving the World's Biological Diversity*, IUCN:Gland

Meadows, D H, Meadows, D L, Randers, J and Berherns, W (1974) *The Limits to Growth*, Universe Books:New York

Miller, J and Lad, F (1984) 'Flexibility, Learning and Irreversibility in Environmental Decisions', *Journal of Environmental Economics and Management*, 11:161–72

Mittermeier, R (1986) 'Primate Diversity and the Tropical Forest', in Wilson E O (ed.) *Biodiversity*, National Academy of Sciences:Washington, DC

Munasinghe, M and McNeely, J (1994) *Protected Area Economics and Policy*, World Bank and IUCN:Washington, DC

Muscat, R (1985) 'Carrying Capacity and Rapid Population Growth: Definition, Cases and Consequences', in Mahar, D (ed.) *Rapid Population Growth and Human Carrying Capacity*, World Bank Working Paper 690, World Bank:Washington, DC

Myers, A and Giller, P (1988) *Analytical Biogeography*, Chapman & Hall:London

Myers, N (1979) *The Sinking Ark. A Look at the Problem of Disappearing Species*, Pergamon:New York

Myers, N (1983) *A Wealth of Wild Species*, Westview:Boulder

Myers, N (1984) *The Primary Source*, Norton:New York

Norgaard, R (1986) 'The Rise of the Global Exchange Economy and the Loss of Biological Diversity', in Wilson, E O (ed.) *Biodiversity*, National Academy of Sciences:Washington, DC

Norton, B (ed.) (1986) The Preservation of Species, Princeton University Press:Princeton, New Jersey

Norton-Griffiths, M and Southey, C (1995) 'The Opportunity Costs of Biodiversity Conservation in Kenya', *Ecological Economics*, 12(2):125–40

Office of Technology Assessment (1988) *Technologies to Maintain Biological Diversity*, Lippincott Co:Philadelphia

Oldfield, M (1984) *The Value of Conserving Genetic Resources*, US Department of Interior: Washington, DC

Olson, S (1989) 'Extinction on Islands: Man as a Catastrophe', in Western, D and Pearl, M (eds) *Conservation for the Twenty-first Century*, Oxford University Press:Oxford

Olstrom, E (1990) *Governing the Commons*, Cambridge University Press:Cambridge

Panayotou, T (1989) 'The Economics of Environmental Degradation Problems, Causes and Responses', Harvard Institute for International Development,Cambridge:Massachusetts (reprinted in Markandya, A and Richardson, J (eds) (1992) *Environmental Economics*, Earthscan:London)

Panayotou, T (1992) 'Conservation of Biodiversity and Economic Development', paper presented to the Beijer Institute Symposium on Biodiversity Conservation, July

Pearce, D W (1988) 'The Sustainable Use of Natural resources in Developing Countries' in R K Turner (ed.) *Sustainable Environmental Management:Principles and Practice*, Belhaven Press:London

Pearce, D W (1991) 'An Economic Approach to Saving the Tropical Forests' in Helm, D *Economic Policy Towards the Environment*, Blackwell:Oxford

Pearce, D W, Barbier, E, Markandya, A (1990) *Sustainable Development: Economics and Environment in the Third World*, Edward Elgar:London

Perrings, C (1989) 'An Optimal Path to Extinction? Poverty and Resource Degradation in the Open Economy', *Journal of Development Economics*, 30(1):1–24

Perrings, C (1991) 'Ecological Sustainability and Environmental Control', *Structural Change and Economic Dynamics*, 2:275–95

Perrings, C (1992) 'Biotic Diversity, Sustainable Development and Natural Capital', paper presented to the International Society for Ecological Economics, Stockholm, Sweden, August

Peters, C, Gentry, A and Mendelsohn, R (1990) 'Valuation of an Amazonian Rainforest', *Nature*, 339:655–7

Peterson, W and Randall, A (1984) *Valuation of Wildland Resource Benefits*, Westview Press: Boulder, Colorado

Phelps, E (1961) 'The Golden Rule of Accumulation: A Fable for Growth-men', *American Economic Review*, 57:89–99

Plucknett, D L and Smith, N J H (1986) 'Sustaining Agricultural Yields', *BioScience*, 36:40–5

Plucknett, D L Smith, N J H, Williams, J T and Murthi Anishetty, N (1983) 'Crop Germplasm Conservation and Developing Countries', *Science*, 8:163–9

Plucknett, D L Smith, N J H, Williams, J T and Murthi Anishetty, N (1987) *Gene Banks and the World's Food*, Princeton:Princeton University Press

Pharmaceutical Manufacturers Association: Annual Survey Report 1988–1990, cited in World Conservation Monitoring Centre, (1992) *Global Biodiversity 1992*, WCMC:Cambridge

Pindyck, R (1978a) 'The Optimal Exploration and Production of Nonrenewable Resources', *Journal of Political Economy*, 86:841–61

Pindyck, R (1978b) 'Gains to Producers from the Cartelization of Exhaustible Resources', *Review of Economics and Statistics*, 60:238–51

Pindyck, R (1991) 'Irreversibility, Uncertainty and Investment', *Journal of Economic Literature*, 29:1110–48

Pinstrup-Anderson, P and Hazell, P R B (1985) 'The Impact of the Green Revolution and the Prospects for the Future', *Food Reviews International* 1(1):1–12

Porter, R C (1982) 'The New Approach to Wilderness Preservation through Cost-Benefit Analysis', *Journal of Environmental Economics and Management*, 9:59–80

Prescott-Allan, R and Prescott-Allan, C (1983) *Genes from the Wild*, Earthscan:London

Principe, P (1991) 'Valuing the Biodiversity of Medicinal Plants', in Akerle, O, Heywood, V and Synge, V, *The Conservation of Medicinal Plants*, Cambridge University Press:Cambridge

Quian, Y (1992) 'Equity, Efficiency and Incentives in a Large Economy', *Journal of Comparative Economics*, 16:27–46

Ramamohan Rao, T V S (1991) 'Efficiency and Equity in Dynamic Principal-Agent Problems', Journal of Economics, 55(1):17–41

Randall, A (1991) 'Total and Nonuse Values,' in Braden, J B and Kolstad, C D (eds) *Measuring the Demand for Environmental Quality*, Amsterdam:Elsevier

Raup, D (1988) 'Diversity Crises in the Geological Past', in Wilson, E O (ed.) *Biodiversity*, National Academy Press:Washington, DC

Raven, P (1988) 'The Scope of the Plant Conservation Problem Worldwide' in Bramwell, D, Hamann, O, Heywood, V and Synge, H (eds) *Botanic Gardens and the World Conservation Strategy*, Academy Press:London

Ready, R and Bishop, R (1991) 'Endangered Species and the Safe Minimum Standard', *American Journal of Agricultural Economics*, 73(2):309–12

Reid, W et al. (1993) *Biodiversity Prospecting*, World Resources Institute:Washington, DC

Reid, W and Miller, K (1989) *Keeping Options Alive*, World Resources Institute:Washington, DC

Renewable Resources Assessment Group (RRAG) (1989) 'The Impact of the Ivory Trade on the African Elephant Population', in Cobb, S (ed.) (1989) *The Ivory Trade and the Future of the African Elephant*, Report of the Ivory Trade Review Group to the CITES Secretariat

Repetto, R (ed.) (1985) *The Global Possible*, Yale University Press:New Haven

Repetto, R (1986) *World Enough and Time*, Yale University Press:New Haven

Repetto, R (1986) 'Soil Loss and Population Pressure on Java', *Ambio*, 15:14–20

Repetto, R (1988) 'Economic Policy Reform for Natural Resource Conservation', World Bank, Environment Department, *Working Paper No. 4*, Washington, DC

Repetto, R and Gillis, M (1988) *Public Policies and the Misuse of Forest Resources*, Cambridge University Press:Cambridge

Robinson, W and Bolen, E (1989) *Wildlife Ecology and Management*, (2nd edn), Macmillan:New York

Romer, P (1986) 'Increasing Returns and Long Run Growth', *Journal of Political Economy*, 94:1002–37

Romer, P (1987) 'Growth Based on Increasing Returns due to Specialisation', *American Economic Review*, Papers and Proceedings, 77:56–62

Romer, P (1990a) 'Endogenous Technological Change', *Journal of Political Economy*, 98:245–75

Romer, P (1990b) 'Are Nonconvexities Important for Understanding Growth', *American Economic Review, Papers and Proceedings*, 80(2):97–103

Ruitenbeek, J (1990) Evaluating Economic Policies for Promoting Rainforest Conservation in Developing Countries, unpublished PhD dissertation, London School of Economics, University of London

Samuelson, P (1954) 'The Pure Theory of Public Expenditure', *Review of Economics and Statistics*, 36:387–9

Samuelson, P (1976) 'Economics of Forestry in an Evolving Society', *Economic Inquiry*, 14:466–92

Sappington, D (1991) 'Incentives in Principal-Agent Relationships', *Journal of Economic Perspectives*, 5(2):45–66

Schneider, R et al (1992) Brazil: *An Analysis of Environmental Problems in the Amazon*, World Bank: Washington, DC

Scott, A (1955) 'The Fishery: The Objectives of Sole Ownership', *Journal of Political Economy*, 63:116–24

Sharpe, T (1982) The Control of Natural Monopoly by Franchising, mimeo

Simberloff, D (1986) 'Are we on the verge of a mass extinction in tropical rain forests?', in Elliot, D (ed.) *Dynamics of Extinction*, John Wiley:New York

Simon, J (1992) *Population and Development in Poor Countries*, Princeton University Press: Princeton

Sinn, H (1982) 'The Economic Theory of Species Extinction: Comment on Smith', *Journal of Environmental Economics and Management*, 9(2):82–90

Smith, V K (1972) 'The Effects of Technological Change on Different Uses of Environmental Resources', in Krutilla, J V (ed.) *Natural Environments: Studies in Theoretical and Applied Analysis*, Johns Hopkins University Press:Baltimore

Smith, V K (ed.) (1979) *Scarcity and Growth Reconsidered*, Johns Hopkins Press:Baltimore

Smith, V K (1987) 'Uncertainty, Benefit-cost Analysis, and the Treatment of Option Value.' *Journal of Environmental Economics and Management*, 14:283–92

Smith, V K and Krutilla, J V (eds) (1982) *Explorations in Natural Resource Economics*, Johns Hopkins University Press:Baltimore

Smith, V L (1975) 'The Primitive Hunter Culture, Pleistocene Extinction and the Rise of Agriculture', *Journal of Political Economy*, 83:727–55

Smith, V L (1977) 'Control Theory Applied to Natural and Environmental Resources: An Exposition', *Journal of Environmental Economics and Management*, 4:1–24

Solbrig, O (1991) 'The Origin and Function of Biodiversity', *Environment*, 33:10–19

Solow, R (1963) *Capital Theory and the Rate of Return*, North Holland: Amsterdam

Solow, R (1974a) 'The Economics of Resources or the Resources of Economics', *American Economic Review*, 64:1–12

Solow, R (1974b) 'Intergenerational Equity and Exhaustible Resources', *Review of Economic Studies*, Symposium Issue on Depletable Resources, 37–48

Southgate, D and Pearce, D W (1988) 'Agricultural Colonisation and Environmental Degradation in Frontier Developing Economies', World Bank, Environment Department, *Working Paper No. 9*, Washington, DC

Spence, M (1975) 'Blue Whales and Applied Control Theory', in Gottinger, H (ed.) *System Approaches and Environmental Problems*, Vandenhoeck:Gottingen

Stern, N (1989) 'The Economics of Development: A Survey', *Economic Journal*, 99:597–685

Swaney, J and Olson, P (1992) 'The Economics of Biodiversity: Lives and Lifestyles', *Journal of*

Economic Issues, 26(1):1–25

Swanson, T (1989a) 'Policy Options for the Regulation of the Ivory Trade', in ITRG, *The Ivory Trade and the Future of the African Elephant*, Lausanne

Swanson, T (1989b) 'A Proposal for the Reform of the African Elephant Ivory Trade', London Environmental Economics Centre DP 89–04, International Institute for Environment and Development:London

Swanson, T (1990a) 'Conserving Biological Diversity', in Pearce, D (ed.), *Blueprint 2: Greening the World Economy*, Earthscan:London.

Swanson, T (1990b) 'Wildlife Utilisation as an Instrument for Natural Habitat Conservation: A Survey', London Environmental Economics Centre Discussion Paper 91–03

Swanson, T (1991a) 'The Environmental Economics of Wildlife Utilisation', in *Proceedings of the IUCN Workshop on Wildlife Utilisation*, IUCN:Gland

Swanson, T (1991b) 'Animal Welfare and Economics: The Case of the Live Bird Trade', in Edwards, S and Thomsen, J (eds) *Conservation and Management of Wild Birds in Trade*, Report to the Conference of the Parties to CITES, Kyoto, Japan

Swanson, T (1992a) 'Policies for the Conservation of Biological Diversity', in Swanson, T and Barbier, E (eds) *Economics for the Wilds: Wildlands, Wildlife, Diversity and Development*, Earthscan:London

Swanson, T (1992b) 'The Economics of a Biodiversity Convention', *Ambio*, 21:250–7

Swanson, T (1992c) 'The Evolving Trade Mechanisms in CITES', *Review of European Community and International Environmental Law*, 1:57–63

Swanson, T (1993) 'Regulating Endangered Species', *Economic Policy*, April

Swanson, T (1994a) *'The International Regulation of Extinction'*, Macmillan:London and New York University Press:New York

Swanson, T (1994b) 'Efficient Conracting for Biodiversity Conservation', paper prepared for the OECD experts' group on biodiversity, OECD:Paris

Swanson, T (ed.) (1995a) *'The Economics and Ecology of Biodiversity Decline'*, Cambridge University Press:Cambridge

Swanson, T (ed.) (1995b) *'Intellectual Property Rights and Biodiversity Conservation'*, Cambridge University Press:Cambridge

Swanson, T (1996) 'Northern Reliance on Southern Biodiversity:Biodiversity as Information', *Ecological Economics*, 17:1–8

Swanson, T and Barbier, E (eds) (1992) *Economics for the Wilds: Wildlands, Wildlife, Diversity and Development*, Earthscan:London

Swanson, T and Pearce, D (1989) 'The International Regulation of the Ivory Trade – The Ivory Exchange', paper prepared for IUCN:Gland

Terborgh, J (1974) 'Preservation of Natural Diversity: The Problem of Extinction Prone Species', *Bioscience* 24:715–22

Vickers, J and Yarrow, G (1988) *Privatisation*, MIT Press:Cambridge

Vitousek, P, Ehrlich, P, Ehrlich, A and Matson, P (1986) 'Human Appropriation of the Products of Photosynthesis', *Bioscience*, 36(6):368–73

Watson, D (1989) 'The Evolution of Appropriate Resource Management Systems', in Berkes, F (ed.) *Common Property Resources: Ecology and Community Based Management*, Belhaven:London

Weitzman, M (1970) 'Optimal Growth with Scale Economies in the Creation of Overhead Capital', *Review of Economic Studies*, 37:555–70

Weitzman, M (1976) 'Free Access versus Private Ownership as Alternative Systems for Managing Common Property', *Journal of Economic Theory*, 8:225–34

West, R (1977) *Pleistocene Geology and Biology*, Longman:London

Western, D (1989) 'Population, Resources and Environment in the Twenty-first Century', in Western, D and Pearl, M (eds) *Conservation in the Twenty-first Century*, Oxford University Press: Oxford

Western, D and Pearl, M (1989) *Conservation for the Twenty-first Century*, Oxford University Press:Oxford

Wijnstekers, W (1988) *The Evolution of CITES*, Secretariat of the Convention on International Trade in Endangered Species:Lausanne

Williamson, M (1988) 'Relationship of Species Number to Area, Distance and other Variables', in Myers, A and Giller, P *Analytical Biogeography*, Chapman & Hall:London

Williamson, O (1975) *Markets and Hierarchies*, Free Press:New York

Williamson, O (1976) 'Franchising Bidding for Natural Monopolies', *Bell Journal of Economics*, 7:73

Williamson, O (1980) 'Transaction Cost Economics: The Governance of Contractual Relations', *Journal of Law and Economics*, 70:336–2

Williamson, O (1983) 'Credible Commitments: Using Hostages to Support Exchange', *American Economic Review*, 73(4):519

Williamson, O (1985) '*Economic Institutions of Capitalism*', Free Press:New York.

Williamson, O (1986) *The Economics of Capitalist Institutions*, Blackwell:Oxford

Wilson, E O (1988) *Biodiversity*, National Academy Press:Washington

Wilson, E O (1988) 'The Current State of Biological Diversity', in Wilson, E O (ed.) *Biodiversity*, National Academic Press:Washington, DC

Witt, S (1985) *Biotechnology and Genetic Diversity*, California Agricultural Lands Project:San Francisco

World Bank (1989) *World Development Report*, Oxford University Press:Oxford

World Bank (1992) *World Development Report*, World Bank:Washington, DC

World Commission on Environment and Development (WCED) (1987) *Report of the World Conference on Environment and Development*, UNEP:Geneva

World Conservation Monitoring Centre (WCMC) (1992) *Global Biodiversity*, Chapman & Hall: London

World Resources Institute (1990) *World Resources 1990- 1991*, Oxford University Press:Oxford

Wright, H (1970) 'Environmental Changes and the Origin of Agriculture in the Near East', *Bioscience*, 20:19–23.

Yang, X and Wills, I (1989) 'A Model Formalising the Theory of Property Rights', *Journal of Comparative Economics*, 14:177–98

INDEX

Adaptive radiation 8
Africa
    agriculture 49
    costs of conservation 2
    elephants *see* African elephant
    protected areas 82
    rhino management 2
    tropical forests 6
    wildlife protection 2
African elephant
    access to 37, 38–9
    CITES Management Quota System
    99–100
    decline of 34–42
    homesteading regimes 40
    investment in 40
    ivory trade 35, 37, 39, 40, 98, 100, 113
    management resources diversion 41–2
    open access regimes 38–9, 40
    overexploitation 35–6, 37, 40
    slow growth rate 36, 38
African leopard 99
Agriculture
    biodiversity problem in 50–4
    in the developing world 49, 50
    development of 28, 32, 49-50, 51
    effects of 32
    Farmers' Rights 81, 102–3
    gene bank system 5
    homogenisation of biological resources
    and 49
    plant genetic resources 81, 101–3
        see also Plant genetic resources
    productivity gains and diversity loss 49
    specialisation
        convergence on specialised
        varieties
        of species 50–4, 55
        dangers of genetic uniformity 67–8
        impact of 66–8
    species-specific capital goods 49
    species-specific learning 49, 51
Akerlof, G 141
Albon, S 2, 39, 84
Americas, the

human-induced extinction in 20, 26, 28
    see also Latin America; North America
Amphibians
    numbers of species 8
Antarctic Treaty System 86
ASEAN Convention
    listing arrangements 85
Asia
    agriculture 49
Atkinson, I 29
Australia
    human-induced extinction in 20, 26

Barbier, E 4, 35, 100, 113, 125, 135, 137, 138
Barton, N 23
Base resource appropriation 31–4, 41
Beckermann, W 44
Biodiversity
    adaptive radiation 8
    agriculture and *see* Agriculture
    alternative development paths,
    creation of 14
    conservation of
        certification of sustainable use 112–
        16, 150
        property right regimes *see* Property
        rights
        transferable development rights
        approach *see under* Property rights
    contracting for 120–2
        see also Property rights
    Convention on *see* Biodiversity
    Convention
    evolutionary process 6, 8, 9–10
    existing species, numbers of 8
    extinction *see* Extinction
    flowering plants 7–8
    global conversion process 11–13
        management of 13–16
    global development and *see* Global
    development
    'global premium', creation of 16
    human depletion of 19–22
    human development and *see* Human
    development
    informational value of 63–5, 71–3, 104
    institution-building for conservation

OTHER RELEVANT
PUBLICATIONS FROM EARTHSCAN

Economics for the Wilds
Wildlife, Wildlands, Diversity and Development
Edited by Timothy Swanson and Edward B Barbier

Leading environmental economists argue that the long term interests of the wilds are best served by appropriate economic management, valuing the wilds' resources and ensuring indigenous management of them. *Economics for the Wilds* includes major case studies on subjects such as wildlife tourism and use of rainforest products.

Published in association with TRAFFIC International

£12.95 *paperback* ISBN 1 85383 124 7 240 pages 1992

Elephants, Economics and Ivory
Edward B Barbier, Joanne C Burgess, Timothy Swanson and David W Pearce

'*a model of how economics can illuminate environmental problems*' The Financial Times

In some parts of Africa, elephants have been hunted almost to extinction in the quest for ivory. The losses to African economies have been catastrophic. This book examines the economics of the conservation and sustainable management of elephant populations, using principles that can be applied to other wildlife resources. The authors look at the overall statistics, including those for countries where the elephant population is stable. Tackling the difficult relationship between people and wildlife, they consider the multiplicity of economic and social functions fulfilled by ensuring that elephant herds survive: tourism, a variety of ecological purposes and, finally, as a source of ivory. They show how the careful management of elephants as a resource can best serve African interests.

£10.95 *paperback* ISBN 1 85383 073 9 176 pages 1990

Social Change and Conservation
Edited by Krishna B Ghimire and Michel P Pimbert

'*This is a powerful book. It is about conflict, rights, process, professionalism, paradigms, power, politics, gender, biodiversity, sustainability, and political economy. It argues a case for radical orientation in the current conservation thinking, and argues it with empirical evidence and moral force. The chapters, individually and cumulatively, pack a formidable punch. There is an alternative paradigm here which is practical, and which simply has to be the wave of the future. The question is not whether this paradigm will prevail, but how soon and how well. There is a wonderful opportunity for a win–win scenario, with gains for people and nature.*'

Professor Robert Chambers, Institute of Development Studies

Protected areas and conservation policies are usually established with only local nature and wildlife in mind. Yet they can have far-reaching consequences for local populations, often undermining their access to resources and their livelihoods. This book is the first comprehensive discussion of the social consequences of protected area schemes and conservation policies. Drawing on case studies from North America, Europe, Asia, Central America and Africa, it reviews current trends in protected area management, and shows how local people have been affected in terms of their customary rights, livelihoods, well-being and social cohesion. The leading authorities who have contributed to this groundbreaking volume argue for a thorough overhaul of conservation thinking and practice.

Published in association with UNRISD

£18.95 *paperback* ISBN 1 85383 410 6 354 pages 1997

The Economic Value of Biodiversity
David Pearce and Dominic Moran

Economic forces drive much of the extinction of the world's biological resources and biodiversity. It is the failure of economics to 'capture' the actual value of the resources that results in skewed economic decisions and destructive policies. Yet, as this book argues, that doesn't have to be the case. The values of biodiversity and conservation activity can be captured, and once they are, the basis for economic decision changes. Policies which prevent or reduce biodiversity loss can then be justified on *economic* grounds, and biological diversity can be protected by the market place and institutional mechanisms.

£12.95 *paperback* ISBN 1 85383195 6 172 pages 1994

Forest Politics
The Evolution of International Cooperation
David Humphreys

Not only is deforestation the outcome of a complex web of national and international political, economic and social dynamics; it also contributes to a wide range of environmental problems such as global warming, biodiversity loss and soil erosion. Moreover, deforestation concerns a diverse array of political actors: governments, businesses and transnational corporations, UN programmes, intergovernmental organisations and non-governmental organisations are all stakeholders, and all have different visions of forest use and forest conservation.

Forest Politics is the first full-length study of the evolution of international cooperation on forest conservation. It traces the emergence of deforestation as an issue on the international political agenda, beginning with an assessment of the causes of deforestation and its environmental and social effects, and considers the problems facing the international community in dealing with the array of issues involved. It provides a detailed review and critical analysis of the main international policy responses over the last 15 years, with comprehensive studies of: the Tropical Forestry Action Programme; the International Tropical Timber Organisation; the forest negotiations that preceded the 1992 Earth Summit and the negotiation of the International Tropical Timber Agreement, 1994. The book then assesses the many post-Rio conservation initiatives and processes, and concludes by outlining the prospects for future international agreements.

£15.95 *paperback* ISBN 1 85383 378 9 224 pages 1996

Blueprint 2
Greening the World Economy
Edited by David Pearce

'*admirably clear-headed in an area where muddle is often king... an excellent introduction to the most pressing environmental issues*' The Financial Times

'*clarity, breadth and level of sophistication make* [this] *ideal for anyone wishing an introduction to the topic*' Ecological Economics

'*puts the case for taking environmental economics seriously, and does a good job at trying to answer the criticisms of the disbelievers*' New Scientist

Extending the application of environmental economics to the management of the global environment, contributors David Pearce, Edward Barbier, Anil Markandya, Scott Barret, Kerry Turner and Timothy Swanson set out a powerful agenda for international action, welcomed by governments, policy makers, economists and students throughout the world.

£10.95 *paperback* ISBN 1 85383 076 3 240 pages 1991

World Directory of Environmental Organisations
Fifth Edition
Edited by Thaddeus C Trzyna and Roberta Childers

'*an essential purchase*' American Library Association

'*should be part of every library's reference collection*' American Reference Books Annual

This is the only fully comprehensive guide to environmental organisations in all parts of the world. First published over 20 years ago and now in its fifth edition, the directory describes over 2600 organisations in more than 200 countries. It includes: profiles of the activities of over 170 intergovernmental agencies and UN programmes; full descriptions of over 400 international non-governmental organisations; over 2000 national governmental and non-governmental organisations; 'who's doing what' in over 50 key areas in environment and resource management; full addresses and phone and fax numbers; and an index and bibliography of databases and directories.
    A vital handbook and reference to organisations at every level working on conservation.

£50.00 *paperback* ISBN 1 85383 307 X 232 pages 1996

World Who is Who and Does What in Environment and Conservation
Edited by Nicholas Polunin, compiled by Lynn M Curme

This is a unique guide to the world's most eminent and active environmental policy makers, campaigners, researchers, authors and academics. The results of many years' research and data-gathering, the book gives details of over 1300 environmentalists and conservationists, in the vast range of environmental disciplines and subject areas, from over 120 countries throughout the world.
    The A–Z biographical listings include information on the biographees' qualifications and affiliations, academic background and work experience, achievements and awards, and specialist interests and publications. Details are also given of entrants' specialist capabilities and language abilities, their willingness to be consulted for advice or by the media or to act as consultants, and their contact addresses, with phone and fax numbers. Fully cross-referenced indexes also list entrants by speciality and by country, so that users can readily identify experts in any given field and in any geographical location.

£50.00 *hardback* ISBN 1 85383 377 0 600 pages 1997

Earthscan Publications Ltd
http://www.earthscan.co.uk